T0319713

Economics, Culture and Education

Mark Blaug

Economics, Culture and Education

Essays in Honour of Mark Blaug

edited by

G. K. Shaw

Rank Foundation Professor of Economics
The University of Buckingham

Edward Elgar

Published by
Edward Elgar Publishing Limited
Gower House
Croft Road
Aldershot
Hants GU11 3HR
England

Edward Elgar Publishing Company
Old Post Road
Brookfield
Vermont 05036
USA

British Library Cataloguing in Publication Data

Economics, culture and education: essays in honour of Mark Blaug.
   1. Economics
   I. Blaug, Mark, *1927–* II. Shaw, G. K. (Graham Keith *1938–*)
   330

Library of Congress Cataloguing in Publication Data

Economics, culture, and education: essays in honour of Mark Blaug/edited by G. K. Shaw.
   p. cm.
   Includes bibliographical references and index.
   1. Economics–History. 2. Economics–Research. 3. Blaug, Mark.
   I. Blaug, Mark. II. Shaw, G. K. (Graham Keith), 1938– .
   HB75.E33 1991
   330′.09–dc20

                                     91–15078
                                        CIP

ISBN 1 85278 383 4

Printed in Great Britain by Galliard (Printers) Ltd, Great Yarmouth

Contents

Tables

Foreword

Mark Blaug was born in The Hague, The Netherlands in 1927 and remained there until 1940 when the onset of war rendered exile a prudent step for anyone of Jewish parenthood. Initially, exile meant London, England, where Mark Blaug attended St John's Wood Grammar School, and then a move to New York where he completed his formal academic education. Having gained his High School Diploma at the Peter Stuyvesant High School, he entered the City University of New York and graduated with a BA in Economics from Queen's College. MA and PhD degrees quickly followed, this time from the prestigious Ivy League campus of Columbia University.

After a short spell as a statistician at the United States Department of Labour in New York City, Mark Blaug was appointed first Lecturer and then Assistant Professor at Yale University in New Haven, Connecticut. The United States might well have become his permanent home, but after a year spent as Visiting Reader in Economic Thought at the University of Manchester, he was persuaded to return to England where he became successively Senior Lecturer, Reader and Full Professor at the University of London Institute of Education. Since 1984 he has been Professor Emeritus of the Economics of Education at London University as well as Consultant Professor of Economics at the University of Buckingham. In 1989 he accepted a Visiting Professorship of Economics at the University of Exeter, close to the bleak but beautiful countryside of Dartmoor where he has now made his home.

Of course, a potted history such as the above can do no more than sketch the bare outlines of what has been an outstanding academic career. It says nothing of the many distinguished contributions Professor Blaug has brought to economics generally especially in the areas of the history of economic thought, the methodology of economics, cultural economics, the economics of education and nineteenth-century British economic history. This is not the place to give details of such achievements; a complete listing of Professor Blaug's many and varied publications is included as an appendix to this volume. It also fails to do justice to his excellence as a teacher and communicator to students. Nor does it hint at the international recognition borne out by visiting university appointments world wide; and numerous consultancies to international organizations and public bodies in Britain and elsewhere.

By far the best recognition of Mark Blaug's talents and achievements is catalogued here in the very distinction and eminence of the contributors to this *Festschrift*. In each and every case, the participants responded warmly to the invitation to take part. Their tribute to Professor Blaug, expressed in these thoughtful and thought-provoking essays, is a fitting testimony to his achievements as an economist and to the respect which he commands within the profession. There is ample evidence here of Professor Blaug's contribution to scholarship. But equally, it has been made clear to the present editor how many contributors have been influenced and inspired by Professor Blaug's example and guidance over the years. In many cases also, these essays are an appreciation of his virtues as a friend and valued colleague.

Not surprisingly, many of the contributions here focus upon the history of economic thought and the evolution of economic research. Thus, Part I of the volume begins with a remarkably wide ranging discourse by Professor Paul Samuelson defending his views on economic thought and ends with a much more specific analysis by Professor Denis O'Brien upon the macroeconomics of the comparatively unknown (if undeservedly so) British economist Thomas Joplin. Interspersed between these two diverse contributions, Professor Don Patinkin discusses the economics of Keynes's *General Theory*, Professor William Baumol offers a distinctive interpretation of Adam Smith's Invisible Hand, Professor Meghnad Desai pursues the distinction between heresy and heterodoxy, and Professor George Stigler offers a fascinating insight into the direction of economic research.

Part II is altogether more far-ranging in its scope. It begins with a persuasive analysis of the costs of inflation by Professor Walter Eltis. This is followed by four distinctive contributions on methodology. Professor Bruce Caldwell examines the methodology of scientific research programmes in economics generally, a paper which is complemented by Professor D. Wade Hands writing on Popper and the Rationality Principle. Professor Rosenberg offers a critical appraisal of General Equilibrium Theory and finally Professor Arjo Klamer argues the case for an interpretative approach to economics linking it, topically, with the criticisms of feminist economics. Education and the topical questions of charging the full cost of fees for overseas students and the provision of income contingent student loans are respectively analysed by Ms Maureen Woodhall and Dr Nicholas Barr. Finally, the volume concludes with a joint paper by Professors Alan Peacock and Ilde Rizzo returning to the area of government expenditure growth.

It perhaps remains to explain why this *Festschrift* should emanate from its present source and especially from a young University possessed of less than a thousand students. The simple fact is that Professor Blaug has maintained a long and valued association with the University of Buckingham, Britain's *only* independent university. He was a member of the original Planning Board and when the University of Buckingham finally opened its doors in 1976, Mark Blaug became the first external examiner in Economics and thereby made an invaluable contribution, helping to maintain that department's external credibility long before the award of the Royal Charter. Apart from the desire to honour a valued and distinguished colleague, therefore, there are sound reasons why the present *Festschrift* should have its origins in the University of Buckingham.

Those who know Professor Blaug will testify to his ready wit, conviviality and, above all, to his incisive ability to home in on the essence of a question. His participation in University seminars invariably promotes comprehension and further insight. Recently these talents have found expression in a new venture, an impressive hour-long video on the life and work of John Maynard Keynes.

Tribute must also be paid to the amazing catholicism of Professor Blaug's interests. There can be few people, for example (perhaps only one!), who can claim to have been in the London audience of the Karpov–Kasparov chess encounter and also of the 1990 World Cup Soccer final between Argentina and West Germany. This must give him a unique opportunity to judge which was the more enjoyable or tactically impressive event.

As editor of the present volume I wish to thank the contributors for their willingness to take part and for the excellence of their contributions. For myself, for Mrs Linda

Waterman who willingly undertook the secretarial chores involved, and last but not least for Edward Elgar, it remains a great personal pleasure to see Professor Mark Blaug honoured in this way.

G. K. S.

Contributors

Nicholas Barr is Senior Lecturer in Economics, London School of Economics (University of London).

William J. Baumol is Professor of Economics at Princeton and New York Universities and Director of the C. V. Starr Center for Applied Economics, New York University, New York.

Bruce J. Caldwell is Professor of Economics, University of North Carolina at Greensboro, USA.

Meghnad Desai is Professor of Economics, London School of Economics (University of London).

Walter Eltis is Director General, National Economic Development Office, London; and Emeritus Fellow, Exeter College, Oxford.

D. Wade Hands is Associate Professor of Economics, University of Puget Sound, Tacoma, Washington, USA.

Arjo Klamer is Associate Professor of Economics, George Washington University, Washington, D.C., USA.

Denis O'Brien is Professor of Economics, University of Durham, England.

Don Patinkin is Professor of Economics, The Hebrew University of Jerusalem.

Sir Alan Peacock is Executive Director, The David Hume Institute, George Square, Edinburgh.

Ilde Rizzo is Professor of Public Finance, University of Reggio Calabria, Italy.

Alexander Rosenberg is Professor of Philosophy, The University of California, Riverside, California, USA.

Paul A. Samuelson is Institute Professor Emeritus, Department of Economics, Massachusetts Institute of Technology.

George J. Stigler is Director, Center for the Study of the Economy and the State, The University of Chicago, Chicago, USA.

Maureen Woodhall is Senior Lecturer in Higher Education Finance, Institute of Education, University of London, and Consultant Fellow, International Institute for Educational Planning, Paris.

Part I

1. Conversations with my History-of-Economics Critics

Paul A. Samuelson

When a lion deviates into the tigers' sector of the jungle, he must expect growls not gratitude. It is the story of my life. Having established my bona fides as a pukka scientist with several score articles and hundreds of equations, I helped make the occupation of textbook writer once again respectable. When I visited Yale to give a lecture on Marx (his 'transformation problem'), the audience feared to respond because of a suspicion that I must be perpetrating a put-on: back then, before the gusher of Marxian matrices, to non-Japanese scholars Marxian prose was as dead as Cicero's orations; but few pats for my resuscitations have been aimed at my back by appreciative Marxians. With the periodicity of the Winter Solstice I receive Christmas cards from Frank Hahn expressing astonishment that I spend so much time writing on Sraffian matters while real-world problems still cry out for solution; but I am not aware that graven images of my likeness are being erected in India, Italy or the minor Colleges of East Anglia.

It is the 5 per cent of my published papers that deal with the history of economic science that I discuss on this occasion. However much these please their author, they do seem to gore the oxen who trod in the fields of *Dogmengeschichte*. Even Mark Blaug, whose mode of writings I have envied and for whom I might be regarded as a bush league John the Baptist, rises to my fly. Don Patinkin, reared in the Chicagoland of my remote youth, has similarly found me out. The way of the amateur in the professional ring is indeed hard. And George Stigler, my prefect when a boy on the Midway, goes whole hours without annihilating me with a wisecrack. Water cannot even rise to its own source. Viner and Schumpeter were my teachers, so I really have no excuse for my sins.

When meeting St Peter my worst crime will be the espousal of a Whig-History approach to the history of science. But that is a late-in-the-day heresy, exempt under the Statute of Limitations that applies to scholars over the age of 69 – except that, to the omniscient eye, this approach may be discerned to have been there back from my very beginnings.

Actually, these are mock complaints. My occasional doctrinal writings have received due notice and have left their mark on the literature. Argumentation is the staple of *Dogmengeschichte*. To paraphrase Shaw, practitioners of live science do, historians of thought argue. In this present brief offering to Mark Blaug, I want to argue some subtle issues in the history of economic analysis.

HOW REPUTATIONS RISE AND FALL

It will help to start off the discussion to provide some concrete materials to talk about. An anthropologist who applies contents analysis to the five embalmed volumes of my

Collected Scientific Papers and several book contributions will record repeated roguish reappraisals of reputations among past great economists. To prime the pump of discussion I sample a few of them:

1. Alfred Marshall, whose stock quotations were forming a head-and-shoulders peak when I entered economics on 2 January 1932, has sunk down to being just a great economist and one who for reasons of temperament and health never lived up to his superlative potential. I early placed my short sales.[1]
2. Knut Wicksell, who used to be the Scandinavian Marshall, has enjoyed a Kondratief bull cycle. I realized my capital gains in him after his canonization but still hold him in high esteem, even though it was a figment of Bertil Ohlin's 1937 imagination that Jean-Baptiste Wicksell was ever an anticipator of Keynes's 1930s notions of effective demand.
3. Francis Edgeworth, who cowered in Marshall's shade, grew all his life in mathematical insight and statistical originality. One wonders how much the wily R. A. Fisher gleaned from him and wonders that Karl Pearson gained nothing. I once described Edgeworth as my pin-up boy in economics. A young scholar researching the origins of my *Foundations* wrote me that I had stolen it all from Edgeworth. My modest reply was that I had not been that smart, having to do much of it the hard way. (It is a matter of self-reproach that, until Martin Shubik recognized the concept of the *core* in the 1881 *Mathematical Psychics*, I overlooked completely this great Edgeworthian innovation.)
4. Léon Walras, yes, I must agree with Joseph Schumpeter, is the greatest of our great economists. Paraphrasing what Lagrange wrote about Newton, I have expressed Schumpeter's case thus: Walras is the greatest of the economists and also the *luckiest*, for he discovered the (general equilibrium) system of the world and, alas, there is only one system of the world to be discovered. But I cannot deny that Walras is so thorough as to be a bit dull; translation into English did not bring him to sparkling life; and he did resemble Irving Fisher in being something of a do-gooder. Like Max Planck and Marx, Walras never completely understood his own system.
5. Vilfredo Pareto, when I was a kid, was the genius who was supposed to have gone way beyond Walras. Now that I have read all of him in English, I do value his merits. But, paradoxically, it was his contempt for welfare economics that led him by the back-door to make his greatest contribution in identifying certain necessary conditions that a welfare optimum must satisfy (so-called Pareto optimality, a mid-twentieth-century coinage). His distribution of income and his sociology have not weathered so well. Pareto was too impatient a scholar and lacked competent critics and pupils. Also, though he was prolific, he was repetitive. Though Pareto purported to be coolly objective, ideologically he was incontinent. Too little recognition has been made of the similarity of Schumpeter's political credo to Pareto's.
6. John Maynard Keynes can be characterized briefly. With Léon Walras and Adam Smith, he belongs to the greatest of our great, albeit with warts aplenty.
7. Irving Fisher was born late to be a pioneer in value theory, but his paradigm for capital theory earns him a rating as the greatest of the American economists, outstripping J. B. Clark, Francis Walker, Henry Carey, Frank Taussig and the usual suspects. His do-goodism and unmerited self-confidence as a picker of common stocks masked recognition of his scientific merits.
8. Karl Marx I once described as a minor post-Ricardian, a not-unworthy predecessor

of Leontief. Maurice Dobb could never take me seriously after that. Alas, I was right. As I wrote in the 1974 Lloyd Metzler *Festschrift*, Marx did his best economics in his Volume II 'Tableaux of Steady and Expanded Reproduction'. Like Max Planck and his 1900 Quantum Theory, Marx never quite understood his own accomplishments. I took Marx seriously because one out of four billion humans used to do so.

His 1867 novelties concerning rates of surplus value and exploitation represented a sterile detour that renders zero or negative insight into the laws of motion of real-life capitalism and into the forces that create inequality of wealth and income. (Example: To understand the inequalities in the distribution of incomes for Europe, North America, and the 1776–1990 developing world, you must combine (a) analysis of Henry George resource endowments with (b) analysis of Schumpeterian entre-preneurial rents, and (c) analysis of Knightian uncertainty, three vital processes that none of Marx's paradigms at all illuminate! To understand the laws of motion of growth and decay you must similarly look elsewhere than in the Marxian corpus.) What has to be understood is that my devastating critique has *naught to do with Clarkian neoclassicism*. The testimony of von Neumann–Sraffa discrete technologies is equally harsh on Marx's proposed economic paradigms of *mehrwert* (or equalized rates of 'surplus value'). Piero Sraffa's growling against marginalism provided that Trojan horse within which the generation of Steedman-like Marxists were led to realize that the *mehrwert* paradigm was wrong normatively and positivistically.

Now that only the population of North Korea takes Marx so seriously as an economist, perhaps scholars will realize my literal truth in saying: the Bortkiewicz–Marx transformation procedure from 1867 'values' to 1895 'prices' is precisely a procedure of 'erase and rewrite', replacing the 1867 axiom system by the conventional 1776–1895–1990 axiom system of competitive pricing. The Child at the Emperor's Court in Hans Christian Andersen's tale was instantly believed by all; I have yet to be told by two people that they can describe what I proved in my literary and mathematical exposition of the transformation problem and that they do agree with it. Oh well, as Milton Friedman used to say, 'One man with the truth is a majority.' All we cranks say that.

Bortkiewicz's 1907 critique of Marx, politically not unsympathetic to him, is worth all the other commentaries put together. As a shining example of Whig History, the Bortkiewicz instance could not be bettered.

A BETTER NAME THAN 'WHIG HISTORY'?

This haphazard glance at re-evaluations emphasizes the point that each generation perceives a particular earlier generation in its own way. As time passes, as we learn more, as lost documents surface, it is not the case that there is a convergence toward the one true account of history. 'History as it happened' is neither attainable in principle nor, where the history of a *cumulative* science is concerned, is it a desirable end. This definitely does not mean that each generation is encouraged to fabricate its own fictional versions of earlier generations. There is no point in calling such exercises history and it is fraudulent to palm them off as being so. The 1838 book by Cournot constantly circulates out of the MIT library while McCullouch's tomes of that period sleep peacefully on the shelves because the Cournot work does advance our understanding of why Marshall cannot validly have a decreasing marginal cost supply schedule for a competitive firm. It enjoys present-day relevance.

Thomas Macaulay believed that his day's Whig society was the latest and best and *final* thing. His history of England knew how to label Stuarts clearly as bad kings and Hanoverians as good ones. That is how Whig history got its name. But that is *not* what scientists mean when they use the term 'Whig history of science'.

Every scientist knows, from experience and reasoning, that today's science will be displaced by tomorrow's. The king is dead; long live the king. But this is not the same thing as the case that today's short skirts will be displaced by tomorrow's low hem-lines. When Tom Kuhn wrote his 1962 *Structure of Scientific Revolutions*, he stressed the elements of subjective controversy between scientific schools. But – as he came to realize but did not choose to stress – his 1962 words underplayed the truth that in the physical and life sciences there is no perpetual cycling and recycling between arbitrary versions of doctrine: cider is not acid in Napoleon's 1803 and Pauling's 1952, and base in Davy's 1803 and Lysenko's 1952; paradigms differ and you takes your choice! That would be bad history, sociology and philosophy of science.

A later paradigm is likely to be a better paradigm and be more lasting. Einstein's 1915 system does not so much reject Newton's 1588 system as give it a *dominating* generalization. In the creative arts Shakespeare is not better than Homer because he comes later. To think that economics is merely like poetry is both to downgrade it as a serious attempt to be a science and is to grossly misdescribe economics.

I know, perhaps more precisely than most, what are the limitations of mainstream economics. I can predict, perhaps a bit less vaguely than most, where the likely changes in economists' beliefs may come in the next two decades. But that doesn't make me fascinated by this mistake or that mistake in 1817 Ricardo. And it certainly does not make me a Pontius Pilate, who rubs his hands and says things like, 'What is truth?' and 'In the classical paradigm, rent is surplus and cannot cause the price ratio of corn and cloth to change when tastes change from food to clothing. In your mainstream paradigm, perhaps the angles of a triangle add up to 180°: how quaint, but in my paradigm they total 377°.'

My previous paragraph used the words 'mainstream economics' to denote what my readers will well understand it to be. I do not mean, even covertly, that what the majority of economists subscribe to is the *true* (Macaulay, Whig) economics of this day (or certainly not of all future times).

Today, as in every day, there is competition between alternative systems and models. The version of Whig economics that I am trying to formulate says:

> That part of the past which is relevant to the present – that is, is relevant to one *or more* of today's competing paradigms – is to be an object of special historical interest. Instead of 'Whig history', it might be better to speak of 'history that is given special importance and attention because of its relevance to the present'. A good, if ugly, title might be 'Presentistic history'.

Here is a good example to illustrate that Macaulayan complacency is not involved in Whig history of science. Sraffians in our day espouse a version of neo-Ricardianism. A Pasinetti, dissatisfied with mainstream economics, wants a return to a classical paradigm. A lost 1815 Ricardo manuscript, which reckons the profit rate as corn earned on corn in a decomposable food sector, interests a Garegnani or Sraffa.

'Right on!' says the Whig-history methodologists. 'If a Samuel Hollander can look in Smith for supply-and-demand mechanisms, why aren't you non-mainstreamers entitled to hunt there for your preferred baubles?' Whoever the modern-day scholars are, when they concentrate attention on past works relevant to their *present* interests, they are being Whig historians and are being bound by the same rules of accurate quotation and documentation.[2]

In point of mid-century fact, much of the revived interest in 1760–1870 writers has come from neo-Sraffian, neo-Marxian and neo-Keynesian camps rather than from neoclassical-Keynesian synthesists. (The new rational expectationists derive their dicta from their own syllogisms and statistical regressions rather than quoting from Say or Mill.)

SCIENTIFIC THEORIES NOT SCIENTISTS

When I read a Smith or a Keynes, it is the system they are formulating that first interests me – the system discernible there and not primarily *their* understanding or misunderstanding of it. (I have retold the story of Tommy Balogh's overhearing an argument about Pareto in the early 1930s between his two room-mates Nicky Kaldor and Paul Rosenstein-Rodan. When he later said to the overpowering Kaldor, 'I didn't realize you knew Pareto's works', Nicky replied: 'I don't. But after Rosie described the matter, I saw how it had to go.' This hints at my point, but I join in warning that an over-confident Kaldor can find himself deducing his own syllogisms and not those of the specified historical author.) The historian of science is interested primarily in the history of various scientific models and understandings, and only secondarily in the history of particular scholars' beliefs and progressions.

Axel Leijonhufvud tries to denigrate Keynesian paradigms and equations in comparison with Maynard Keynes's own intuitions and perceptions, Keynes versus the Keynesians. To those of us who lived through the 1930–46 years his case is not persuasive. Even if Keynes, on his deathbed or before, repudiated his consumption-function cum liquidity-preference behaviour relations, they would remain as the substantive innovation of the *General Theory*, spawning 20,000 subsequent research efforts.

When I discern in 1931 Richard Kahn or J. Maurice Clark parallel income-consumption behaviour equations – or in 1931 Keynes Harris Foundation *Lectures* – I sing out: Here are foreshadowings of the *General Theory*. My good friend Don Patinkin scolds me with words like: 'Paul, you are so brilliant that you recognize logical and empirical equivalences that the oh-so-ordinary authors do not themselves see. If only you were duller and slower, you'd get things more right.' Flattery will not deter me nor will I let Patinkin use the ju-jitsu manoeuvre whereby the opponent's own strength is used against self.

Patinkin makes another point, presumably intended to apply against me or my position in some regard. Whether or not Paul A. Samuelson is a perfect logic machine who never contemplates simultaneously incompatible propositions and who always perceives clearly the full implications and corollaries of his postulated systems, Professor Patinkin emphasizes that the economic writers of past and present times are definitely imperfect: they commit errors, believe contradictory things at the same time, progress in correct understanding and also regress. I hear Patinkin. I agree that all of us are indeed less than perfect. While it may be that this consideration strengthens some Patinkin criticisms of me, I suspect that it strengthens some of my characteristic contentions.

Here is an example. Back in 1968 I wrote a paper trying to set down from memory what neoclassical, pre-1936 monetary theory really was. I argued that we recognized the *qualitative* difference between a barter and money system; and that the best Cassel and Schumpeter could do to present à la Walras a formalistic equation system of our long-run neutral-money paradigm, I and other pre-Keynesians recognized to be inadequate to generate our understanding of the qualitative difference between a barter and a money system. I then presented a 1968 equation system that better rendered our definite 1935, *qualitative-money* notions.

Perhaps I am over-sensitive but I was left with the feeling that Don Patinkin judged my 1968 account to be contaminated by post-1935 hindsight(s). Where were my pre-1936 documents and other evidences? Like Copernicus, Galileo and Bruno, in my heart of hearts I felt unrepentant, muttering under my breath, 'But the earth does move. But we did understand that a decomposable barter equational system is not a best rendering of what we believed.'

There matters stood for decades while Don and I amiably corresponded. Recently, not completely by chance, I looked up Cassel's 1925 popular *Fundamental Thoughts in Economics*. There, seven years after Cassel had written in his *Theory of Social Economy* the imperfect barter-dichotomy equation system that Patinkin rightly complained about, Cassel wrote down all the apperceptions I had claimed. When I photocopied the passages to Patinkin, he acknowledged that there was indeed no invalid barter-dichotomy in 1925 Cassel. I felt vindicated.

A Patinkin apprentice might interpret this to be a case where Cassel learned something between 1918 and 1925. That is not my best interpretation. After his early-century borrowings from Walras and others, Gustav Cassel's thought changed remarkably little. Before 1918 when Cassel stayed at the elementary descriptive level, his analysis was more nearly right than any formalization he could contrive, then or later. So it always goes! Businessmen or investors who sound to sophisticated economists like idiots when they frame generalizations are really not that bad in how they actually function. (Shaw was right: Wagner is not so bad as he sounds!)

To sum up: after you have been able to discern in an old author a posed economic model, you should follow Viner's advice to try to find the best-case understanding by him of that model. (I would add: you should also work out his worst-case understandings.)

It is amazing how, when you pursue this procedure, Adam Smith rises in worth and how David Ricardo declines in merit. Partly it is a matter of Ricardo's weakness of exposition. Constantly he fails to distinguish between necessary and sufficient conditions. Chronically, he writes that certain things must be true, when a modern judge can provide multiple exceptions. No pre-1870 writer is free of such blemishes, but for reasons of conservative temperament Smith is more guarded and qualified in his contentions. While editor Sraffa has focused new light on Ricardo, we discern at second looks so many new warts and pimples. Unfortunately, both neo-Ricardian radicals and conventional main-streamers still glorify some of the pimples as beauty spots!

BLAUG, HOLLANDER AND STIGLER

This being the two hundredth anniversary of Adam Smith's death, I discuss in another place the obvious and merited rise in Smith's reputation as an economic theorist – absolutely and in comparison with Ricardo's reputation. Here I want to talk about a critique used in common by Mark Blaug and Samuel Hollander, in which they invoke the authority of George Stigler to discount the importance of what all agree are certain innovations buried in the *Wealth of Nations*. My purpose is not to argue for victory. Some interesting points are raised.

My 1978 canonical model of classical economists' growth analysis occurs, I asserted, in the 1776 *Wealth of Nations* as well as in 1817 Ricardo, 1848 Mill and 1867 Marx. Salim Rashid (1989) objected: we all coddle Smith the plagiarist; Samuelson reads into him goodies from Samuelson's own mind; anyway all those goodies are already stolen from Cantillon, Turgot and several others. Cigdem Kurdas (1988) objected that the model I attribute to Smith does not contain the Smith, Allyn Young and Ohlin phenomena of division of labour and increasing returns to scale – as if an author can't have two different ideas in one lifetime and one book, as if an author is allowed only one 'central message' à la Patinkin.

Samuel Hollander (1980) is more judicious. He makes out for me the documented case that I had not already set out: Yes, when Hollander reads all of the *Wealth of Nations*, he can find definitely there *every* element involved in the canonical growth model. Mark Blaug agrees with Hollander.

> 'But,' they each somewhere say in print or correspondence, 'the reader must do a lot of work and look in a lot of different places in Smith's book for those vital elements. Smith's eighteenth and nineteenth century readers failed to recognize these axioms, theorems, and corollaries in Smith. A tree that falls in the forest where no one can see or hear it . . . As Stigler has well said (I am still paraphrasing), a Gossen may have been as original as all get out before the Jevons–Menger–Walras marginal-utility revolution, but since we know that no one read his published book, Gossen is properly to be reckoned as a cipher in the development of the history of ideas. The failure of Smith's successors to detect the diminishing returns and other elements of his canonical growth model is a *central fact* in the history of economic analysis and by Stiglerian *ipse dixit*, that's that.'

My paraphrase is purposely a caricature, but is made so for expositional brevity. Let me now provide pro-and-con commentary.

1. Stigler has a point. But it must not be misunderstood. The Gossen that was not read had *at that time* zero influence. By 1880 competent scholars knew of his work; in 1904 and 1954 and 1990, the importance awarded Gossen's 1854 effort is and ought to be a different one. Even a non-Whig historian will concede that. Clerk Maxwell is the greatest physicist between Newton and Einstein. But few understood or agreed with his early works on electromagnetism. He was second choice for all honours then. Willard Gibbs's thermodynamics was at first a stone thrown in a pond that displayed no ripple. But then Maxwell and Rayleigh and Ostwald and . . . began to digest it and eventually it became the keystone of macroscopic thermodynamics. Even today new insights are still discovered in it. Neither Stigler nor I would want to deny that Eugen Slutsky's synthesis of demand theory around the concept of compensated demand, undiscovered in its wartime Italian journal from 1915 to 1935, completely anticipates the stellar (and independent) achievement of 1934 Hicks-Allen. My MIT students were assigned both Slutsky and 1939 *Value and Capital* because the 1934 item had (in Robert K. Merton's phrase) been 'obliterated by incorporation' – the finest fate our brainchildren can achieve.

2. There is no excuse for failing to give credit in 1990 for what Smith deserves. My gentle beef with both Hollander and Blaug is that their recent expositions do not yet do justice to Smith and do not mete out precise algebraic justice to Ricardo. Smith is right, not wrong or incomplete, when he contends that capital accumulation can lower the profit rate *even when land is unlimitedly free*. Yes, Ricardo was right to demonstrate that the profit rate need not ever fall in a model where land supply grows

in balance with labour supply and capital supply's; but no Ricardian should misconstrue this to imply that *only* land shortage can cause a drop in the profit rate. Necessary and sufficient conditions are distinguishable propositions in every epoch.

3.   Just as the American Constitution is a living document, the proper Stiglerian dictum concerning evaluations of reputations and historical importance involves a time-dated evolution. Why should Sraffa in 1951 or any of the modern writers I have named in this article fail to label as error Ricardo's 1817 emendation of 1776 Smith – that the presence of residual rent would in the absence of different time-intensities leave labour-theory-of-value price ratios intact? Ricardo was dead wrong in thinking he could get rid of the complication of land by going to external-margin (or internal-margin) land. Why didn't his editor say so? Why didn't the reviewers of Sraffa's edition say so? Smith's eclectic three-component breakdown of price has brought him patronizing derision instead of praise as a pre-Walrasian. Better to have a not-fully-defined theory than a well-defined wrong one. And better still, as I shall argue again elsewhere, the careful reader of Smith will find in his book a well-resolved endogenous determination of his three components of price. If that were not so, the canonical growth model would not be discoverable in Smith. No commentator has yet been able to specify passages which suggest convincingly that Smith was unaware of the relations we can discern in the *Wealth of Nations*.

4.   In friendly correspondence with some of the experts named, I have warned against the Fallacy of Pedantical Literalness. If 1776 Smith or 1798 Malthus do not write down $\partial^2 Output/(\partial Labour)^2$ is negative or its literary equivalent, they allegedly fail to understand 'The Law of Diminishing Returns' (of 1815 West–Malthus–Ricardo or 1890s Clark–Wicksteed). That is wrong. Cantillon, the Physiocrats and many eighteenth-century readers clearly speak of how crowding the land reduces labours' wages: as Keats would say, that is all you need to know about diminishing returns for the canonical model.

Patinkin speaks of 'noise and signal'. He speaks of 'central messages'. Yes, Kahn in 1931 had the notion that contrived fiscal spending will generate primary employment and also multiplied (finite) secondary employment. But that 1936 central message of the *General Theory* allegedly was not Kahn's 1931 central message, by his own admission in a letter to Patinkin. Pshaw! Like Lewis Carroll, I have oodles of central messages every day before breakfast. When I read Kahn of the 1930s and his 1984 Mattioli lectures, I am renewed in the belief that 1931 Kahn is an important foreshadower, temporally and causally, of 1933 and 1936 Keynes.

So with Smith. When he speaks of more capital as causing 'more competition', or as meeting limited opportunities for investment (at the old interest rate), he should not be construed as lapsing from his belief in Say's Law or departing from a supply-and-demand determination of the interest rate. In those days he and others expressed many of our things *their* way. I repeat this does not give us licence to read what we want in their usages.

5.   Mark Blaug (1985c) properly distinguishes a 'rational reconstruction' of an earlier theory from a 'historical reconstruction'. Samuelson he accuses of sometimes palming off consciously or unconsciously the former for the latter. To be convicted of that would be, I agree, to be caught in crime. But the case must be made.

Often, my careful modern analysis testifies in defence of ancient authors rather than tending to make them look bad. Here is an example. Hollander and Blaug write as if the Smithian natural price of goods readily reproducible must obey the special case of constant cost. 'Implicitly', it is opined, Smith must be assuming uniform organic compositions of capital (land and labour). This is a gratuitous supposition. Why pretend that his natural prices of two goods keep the same ratio when their relative outputs vary? A bad rational reconstruction is worse than none, particularly when you saddle the author with it as allegedly his historical reconstruction. Sometimes Ricardo deserves such justice but it is hard cheese to lump Smith with Ricardo (or to praise the latter for criticizing the former for failure to agree in the error).

COMMENTATOR'S CODE OF DUTY

What ought to be expected of an editor who presents to a later-day age the works of an earlier scholar – a Sraffa on Ricardo, a Cannan on Smith, a Stigler surveying the developing of utility notions? What ought to be expected of a reviewer of such efforts and of a commentator on an earlier writer – a Stigler reviewing Sraffa or summing up on Ricardo, a Baumol purporting to describe how Marx believed that he could explain the macrototal of profits by means of his novel analysis of the macrototal of surplus value?

The discreet editor presents the textual data, staying out of the act as much as possible. Some information helpful to later-time readers is succinctly presented. It is gauche to pepper the sacred text with bracketed '*sics*' and later-century opinions. Nevertheless, where an editor is presenting a clearly demarcated introduction and set of explanatory footnotes, there is in my opinion a minimal duty that should be performed.

Let me illustrate. I am editing the correspondence of Harold J. Laski. He writes a 1 June 1919 letter to Justice Oliver Wendell Holmes Jr saying: 'Ran into Winnie in Piccadilly. He was in good form, saying, "Man is the only species to feel shame – or have need to." Rather good, what?' This is a made-up example but let me play the hand. At the first mention of 'Winnie' the editor identifies Winston Churchill as one-time Lord of the Admiralty and descendant of the Duke of Marlborough. He forbears to identify Piccadilly. If research confirms that Churchill was away in Australia from 15 May 1919 to 3 August he mentions that fact. The consummate editor might appropriately add, 'The bon mot in question was uttered by Mark Twain in 1899, but Samuel Clemens was ascertainably dead throughout the summer of 1919.' When you edit a personality like Laski you do risk tiring your reader, but duty is duty.

Similarly, as Blaug has gone on record in agreeing with me, when a Baumol attributes to Marx the attempt to explain total profits by equating it to total surplus value, if no such explanation could be cogent, it is non-optimal not to mention that. To fail to do so is like writing on successive pages of a Goethe commentary, 'On Monday he finished Faust II; on Tuesday morning he squared the circle, leaving to twilight the trisecting of the angle.' Samuelson (1990) raised a pejorative eyebrow at editor Sraffa's failure to point out that Ricardo's belief was erroneous that he could, by going out to the external margin of no-rent land, get rid of deviations from the labour theory of value. I will not saw sawdust further here.

What I shall do is to find perfectionist's fault with George Stigler's account of David Ricardo's 93 per cent labour theory of value. Stigler correctly declares that Ricardo admitted that differences in the intensity of time-phasing in production can vitiate the 100 per cent accuracy of the labour theory of value. Then Stigler gives an accurate account of the primitive exercise by Ricardo in what we would today call *sensitivity analysis*.

Ricardo specifies a numerical example in which two hypothetical goods differ in their wage-profit intensities; specifying what Ricardo considers to be a realistic range of profit rates, Ricardo calculates arithmetically that the variation in those goods' price ratio works out only to about 7 per cent; *ergo* until the end of time the literature is going to be burdened with the concept of Ricardo's 93 per cent labour theory of value. (Already from Oxbridge I have received a paper to comment on entitled 'Samuelson's 93 per cent Theory of Scarcity'. Later we can expect 'The 93 per cent Theory of Phlogiston' and 'The 90.17 per cent Theory of Fire-Stone-Air-and-Water'.)

Where has Dr Stigler failed us? Ricardo's sensitivity analysis is *ad hoc* humpty-dumptyism. Had he chanced that day to pick a numerical example concerning corn that is produced by means of corn, his arithmetic could easily have resulted in a 200 per cent change in price ratio of velvet to corn from a change in the profit rate from 9 per cent to 10 per cent. If that possibility escaped the attention of an 1817 writer, we cannot accord to a twentieth-century writer the same absolution. See Samuelson (1990: 277–8) for arithmetic debunking of the robustness of Ricardo's arithmetic.[3]

I hold today's Samuel Hollander to a higher standard of accuracy than 1907 Jacob Hollander. If that be Whig history, so be it. Blaug, Stigler, Samuelson and the rest of the troops have their work cut out for them. Both the sacred texts and the recent commentaries on them, in my view, are replete with non-optimalities that need still to be recognized and elucidated. This does not mean that I admire old Edwin Cannan for his supercilious contempt for predecessors. (He was not more tolerant of his contemporaries and successors!)

FINALE

When Samuelson (1987) proclaimed a manifesto for Whig history of economic science, the argument was made that old-fashioned antiquarians had lost their market and maybe something different would sell better. Kurdas reminds me that empirical experience showed that the market for history of economics remains small despite the shift toward using present-day tools in that area. I shall say, *'touché'* rather than take defence in the observation that the field might well have shrunk even worse under the older techniques.

Now I shall base my case on the brute fact that economics is in some degree a cumulative science. If study of the past is worth doing, it is worth doing as well as we can. When Mark Blaug likes to quote T. S. Eliot – 'We know more than the Ancients. Yes, it is the Ancients that we know' – do his readers realize that Eliot means to say that we really don't know more than olden-day folk? This poet, whose prose said a few wise things and many foolish ones, would be laughed out of every hospital and freshman laboratory. I suggest we add the economic classroom to the list, humbly but firmly.

NOTES

1. To help celebrate the one hundredth anniversary of the Royal Economic Society and of Marshall's *Principles*, I wrote by invitation a brief account of the controversies over Marshall's consumers surplus, involving him, Neville Keynes, Nicholson, Cannan, Allyn Young, Barone and many others. Steeping myself momentarily in Marshall's writings, I was struck by how little he did from 1875 to 1924 to understand and improve on what he knew well were deficiencies in his approximations. The case of an Euler, who spent a long and busy life in developing and perfecting his brainchildren, provides a sharp contrast. See Samuelson (1990b).

2. The validity of my exposition is not affected by the happenstance that my own search in Ricardo, Smith and Mill fails to find there an alternative paradigm that can perform better than the Walras–Chamberlin–Neumann–Debreu–Keynes paradigm of mainstream economics. If a Garegnani disagrees with a Samuelson on best 1990 analyses, why should those two agree on judging an 1817 text? Herbert Butterfield (1949) coined the term 'Whig history' in connection with the history of science and intends it to have a pejorative meaning. Preferring Christianity, God help us, to it as a unifying theme for history, he set up a straw man for demolishment: Whig historians allegedly describe Galileo as honing in on Newton's later theory of gravitation and they allegedly ignore his false gyrations. Who espouses that?

3. By the usual Mertonian coincidence, just as I was penning these lines the mail brought me from Australia William Coleman (1990), which nicely demonstrates by elementary Australian arithmetic the non-robustness of Ricardo's arithmetic.

2. On the *General Theory***** ** 1

Don Patinkin

In our profession, Keynes (who was a man of many parts[2]) is known primarily for his contributions to monetary theory. These were embodied in his interwar trilogy, which began with his *Tract on Monetary Reform* (Keynes 1923), in which he expounded the quantity theory tradition that he had inherited from his teachers, Marshall and Pigou, at Cambridge; continued with his two-volume *Treatise on Money* (Keynes 1930a,b) (henceforth, *Treatise*), in which – still an advocate of the quantity theory – he supplemented the comparative-statics properties of this theory with a Wicksellian dynamic analysis of the interaction between the rate of interest and the price level – an analysis which Keynes carried on by means of his so-called 'fundamental equations for the value of money'; and concluded with his *General Theory of Employment, Interest and Money* (Keynes 1936) (henceforth, *General Theory* or *GT*). This was the revolutionary work (as Klein (1947) in his classic study so rightly termed it) which he wrote under the constant stimulus and criticism of his colleagues and students – and with which he changed the face of monetary theory, laid the foundation for its development into macroeconomic theory, and defined the analytical framework and research programme of this theory for decades to come.

It is frequently said that the *General Theory* was the product of the mass unemployment of the 1930s. This, however, is a half-truth: it fails to take account of the fact that Britain of the 1920s (unlike the United States and most European countries at that time) was also suffering from severe and prolonged unemployment. The point, however, is that this unemployment did not in Kuhn's (1970: chs 6–8) term[3] constitute an 'anomaly' or 'puzzle' for the prevailing theory, which explained unemployment as the consequence of too high a wage rate: indeed, this was the explanation Keynes himself advanced in his *Economic Consequences of Mr Churchill* (1925). Specifically, he explained that the return of Britain to the gold standard in April 1925 at prewar parity had overvalued the pound relative to the existing level of money wages, and it was this that had generated unemployment, first in the export industries and then elsewhere. Thus, in theory, the way to restore full employment was to reduce money wages; but in practice, the resistance of labour made such a policy impossible to carry out, thus making it necessary to adopt alternative policies (1925: 208–12, 227–9). And in his 1930 *Treatise* (1930b: 162–5) Keynes repeated this analysis.[4]

In contrast, the unemployment of the early 1930s created doubts about the existing theory not only because of the persistence and worsening of unemployment, but because it constituted an anomaly for this theory, and this for two reasons. First, unemployment had become a worldwide phenomenon, and so could not be explained as the result of the specific circumstances of Britain. Secondly, and this was a point to which Keynes alluded in the *General Theory* (p. 9), money wages in the early 1930s had fallen sharply in the United States, but to no avail in so far as unemployment was concerned.[5] True, the price level had fallen even more. But this too was part of the anomaly that concerned Keynes: namely, that labour controlled only its money wage and might not have any way of reducing its real wage (1936: 13). Thus the unemployment of the 1930s was of a kind which the classical theory could not explain and which, therefore, called for a new theory.

The nature of this new theory – the central message of the *General Theory* – was identified by Keynes in a 1936 letter to Roy Harrod (reproduced in *Collected Writings* XIV: 85) as his theory of effective demand; and he went on to emphasize that a crucial element of this theory was 'the psychological law that, when income increases, the gap between income and consumption will increase' – that is, that the marginal propensity to consume is less than unity. That this is the central message of the book is also clear from the preface to it, in which Keynes tells us that, in contrast to his *Treatise* (whose primary concern was the interaction between the rate of interest and the price level), his new work is 'primarily a study of the forces which determine changes in the scale of output and employment as a whole.' In Chapter 3: 'The Principle of Effective Demand' of Book I: 'Introduction', Keynes then presents a 'summary of the theory of employment' that he will develop in the book (1936: 27), and he devotes most of the remaining chapters of the *General Theory* to this development.

Figure 2.1 reproduces the familiar 'Keynesian-cross' diagram which has served to transmit the central message of the *General Theory* to generations of economics students.[6] I wish, however, to refine the usual analysis which accompanies this diagram in one

Figure 2.1

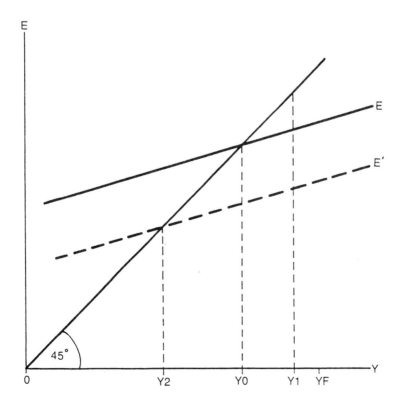

respect. In particular, what I mean by the theory of effective demand is not only that the intersection of the aggregate-demand curve $E = F(Y)$ with the 45° line determines equilibrium real output Y_0 at a level that may be below that of full employment Y_F; not only (as Leijonhufvud (1968) has also emphasized) that disequilibrium between aggregate demand and supply causes a change in output and not price; but also (and this is the distinctively novel feature) that the change in output (and hence income) itself acts as an equilibrating force. That is, if the economy is in a state of excess aggregate supply at (say) the level of output Y_1, then the resulting decline in output, and hence income, will depress supply more than demand and thus eventually bring the economy to equilibrium at Y_0. Or, in terms of the equivalent savings = investment equilibrium condition, the decline in income will decrease savings while leaving investment unchanged, and thus eventually eliminate the excess of savings over investment that exists at Y_1. In Keynes's words, 'The novelty in my treatment of saving and investment consists, not in my maintaining their necessary aggregate equality, but in the proposition that it is, not the rate of interest, but the level of incomes which (in conjunction with certain other factors) ensures this equality' (Keynes 1937: 211; cf. also 1936: 31, lines 16–23; 179, lines 2–6). In more formal terms (which, like the diagram, Keynes did not use), the theory of effective demand is concerned not only with the mathematical solution of the equilibrium equation $F(Y) = Y$, but with demonstrating the stability of this equilibrium as determined by the dynamic adjustment equation $dY/dt = \phi[F(Y) - Y]$, where $\phi' > 0$.

Correspondingly, as Keynes emphasizes in his letter to Harrod and elsewhere, a crucial assumption of his (Keynes's) analysis is that the marginal propensity to consume is less than unity, which in turn implies that the marginal propensity to save is greater than zero. For, if the marginal propensity to consume were equal to unity, no equilibrating mechanism would be activated by the decline in output. Specifically, as income (output) decreased, spending would decrease by exactly the same amount, so that any initial difference between aggregate demand and supply would remain unchanged. Alternatively, as income decreased, the initial excess of desired saving over investment would remain unchanged. Thus the system would be unstable.

This, then, is the major novelty of the *General Theory* and its central message: the theory of effective demand as a theory which depends on the equilibrating effect of the decline in output itself to explain why 'the economic system may find itself in stable equilibrium with N [employment] at a level below full employment, namely at the level given by the intersection of the aggregate demand function with the aggregate supply function' (1936: 30). Here was an explanation of the 'paradox of poverty in the midst of plenty' (ibid.) that then beset the Western world.

The foregoing analysis has been the stuff of introductory textbooks in economics for so many years that it is difficult today to conceive of the intellectual shock-wave that it first created. This shock – the radically different conceptual framework that the *General Theory* required of the profession – was due in good part to the very notion of an aggregate demand curve. For one of the points that had been greatly emphasized in Marshall's *Principles* – which then still served as a basic text – was that the demand function for a good could be defined only under the assumption of 'ceteris paribus'. Indeed, in order to insure that this assumption was fulfilled in practice, the more punctilious economists of those days were only willing to speak of the demand function for a good the total expenditure on which was small, so that variations in these expenditures as price varied would not significantly affect what Marshall called the 'marginal utility of money' (that is, the marginal utility of money expenditures: see

Marshall 1920: Book iii, chs iii and vi). How then could one validly speak of a demand function for the aggregate of all goods? How was it possible in such a case for 'other things to be held constant'? And even if this problem could be solved, how was it possible to talk about a demand for aggregate output as a whole that was in some way conceptually different from actual aggregate income, as if national income expended could somehow differ from national income received?

That is the way of science: that new ideas which at first seem strange and controversial ultimately percolate down to the textbooks and become commonplace.

The novelty of the foregoing analysis at the time that Keynes presented it can also be seen by contrasting it with the one he himself had presented only a few years earlier in the *Treatise*. Here – in his famous 'parable of the banana plantation' – Keynes considered an economy in an initial state of full employment in which a 'thrift campaign' is initiated. In the analytical framework of the *General Theory* as represented by Figure 2.1, such an increase in savings would be represented by a downward shift of the aggregate-demand curve in Figure 2.1 to E′; and the resulting decline in output would then cause a corresponding decline in the amount consumed (as well as in the amount saved) until a new equilibrium is necessarily reached at Y_2 (cf. 1936: 82–5, 183–4). In the *Treatise*, however, Keynes applied his 'fundamental equations for the value of money' to conclude that the resulting increased savings, unmatched by increased investment, will generate a downward spiral of employment, wages and output; and that

> there will be no position of equilibrium until either (a) all production ceases and the entire population starves to death, or (b) the thrift campaign is called off or peters out as a result of the growing poverty; or (c) investment is stimulated by some means or other so that its cost no longer lags behind the rate of saving.   (1930a: 159–60)

Though we should not take this first alternative seriously (a clear example of Keynes's propensity to shock his readers), the fact remains that none of these alternatives indicates that Keynes of the *Treatise* understood that the decline in output itself acts directly as a systematic endogenous equilibrating force. Instead, equilibrium is restored either by an exogenous decrease in savings or an exogenous increase in investments.

Figure 2.1 (the 'Keynesian-cross') depicts the essence of the theory of effective demand as presented in Book I of the *General Theory* under the explicit simplifying assumptions of a constant level of investment (which presupposes a constant rate of interest) and a constant money wage-rate (1936: 27–9). After elaborating on the various components of this simplified version of this theory in Books II and III, Keynes proceeds in Book IV to drop the assumption of a constant rate of interest and to explain its determination by means of his theories of liquidity preference and the marginal efficiency of capital, respectively. His theory at this point of the book is most conveniently represented by Hicks's (1937) famous IS–LM diagram, which explains the determination of the equilibrium levels of income and the rate of interest as the result of the interaction between the markets for commodities and money balances.

Finally, in Chapter 19 of Book V, Keynes drops the assumption of a constant money-wage rate and analyses the effects of a decline in it. His basic argument in this chapter is that a decline in money wages (which in practice would, because of the resistance of workers, take place only very slowly: 1936: 267; see also ibid.: 9, 251, 303) can increase the level of employment only by first increasing the level of effective demand; that the primary way it can generate such an increase is through its effect in increasing the quantity of money in terms of wage units, thereby decreasing the rate of interest and stimulating investment; that accordingly the policy of attempting to eliminate unemployment by reducing money wages is equivalent to a policy of attempting to do so by increasing the quantity of money at an unchanged wage rate and is accordingly subject to the same limitations as the latter: namely, that a moderate change 'may exert an inadequate influence over the long-term rate of interest', while an immoderate one (even if it were practicable) 'may offset its other advantages by its disturbing effect on confidence' (1936: 266–7). Hence Keynes's major conclusion – and indeed the negative component of his central message – that 'the economic system cannot be made self-adjusting along these lines' (1936: 267).

Thus Chapter 19 is the climax of the *General Theory*: it applies the analysis of the earlier chapters to demonstrate the basic proposition proclaimed at the beginning of the book: namely that, contrary to the 'classical' view, 'a willingness on the part of labour to accept lower money-wages is not necessarily a remedy for unemployment' – a claim that Keynes had promised would be 'fully elucidated . . . in Chapter 19' (1936: 18; see also bottom of 11).

Correspondingly, the analysis of Chapter 19 provides the explanation of Keynes's oft-cited enigmatic statement at the beginning of the *General Theory* that 'there may exist no expedient by which labour as a whole can reduce its *real* wage to a given figure by making revised *money* bargains with the entrepreneurs' (1936: 13, italics in original). For while in Chapter 2 of the *General Theory* Keynes rejected the 'second classical postulate' that 'the utility of the wage when a given volume of labour is employed is equal to the marginal disutility of that amount of employment' (which postulate means that workers supply all the labour that they would like to at any given real wage rate and are thus on their supply curve: that is, that full employment always exists), he accepted the first one that 'the wage is equal to the marginal product of labour' (which means that entrepreneurs are always on their demand curve for labour). And he also accepted the 'classical' law of diminishing returns, which implies that 'the real wage earned by a unit of labour has a unique (inverse) correlation with the volume of employment' (1936: 5, 17). Thus if a reduction in money wages does not succeed in affecting the level of effective demand, it will also not affect the level of output, hence the level of labour input, hence the marginal product of labour, and hence the real wage rate.

I must at this point emphasize that though I maintain the validity of IS–LM as an interpretation of the *General Theory*, I reject two contentions that have frequently been made about it in this connection: namely, the contentions that the validity of the argument of the *General Theory* is crucially dependent on the assumptions of absolute wage rigidity and/or the 'liquidity trap'. (For the *loci classici* of these contentions, see Hicks (1937) and especially Modigliani (1944).) The first of these contentions is refuted by Keynes's analysis in Chapter 19 discussed above. Furthermore, were the *General Theory* to depend on the assumption of wage rigidity, there would be no novelty to its message: for the fact that such a rigidity can generate unemployment was a commonplace of classical economics. Indeed, Keynes began the *General Theory* (p. 16) with a rejection of this explanation of involuntary unemployment. Needless to say, this does not mean that Keynes went to the opposite extreme of assuming wages to be perfectly flexible. Instead, his view of the real world was that 'moderate changes in employment are not associated with very great changes in money-wages' (1936: 251). At the same time, Keynes emphasizes that there exists an 'asymmetry' between the respective degrees of upward and downward wage flexibility: that, in particular, 'workers are disposed to resist a reduction in their money-rewards, and that there is no corresponding motive to resist an increase' (1936: 303). In so far as the 'liquidity trap' is concerned, here we have Keynes's own statement that 'whilst this limiting case might become practically important in the future, I know of no example of it hitherto' (1936: 207).

Both of the foregoing contentions stem from the mistaken attempt to interpret the *General Theory* as being concerned with a position of 'unemployment equilibrium' in the fullest sense of the term. For by definition there cannot be a state of long-run unemployment equilibrium in the sense that nothing in the system tends to change unless wages are rigid. Alternatively, if money wages are not rigid, then a necessary condition for equilibrium – in the sense of the level of unemployment remaining constant over time – is that the rate of interest remain constant; and a necessary condition for the rate of interest to remain constant in the face of an ever-declining money-wage and hence ever-increasing real quantity of money is that the economy be caught in the 'liquidity trap'. Once, however, we view the *General Theory* as being concerned with a succession of short-term Marshallian equilibrium positions as essentially described in its Chapter 19, then neither of the foregoing assumptions is necessary.

Thus in the strict sense of the term, the *General Theory* is, to my mind, a theory of unemployment *dis*equilibrium: it analyses the dynamic workings of an economy in which money wages and hence the rate of interest may be slowly falling, but in which 'chronic unemployment' (1936: 249) nevertheless continues to prevail, albeit with an intensity that may be changing over time (cf. Patinkin, 1956: chs xiii:1, xiv:1, and Supplementary Note K:3, reproduced unchanged in the 1965 edition; 1976a: 113–19).

This interpretation would seem to be in contradiction to Keynes's emphasis that one of his major accomplishments in this book was to have demonstrated the possible existence of 'unemployment equilibrium' (1936: 30, 242–3). I would like to suggest that the answer lies in a letter that Keynes wrote to Roy Harrod in August 1935, in reply to the latter's criticism that Keynes's discussions of the classical position were carried out in an unduly polemical style that exaggerated the differences between the two positions. In Keynes's words:

> the general effect of your reaction . . . is to make me feel that my assault on the classical school ought to be intensified rather than abated. My motive is, of course, not in order to get read. But it may be needed in order to get understood. I am frightfully afraid of the tendency, of which I see some signs in you, to appear to accept my constructive part and to find some accommodation between this and deeply cherished views which would in fact only be possible if my constructive part has been partially misunderstood. That is to say, I expect a great deal of what I write to be water off a duck's back. I am certain that it will be water off a duck's back unless I am sufficiently strong in my criticism to force the classicals to make rejoinders. I *want*, so to speak, to raise a dust: because it is only out of the controversy that will arise that what I am saying will get understood. (*Collected Works*, xiii: 548; italics in original)

And what could 'raise more dust' than a seemingly frontal attack on the 'deeply cherished' classical proposition that there could not exist a state of unemployment equilibrium? Conversely, what could be more easily 'accommodated' within the classical framework than the statement that a sharp decline in aggregate demand would, despite the resulting decline in the wage-unit, generate a prolonged period of involuntary unemployment and hence disequilibrium, but that true equilibrium would obtain only in a state of full employment?

Though the major concern of the *General Theory* is theory and not policy, its view on the latter is unmistakably, albeit most briefly, set out. Since one cannot depend on the 'self-adjusting character of the economic system' (1936: 257) to assure full employment, the government must undertake the responsibility for doing so by itself carrying out or subsidizing investment in order to assure the necessary level of aggregate demand. This is all that Keynes meant in his oft-quoted statement that 'a somewhat comprehensive socialisation of investment will prove the only means of securing an approximation to full employment' (1936: 164, 378).

In this connection I would like to emphasize three frequent misconceptions about Keynes's policy views. First, the *General Theory* advocates fiscal policy not as an alternative to monetary policy, but as one to be used together with it. Secondly, in sharp contrast to present-day monetarists, Keynes – in the *General Theory* as in the *Treatise* – meant by 'monetary policy' a policy whose target variable is, not the quantity of money, but the rate of interest. Thirdly, as hinted in the preceding paragraph, Keynes restricted the role of government to that of assuring full employment by proper monetary and fiscal policy; once this was achieved, the composition and distribution of this full-employment output could be left to be determined by market forces (1936: 378–9; see also his posthumously published 1946 article on 'The Balance of Payments in the United States').

Despite the many criticisms and discussions of the *General Theory* that followed its publication (cf., for example, the review articles by Harrod, Hicks, Leontief, Lerner, Meade, Pigou, Viner *et al.* reprinted in Lekachman, 1964, and Wood, 1983), its basic analytical structure not only remained intact, but also defined the research programme for both theoretical and empirical macroeconomics for decades to come. Truly a scientific achievement of the first order. The past two decades, however, have seen the emergence of basic criticisms of Keynesian economics from the viewpoint of both theory and policy. But before turning to these criticisms, let me first briefly indicate three important extensions that have been made of Keynesian economics in the years since the Second World War.

The first such extension was to growth theory. It was only natural that during the depression years of the 1930s few economists (and Keynes was no exception) were concerned with this problem. But when in the 1950s and 1960s economic growth became a major concern, the analytical framework of the *General Theory* served as the point of departure for many of the growth models which were then developed. In this context it is interesting to note the transformation that took place over the years in the attitude toward saving: whereas the spirit of the *General Theory* hovers over the early contributions by Harrod (1939) and Domar (1946), which regard the increase in potential savings generated by increasing income as a threat to full employment, and growth as the means (via the acceleration principle) of generating the level of investment necessary for absorbing these savings and thus eliminating this threat, the later contributions regard saving as a socially desirable act which provides the crucially necessary financing for the additional investment required for growth. Correspondingly, growth was transformed from being a means to an end to being an end in itself.

The second extension was to an open economy. Both before and after the *General Theory* – both in the *Tract* (1923) and *Treatise* (1930), on the one hand, and in the discussions toward the end of the Second World War which led to the Bretton Woods agreement, on the other – Keynes played a major role in dealing both theoretically and practically with the problems of international trade, finance and reserves in a world of fixed exchange rates and relatively free trade. There is, however, practically no reference to these problems in the *General Theory*. The explanation of this fact lies in the situation that prevailed in the Western world during the period that the *General Theory* was being written. In particular, this was the new world ushered in by England's abandonment of the gold standard in 1931: a world of flexible exchange rates and/or severe restrictions on the flow of international trade, in which the aforementioned problems had accordingly largely lost their relevance. Correspondingly, the analysis of the *General Theory* is carried out almost entirely on the implicit assumption of a closed economy.

The generalization of the *General Theory* to an open economy began almost immediately after its publication with Joan Robinson's (1937) well-known essay on 'Beggar-My-Neighbour Remedies for Unemployment'. The opening statement of this essay is that 'an increase in the balance of trade is equivalent to an increase in investment' and therefore has a similar multiplier effect on the equilibrium levels of income and employment. Shortly afterwards, Machlup (1939: 21–2) took account of the effect on the multiplier of the 'leakage into imports' generated by the increase in income. But several years were to pass before account was also taken of the effects on income and interest, via their effect on the domestic money supply, of international capital movements. Indeed, even though this question had been analysed by Meade (1951), and by Mundell (1963) and Fleming (1962), it was only in the 1970s, when such capital movements became of great importance in a Western world in which a regime of flexible exchange rates had replaced one of fixed rates, that this analysis was fully integrated into Keynesian economics. In terms of Hicks's famous diagram, one can thus roughly say that the extension of the *General Theory* to an open economy occurred in two stages: first, in taking account of such openness on the IS curve; secondly, and significantly later, in also doing so with respect to the LM curve. In any event, Keynesian economics today is unmistakably open macroeconomics in the fullest sense of the term.

The third extension was to problems of inflation. Here too was a problem that was of great interest to Keynes both before and after the *General Theory*. However, undoubtedly because of the deflationary conditions that then prevailed, it was not of much concern in that book, though Keynes did emphasize the undesirability of 'great instability of prices' (1936: 269). More generally, and in sharp contrast to the *Treatise* (whose central message revolved about the 'fundamental equations for the value of money': see Patinkin 1976a: chs 4–5), Keynes of the *General Theory* stated that 'the Theory of Prices falls into its proper place as a matter which is subsidiary to our general theory' (1936: 32).

In the case of inflation, Keynes himself, in his later *How to Pay for the War* (1940), played an important role in extending the analysis of the *General Theory* to one aspect of the problem, namely, demand inflation. I should also note that a recurrent theme of the *General Theory* (pp. 173, 249, 253, 296 and 301) is that as the level of employment in an economy increases as a result of an increase in effective demand, the money-wage rate begins to rise even before full employment is reached with consequent upward pressure on prices. In this theme there is some adumbration of the post-Second World War discussions of cost inflation generated by wage increases. It might also be interpreted as something of an adumbration of one aspect of the later Phillips-curve analysis: namely, the coexistence of inflation and unemployment (Phillips, 1958).

In the decade which followed Phillips's presentation of his empirically based curve, the inference that Keynesian economists drew from it was the inverse one: namely, that there was a tradeoff between the rate of inflation and the rate of unemployment, and that by increasing the former, one could decrease the latter (cf., for example, Samuelson and Solow 1960). As is well known, Friedman (1968b) and Phelps (1967, 1972) subsequently and quite rightly criticized this inference on the grounds that workers are concerned with their real, and not nominal, wage, so that the position of the Phillips curve depends on their price expectations (the expectations-augmented Phillips curve). Correspondingly, as these expectations are adjusted to the rate of inflation, the tradeoff disappears and the economy returns to the 'natural rate of unemployment', which is the term that Friedman coined to denote what had hitherto been called 'frictional unemployment', and which is accordingly the rate that corresponds to 'full employment'.

What must, however, be emphasized is that though this has generally been the long-run effect of inflation, there has generally also been a prolonged short-run period during which a tradeoff has taken place. Thus the expectations-augmented Phillips curve can be incorporated into the Keynesian system as interpreted above: namely, as a dynamic system whose level of unemployment varies over time.

In this connection I should like to point out that the term 'natural rate of unemployment' (which has long since become established in the literature) is misleading: for it has the connotation of a rate that is 'naturally' – that is, in the natural course of events and without too much difficulty – established by the automatic workings of the economic system. But this implication is at variance with the empirical evidence of prolonged periods of unemployment at rates significantly higher than the one that would result from frictional unemployment alone (cf., for example, Murphy and Topel, 1987). Thus the term 'natural rate of unemployment' begs the basic policy question which Keynes raised in the *General Theory*: namely, whether one can in practice rely on the 'self-adjusting quality of the economic system' for the achievement of full employment, a question which (for reasons exposited in Chapter 19 of the book) Keynes answered in the negative.

During the first two decades after the Second World War, Keynesian economics became increasingly accepted and by the end of the 1950s it reigned supreme in both theory and practice. The policies it advocated resulted in the United States in low rates of unemployment and inflation and high rates of growth. This situation changed sharply in the early 1970s, at which time the economy began to experience what was a contradiction to the teachings of Keynesian economics: high rates of both unemployment and inflation, or what was frequently called 'stagflation'. This was the basic cause of a 'crisis in Keynesian economics' which in turn generated basic criticisms of both its premises and conclusions.

I have already discussed the way in which those criticisms manifested themselves in connection with the Phillips curve. There are two other major criticisms that I should now like to comment upon briefly: namely, those that have emanated from monetarism and from the rational-expectations approach, respectively.

With respect to policy, the claim of monetarism has been that the functional relation between the quantity of money and the level of national income (the velocity of circulation) is more stable than that between government spending and national income (the multiplier), and that accordingly monetary policy whose target variable was the quantity of money was preferable to fiscal policy. The validity of this claim is thus crucially dependent on the stability of the demand curve for money in the real world. Though empirical studies showed that such stability did exist for many years in the United States, this has not been the case since the mid-1970s (see, for example, Judd and Scadding, 1982; Roley, 1985; and references there cited).

Over the years there has been a narrowing of the distance between Keynesians and monetarists as the former – undoubtedly under the influence of the latter, as well as of the force of contemporary economic developments – have attached more importance to the role of the quantity of money in both theory and practice. (I must, however, remind the reader that Keynes himself continued to attach great importance to monetary policy – in his sense of the term – even in the *General Theory*: see above.) From this viewpoint one can rightly say that (except for the real-business-cycle theorists) 'we are all monetarists now'. But to this I must immediately add that from the viewpoint of the theory of the demand for money, 'we are all Keynesians' – not only now, but since the beginnings of the 'monetarist counterrevolution' as marked by Friedman's 1956 article. For though Friedman based his views in that article (as well as in his 1968 encyclopaedia article) on what he called 'a reformulation of the quantity theory' – and what has come to be called 'the modern quantity theory' – this 'reformulation' is more closely related to Keynes's liquidity-preference theory than to the traditional quantity theory (Patinkin 1969, 1972, 1974).

Might I also observe that today there seems to be fairly wide agreement that Keynesianism and monetarism share another characteristic: namely, that neither has provided an adequate explanation of, and corresponding policy proposals for, the macroeconomic problems of unemployment and/or inflation of recent years. Thus what we have really been confronted with in these years is not only a 'crisis in Keynesian economics' but a 'crisis in macroeconomics'.

Let me finally make a few remarks about 'the new classical macroeconomics'.[7] Here I must distinguish between two of its aspects: the assumption of rational expectations and the assumption of market equilibrium. While I feel that in the hands of some of its advocates the assumption of rational expectations has led to irrational extremes (for example, the short-run vertical Phillips curve; more generally, the complete neutrality of anticipated policy), it rightly emphasizes the point that government policy is not exogenous to the economy; that agents do form expectations with respect to it, and especially with respect to its credibility; and that these most rational expectations have an important influence on the success with which such policies can be carried out. I should, however, point out that this is a valid criticism not only of Keynesian policy proposals, but of practically all proposals that preceded the 'rational-expectations revolution'. And much the same can be said for the criticism that has been based on the danger that the purposes of policy can be thwarted by destabilizing lags, a danger that has been analysed and rightly emphasized by Friedman in his influential 1961 article. In brief, the economic realities of the past two decades, and the theoretical developments which they stimulated, have dispelled what we now see to be the naïveté of the earlier approach to policy that characterized our profession as a whole. And this should be cause for humility with respect to the approaches that are today being espoused.

In so far as the assumption of market equilibrium is concerned, this is clearly the antithesis of Keynesian economics and – except in the tautological sense that 'everyone "wants" to do whatever he is doing at the moment; otherwise he would not do it' (Patinkin 1956: 211–12; 1965: 313–14) – is contradicted by the significant levels of unemployment that frequently characterize the real world. The alternative analytical approach (manifested in the interpretation of the *General Theory* above) is that of market disequilibrium generated by quantity constraints (see Patinkin 1956: ch. 13; 1965: *idem*; Barro and Grossman 1971 and 1976; Benassy 1987, and references there cited). Indeed, one of the major issues of macroeconomic theory today is the choice between these two approaches.

In this connection I should like to conjecture that, as one who had seen how the most civilized countries of the world engaged for four long years of stalemated trench warfare in the mutual slaughter of the best of their young men, Keynes was not predisposed to believe in natural forces that always brought agents to generate a mutually beneficial situation. Because of the co-ordination problem generated by the uncertainty of how others react to our actions, the actual world for Keynes was one that – in a macroeconomic context – could readily lead to mutually destructive results of the Prisoner's Dilemma; not to the mutually satisfactory ones of the Walrasian auctioneer.[8]

In this context I should like to make two further observations. First, a recurrent theme of Keynes's writings was that if only economy-wide co-ordination could be achieved, a simultaneous equi-proportionate reduction in all wages could be a solution to the problem of unemployment. This theme first appeared in his *Economic Consequences of Mr Churchill* (1925: 211, 228–9), where Keynes explained that a simultaneous 10 per cent reduction in all money wages – and in this case, in all prices as well – could in principle effect a devaluation in real terms and thus solve the problem of unemployment that had been created by Britain's return to the gold standard at prewar parity, thus overvaluing the pound. It appears again and repeatedly in the *Treatise* (1930a: 141, 151, 244–5, 265 and 281), where a simultaneous equi-proportionate reduction of money wages (prices being held constant) is described as a hypothetical way of reducing real wages and thus eliminating the losses of firms and consequent unemployment. And it also appears in the *General Theory* (1936: 265, 267 and 269). Indeed, in a passage which reminds one of the basic point of departure many years later of Lucas's 1973 article (that classic of the 'new classical macroeconomics') about the practical difficulty that an economic agent faces in deciding whether a change in the price of a good with which he is concerned constitutes a change in its relative price (which calls for a reaction on his part) or whether it is part of a change in the general price level (which, if generated by a monetary expansion, does not), Keynes explained that

> any individual or group of individuals, who consent to a reduction of money-wages relatively to others, will suffer a *relative* reduction in real wages, which is a sufficient justification for them to resist it. On the other hand it would be impracticable to resist every reduction of real wages, due to a change in the purchasing-power of money which affects all workers alike; and in fact reductions of real wages arising in this way are not, as a rule, resisted unless they proceed to an extreme degree.   (1936: 14, italics in original)[9]

And the same would (in Keynes's view) be true for a reduction in real wages generated by a simultaneous and instantaneous reduction in all money wages. Furthermore such a reduction would be over before any adverse expectations could be generated.

This was the rationale of Keynes's statement in the *General Theory* that:

> To suppose that a flexible wage policy is a right and proper adjunct of a system which on the whole is one of *laissez-faire*, is the opposite of the truth. It is only in a highly authoritarian society, where sudden, substantial, all-round changes could be decreed that a flexible wage-policy could function with success. One can imagine it in operation in Italy, Germany or Russia, but not in France, the United States or Great Britain.   (1936: 269)

The experience of Eastern European countries in the last two decades has shown us that this is a somewhat naïve notion of what even a totalitarian government can do. In any event, this passage – and the context in which it and the other passages cited above appear – makes it clear that Keynes's purpose was not to advocate wage flexibility as a means of eliminating unemployment, but to provide a 'negative proof' of the impracticability of such a policy for a democratic society, which by its very nature cannot enforce the simultaneous economy-wide co-ordination necessary to achieve this mutually beneficial end.

My second observation is that the above is not intended to deny that the 'new classical macroeconomics' has made an important contribution in insisting that we should try to provide a rigorous theoretical explanation of the existence of wage stickiness as well as of long periods of unemployment at levels significantly higher than the frictional one. This remains a problem at the frontiers of research on'which much work is now being done.[10]

In order to understand why the *General Theory* had such a revolutionary'impact on the profession – and indeed on the general public – we must take account of the circumstances that prevailed when it burst on the scene. It was a time of fear and darkness as the Western world searched desperately for an explanation of the unprecedented and seemingly endless depression that was creating untold misery for millions of unemployed and even threatening the viability of its democratic institutions. Indeed, largely as a result of the widespread social unrest caused by the mass unemployment, a totalitarian government had already taken power in Italy and a far more evil and oppressive one was doing so in Germany. And the appearance of the *General Theory* in 1936 offered not only an explanation, but also a confident and theoretically supported prescription for ending depressions within a democratic framework by proper government policies. Thus the *General Theory* provided an answer not only to a theoretical problem but to a burning political and social one as well.

At the same time, the fact that the theoretical revolution embodied in Keynes's *General Theory* took place concurrently with the Colin Clark–Simon Kuznets revolution in national-income measurement further increased its impact on the profession: for those measurements made possible the quantification of the analytical categories of the *General Theory*, hence the empirical estimation of its functional relationships, and hence its application to policy problems (Patinkin 1976b).

Let me finally say that the work over the years of students of Keynes's thought has deepened our understanding of the *General Theory*, but has also pointed out deficiencies and errors. Some of these are due to stylistic excesses; some are inconsequential mathematical ones; but some are more significant (cf. Patinkin 1987: sec. 10). But even these last should be regarded as the kind that naturally occur in a pioneering work that breaks new ground and develops a radically different analytical framework. We do no service to Keynes's place in the history of economic thought – and *a fortiori* not to the history itself – by ignoring or trying to explain away these errors. At the same time, they do not change the basic fact that this is the book that made the revolution which has continued to mould our basic ways of thinking about macroeconomic problems. And so the reading of it, at least in part, is an intellectual experience that no aspiring economist even today can afford to forgo.

To this I add the following related plea. In reading the *General Theory*, let us do so in order to acquaint ourselves with one of the classics of our discipline and, more generally, in order to enjoy the pleasures of intellectual history: not in order to invoke Keynes's alleged authority with respect to further developments in macroeconomic theory. By making a clear distinction between this objective and that of the history of thought we do a service to both: for we then permit the study of Keynes's thought to concern itself not with what Keynes might have said or should have said about current theoretical questions, but with what he actually did say; and we permit the attempts to improve upon the current state of macroeconomic theory to be judged substantively, on their own merits, without confusing the issue with arguments about 'what Keynes really meant'. As Keynes said in concluding a long and tiresome correspondence in 1938 on a note that some economist had sent him on an aspect of the *General Theory*, 'the enclosed, as it stands looks to me more like theology than economics! . . . I am really driving at something extremely plain and simple which cannot possibly deserve all this exegesis' (*Collected Works* XXIX: 282).

NOTES

*   This article was originally published in German translation in H. C. Recktenwald (ed.), *Lord Keynes – Opus und Vita Heute* (Düsseldorf: Verlag Wirtschaft und Finanzen 1989). It appears here with the kind permission of the publishers.

** I wish to acknowledge with thanks the support of the Central Research Fund of the Hebrew University of Jerusalem. This paper was completed whilst I was serving as Visiting Professor at the University of California, Los Angeles during the academic year 1988–9. In this connection I am indebted to Sebastian Edwards, Roger Farmer, Seonghan Oh and Guido Tabellini for valuable comments on an earlier draft. I have a similar debt to Alan Blinder, Stanley Fischer, Peter Howitt and David Laidler. Needless to say, the usual proviso obtains with respect to the sole responsibility of the author for the view expressed.

1. I have in this essay drawn freely on the material in Patinkin 1976a, 1982, 1984 and 1987, to which the reader is referred for further details. References to the *General Theory* are to any of the various printings of this book, all of which are paginated in the same way. All other references to Keynes's writing are to the form in which they appear in the relevant volumes (most of which were edited by Donald Moggridge) of the Royal Economic Society's edition of his *Collected Writings*. This 30-volume edition – to paraphrase one of the famous passages of the *Treatise* (1936a: 125) – is verily a widow's cruse from which students of the development of Keynes's thought will continue to draw materials for years to come, without diminution in the profits of scholarship.

2. See the full-length biographies by Harrod (1951), Moggridge (1980), and Skidelsky (1983 and 1989).

3. See also Laudan (1977: ch. 1).

4. As Hutchison (1968: 277–9) has emphasized, other British economists at the time also distinguished between theory and policy when it came to reducing money wages.

5. From 1929 to 1933, money wages (as measured by average hourly earnings) fell in the United States by 28 per cent (US Department of Commerce, *Historical Statistics of the United States* (1960: 92)).

6. Though in its use of income instead of employment this diagram differs from the presentation in Chapter 3 of the *General Theory*, it captures its essence.

7. On this question, see the excellent articles by Peter Howitt (1986a,b).

8. For a game-theorètic approach that explains how lack of co-ordination can generate Keynesian unemployment, see Cooper and John (1988) and references there cited. This paper is an example of the 'New-Keynesian Revival' which attempts to rationalize the Keynesian theory of unemployment in a way that deals with the criticisms levelled by the 'new classical macroeconomics'. See Fischer (1988: 315–25) and the references there cited; see also Howitt (1986b).

9. Keynes made a similar distinction in his *Economic Consequences of Mr Churchill* (1925) (see Keynes 1925: 211).

10. Cf. the literature cited in the survey articles by Fischer (1988), Mankiw (1988) and Katz (1988).

3.   A Glimpse of the Invisible Hand

William J. Baumol

> As every individual endeavours as much as he can . . . to employ his capital . . . that
> its produce may be of the greatest value; every individual necessarily labours to render
> the annual revenue of the society as great as he can. He generally, indeed, neither intends
> to promote the public interest, nor knows how much he is promoting it . . . by directing
> that industry in such a manner as its produce may be of the greatest value, he intends only
> his own gain, and he is in this, as in many other cases, led by an invisible hand to promote
> an end which was no part of his intention. Nor is it always the worse for the society that
> it was no part of it.
>
> Adam Smith 1776: 423

This chapter undertakes to show that the message of the invisible-hand passage and, consequently, that of *The Wealth of Nations* more generally, is often misconstrued, that its relationship to the Arrow–Debreu theorem on the optimality of perfectly competitive general equilibrium is quite distant, and that its philosophical orientation is in *some* respects quite foreign to that of a modern welfare theorist, though in other ways the two are entirely compatible. Some of what will be reported here has already been said quite definitively by those giants of the field, Professor Viner and Lord Robbins, but their evidence and conclusions do not seem to have entered the consciousness of economists unspecialized in the history of economic ideas. Nevertheless, there are several ways in which the discussion that follows may add to their contribution, and it may perhaps even help in the dissemination of their ideas.

Specifically, this chapter will undertake to demonstrate four conclusions:

1. That the welfare theory of Smith's book is primarily a doctrine about the incentives for the maximization of the value of total output, interpreted as an undisaggregated macro entity, rather than an analysis claiming to demonstrate optimality in the *composition* of that aggregate, that is, optimality in the *allocation of resources among the various individual outputs* that constitute that aggregate;

2. that the theory is not intended as an argument for minimization of the economic role of government – favouring a state of 'anarchy plus the policeman', and that Smith actually called for a very considerable level of economic activity on the part of the state, and explicitly used both the externalities and the public-goods arguments;

3. that the invisible-hand doctrine was one in which religious elements were involved deeply and explicitly, representing the culmination of a two-century philosophical debate, and that Smith's viewpoint was, as a result, quite foreign to the determinedly secular orientation of economics since the beginning of the nineteenth century;

4. that Smith's basic conclusion was the reliability of the pursuit of self-interest – of the 'profit motive' – as an instrument for the promotion of public interest, and of the

unreliability of appeals to voluntary exercise of virtue as a primary means to achieve that purpose. In effect, then, Smith's main message, on this interpretation, was the predictability of the failure of economies like those of Eastern Europe under communism to produce living standards comparable with those of the market economies.

Except for the third of these items – Smith's view on the appropriate role of government in the economy – we shall find part of the evidence in the invisible-hand passage itself. But in each case the evidence goes well beyond that, and indicates clearly that the doctrine's intended moral is very different from that which nonspecialists appear to believe it to be.

THE INVISIBLE HAND AND OPTIMALITY IN RESOURCE ALLOCATION

The welfare-maximizing properties of perfect competition are often described, quite illuminatingly, as optimality in resource *allocation*; that is, the picture is that of a stock of resources with a set of alternative uses available to it, and a market mechanism that automatically shifts those resources from one use to another until there remains no unused opportunity for increasing one output without decreasing any other, or for increasing the welfare of any person without damaging that of another. In sum, the modern welfare doctrine entails a subtle analysis of the available alternatives, of the *allocation* of resources among outputs, and of the forces shifting the resources from one use to another, toward an equilibrium in which the optimal usage pattern is achieved.

The point here is that Smith's welfare analysis reached no such level of sophistication. It is true that the shifting of resources among alternative uses does play a clear and critical role in his analysis. This is so, in particular, in the allocation of capital resources, which is assigned the role of elimination of abnormally high profits in any particular field of enterprise, and of bringing the prices of all commodities in competitive fields to their equilibrium levels; that is, into equality with average costs, including the cost (the normal rate of profit) of the required capital.

Yet Smith does not make much of this as the way in which, in his view, the market mechanism serves the general welfare. His point here is considerably more simple-minded. It asserts that the market mechanism elicits from each individual the unstinting expenditure of effort, and effort carried out in a way that is calculated to yield the combination of outputs that is valued most highly by the market. In other words, his conclusion is that the market mechanism elicits a maximal *value of aggregate output*, with little attention devoted to subtleties about the composition of that output.

Here, the invisible-hand passage, quite rightly accepted as the centrepiece of Smithian welfare analysis, is indeed the place to look for confirmation of this conclusion. And a careful reading reveals no hint of any preoccupation with resource *allocation*. Rather, we find only the bald and categorical statement that

> as every individual endeavours as much as he can . . . to employ his capital that its produce may be of the greatest value; every individual necessarily labours to render the annual revenue of the society as great as he can.

The meaning of that assertion seems sufficiently unambiguous.

I know of only one passage in which Smith associates the welfare properties of the market mechanism with resource allocation:

> the private interests and passions of individuals naturally dispose them to turn their stock towards the employments which in ordinary cases are most advantageous to the society. But if from this natural preference they should turn too much of it towards those employments, the fall of profit in them and the rise of it in all others immediately dispose them to alter this faulty distribution. Without any intervention of law, therefore, the private interests and passions of men naturally lead them to divide and distribute the stock of every society, among all the different employments carried on in it, as nearly as possible in the proportion which is most agreeable to the interest of the whole society.   (1776: 594–5)

However, this is an isolated passage devoted not to welfare issues in general but to a particular topic relating to international trade (the allocation of capital between 'a distant [and] a near employment'). It is no more appropriate to rely on this as a description of Smith's welfare theory than it is to use his remarks on the differential returns to mines as the basis for a claim that he had mastered the 'Ricardian' model of differential rent. It is perhaps true that if Smith had been offered a general description of the resource allocation structure of today's welfare theory he would not have found it uncongenial. But that is far from saying that Smith's very simple model encompasses much more than his discussion explicitly describes.

SMITH AND THE ECONOMIC ROLE OF GOVERNMENT

Lord Robbins (1952: Lecture II) has documented effectively the extensive economic role that Smith assigned to the state. Actually, as Robbins emphasized, this should come as no surprise to anyone who has read *The Wealth of Nations* even with minimal care. When Smith comes to his discussion of the proper role of the state (Book V) he tells us that there are three broad tasks that fall within this category. Two of them are not likely to be considered economic – national defence and the administration of justice both have their economic implications, but governmental activity in either arena can hardly be interpreted as economic intervention or as curtailment of the workings of the market. However, the third of the great tasks Smith assigns to government is so broad and prospectively of such magnitude as to be consistent with a public sector of the economy that is enormous – of the sort that one observes in the most socialistic of the mixed economies of today's Western Europe. Indeed, Smith's description of the task is so permissive that one can only wonder at the small number of writers who have remarked upon it. In Smith's words it is

> the duty of erecting and maintaining certain public works and certain institutions, which it can never be for the interest of any individual, or small number of individuals, to erect and maintain; because the profit could never repay the expense to any individual or small number of individuals, though it may frequently do much more than repay it to a great society.   (1776: 651)

There are two points to be noted here. First, there is Smith's recognition that there are economic activities which generate net benefits to society and yet which can never be profitable to private enterprise. In other words, he recognizes that the fact that a project contributes to the social welfare does not automatically make it, even prospectively, into a source of profit. Secondly, Smith has no hesitation about government undertaking the provision of such privately unprofitable goods or services.

It is true that Smith does not tell us at this point why such divergences between the public interest and the pursuit of profit may arise. But elsewhere Smith indicated that his understanding of the issue was strikingly modern. Lord Robbins (1952: 31) drew our attention to a passage in which the externality argument for intervention is laid out quite explicitly, *and generalized beyond the particular issue that gives rise to Smith's discussion at that point in the book*:

> Such regulations [prohibiting small bank notes] may, no doubt, be considered as in some respect violation of natural liberty. But those exertions of the natural liberty of a few individuals, which might endanger the security of the whole society are, and ought to be, restrained by the laws of all governments . . . the obligation of building party walls, in order to prevent the communication of fire, is a violation of natural liberty, exactly of the same kind with the regulations of the banking trade which are here proposed.   (1776: 308)

There are several things to be noted about this passage. First, though the notion of externalities is introduced as part of a discussion of a narrow banking issue, Smith is emphatic in pointing out that he is dealing with a general principle with broad application to matters as remote from banking as rules requiring the construction of fire-resistant walls to prevent the spread of conflagration. Secondly, Smith recognizes that government intervention here does represent a restriction of 'natural liberty'; but he goes on at once to tell us that it is a restriction of natural liberty such as every government does and *should* impose. In other words, he clearly recognized that the presence of an externality of sufficient severity does call for intervention by government in order to protect the public interest.

In Smith's earlier Glasgow lectures (as reported in the notes of two anonymous students) he also provided a very clear description of the public-goods argument:

> the fish of the sea and rivers are naturally common to all; but the same incroaching spirit that appropriated the game to the king and his nobles extended also to the fishes . . .
> Besides those things already mentioned there are many others that are to be considered as common to all, as they can not be lessened or impaired by use, nor can any one be injured by use of them. Thus the air is necessary to be breathed by all, and is not rendered less fit or less in quality for the use of others. . . . In the same manner the water of rivers and the navigation of them, the navigation or right of sailing on the sea, is common to all. No one is injured by such use being made of them by another.   (1762–3, Anon. 1978: 24–6)

This discussion, it is true, is not directly linked by Smith to the possibility that government intervention will be desirable. However, there is recognition of the 'market failure' that results from the presence of public goods.

It is clear, then, that Smith had recognized and understood, at least at some point, the bulk of the circumstances in which, according to the welfare analysis of today, government intervention may be justified. Moreover, he elevated the economic role of government into an important general principle – into one of the three tasks that fall to a responsible state.

In saying this, however, I must not be misunderstood to be claiming that Smith favoured 'big government', or that he believed government should engage in extensive economic activity and undertake any substantial programme of nationalization. Wherever there was no reason to doubt the ability of private enterprise to contribute effectively to the wealth of the nation Smith clearly preferred the private firm to the public enterprise. Many passages can be cited to this effect. For example, he emphasized the wastefulness of state enterprises: 'The agents of a prince regard the wealth of their master as inexhaustible; are careless at which price they buy; are careless at what price they sell' (1776: 771).

Yet Smith's defence of 'natural liberties' and his advocacy of *laissez-faire* emphatically did not extend to the emasculation of government in its economic roles. Indeed, so far as I have been able to find, he was adamant in seeking to have government abstain *almost* completely from only two activities: from arbitrary restrictions upon imports and other mercantilistic restraints of international trade, and from governmental grants of monopolies to individuals or private firms, the source of monopoly to which all the discussion of the subject in Smith's work seems to have been directed. But even freedom of trade to Smith did not, apparently, preclude intervention by government in this arena when it is justified by considerations of national defence, or the imposition of (non-prohibitive) customs duties when called for by the financial needs of the state. After all, he is reputed to have carried out the duties of his last post as collector of customs with a degree of dedication that was surprising to his contemporaries, who had expected him to treat the position as the sinecure it was intended to be.

THEOLOGICAL BACKGROUND OF THE INVISIBLE-HAND DOCTRINE

The term 'invisible hand' seems generally to be interpreted today as a felicitous metaphor, as a well-chosen phrase describing the impersonal workings of that human institution, the market. But in the eighteenth century those words had a connotation that was entirely different. The unambiguous reference was to the Hand of God. The term was no metaphor, and it is not used in that way by Smith. He does not speak of man being led *as though* by an invisible hand; rather an invisible hand does actually do the leading ('he is in this, as in many other cases, led by an invisible hand'). The term was in common use: it is employed in a similar sense in Smith's *Theory of Moral Sentiments* (1790: Part IV, Chapter 1[1]), it occurs repeatedly in George Washington's letters to his mother, and it is a trivial matter to find it elsewhere in eighteenth-century writings. Readers used to the secular viewpoint of contemporary economists, in whose writings no hint of religious element is to be found, will perhaps find this conclusion implausible and, perhaps, a bit shocking. But this only represents cultural provincialism on our own part, and resistance to the *Weltanschauung* of an earlier era. Jacob Viner, who studied the matter as carefully as anyone has, told us:

> Modern professors of economics and of ethics operate in disciplines which have been secularized to the point where the religious elements and implications which once were an integral part of them have been painstakingly eliminated. . . . However, I am obliged to insist that Adam Smith's system of thought, including his economics, is not intelligible if one disregards the role he assigns in it to the teleological elements, to the 'invisible hand'. (1972: 81–2)

There is more to the story than the fact that in the eighteenth century religion still played a greater role in scholarly thought than it does today. That fact alone might well strike the reader as a curiosum of little relevance to what one should get out of Smith's welfare analysis today. But there is a long history underlying the role of the invisible hand in promotion of the public welfare, a history of which Smith's work can be interpreted as the culmination. Albert Hirschman (1977) has traced this history in a delightful and scholarly volume whose small size disguises its rich contents. A rough summary of the tale, sacrificing accuracy to brevity, is that Renaissance philosophers, having gone beyond reliance on faith alone, began to seek an explanation of the role of human selfishness in a world designed by the deity. Did man's pursuit of self-interest, disregarding the welfare of others, not represent a blemish in the work of the deity, and did it not damage severely the workings of society?

A group of distinguished writers, including Francis Bacon, Pascal and Montesquieu, grappled with the issue and, at least in some cases, resolved it by asserting that the natural order contained a mechanism in which the self-interested 'passions' of one individual served to offset those of another; that is, in which the selfish drives of the different members of society served to neutralize one another. But the mechanism by which the consequences were extinguished tended to be described in terms which constituted better poetry than dispassionate explanation of a concrete mechanism. An example is Bacon's use of simile to explain how the 'passions' or 'affections' of different people can be played off against each other: 'I say . . . set affection against affection . . . to master one by another: even as we used to hunt beast with beast and fly bird with bird' (Francis Bacon, as quoted in Hirschman 1977: 22).

Smith's work can be interpreted as a culminating entry in this literature that improved upon its predecessors in at least two ways. First, it did provide the missing mechanism – the market under competitive conditions, which imposed such severe constraints upon the individual that he could only serve his own interests by doing those things that promote the general welfare.[2] Secondly, in Smith's analysis pursuit of self-interest by different individuals was not merely self-*neutralizing*. Much more than that, it constituted the basis of an incredibly ingenious arrangement, in which self-interest actually supplied the fuel by which the general interest was *promoted*. Without pursuit of self-interest the competitive mechanism would lose its effectiveness.

The theological element in Smith's argument can usefully be caricatured as the observation that God's first-best solution having been undermined with the expulsion from Eden, the deity came up with a masterly second-best arrangement: the competitive mechanism. The fall of Adam and Eve released human selfishness; the market mechanism did not stop at offsetting its evil effects, but actually harnessed it as the prime means for the achievement of well-being for all. Still, the market mechanism is only a second-best solution that universal virtue might have rendered unnecessary.

It seems to me that this last portion of my interpretation is confirmed when Smith, at one point in *The Theory of Moral Sentiments*, offers an unambiguous statement on the relative merits of beneficence enforced by virtue as against beneficence enforced by the market:

> All the members of human society stand in need of each other's assistance. . . . Where the necessary assistance is reciprocally afforded from love, from gratitude, from friendship, and esteem, the society flourishes and is happy . . .
>
> But though the necessary assistance should not be afforded from such generous and disinterested motives, though among the different members of the society there should be no mutual love and affection, the society, though less happy and agreeable . . . may subsist among different men, as among different merchants, from a sense of its utility, without any mutual love or affection; and though no man in it should owe any obligation, or be bound in gratitude to any other, it may still be upheld by a mercenary exchange of good offices according to an agreed valuation. (1790: Part II, Section 2, Chapter III)

In other words, the market *can* serve as a substitute for harmonious pursuit of virtue and mutual promotion of one another's welfare by the members of society. But the market solution is only second-best. That is the view of *The Theory of Moral Sentiments*.[3] Unfortunately, *The Wealth of Nations* adds, the non-market solution, even if superior in principle, is unworkable, indeed Utopian.

The preceding discussion is not meant to deal only with the theological side of Smith's position. Rather, it is intended to lead us up to the secular implications of the doctrine, to the key elements in Smith's welfare analysis, elements that continue to be pertinent today. It is to these that I turn next.

SELF-INTEREST VERSUS VOLUNTARISM AS INSTRUMENTS OF PUBLIC WELFARE

The first chapter of *The Wealth of Nations*, with its renowned description of the division of labour in a pin factory, is followed immediately with a discussion of equally merited fame of the means by which individuals arrange for their wants to be met. It is this second chapter which is crucial for comprehension of the fundamental message of the invisible-hand passage.

> man has almost constant occasion for the help of his brethren, and it is in vain for him to expect it from their benevolence only. He will be more likely to prevail if he can interest their self-love in his favour, and shew them that it is for their own advantage to do for him what he requires of them. Who ever offers to another a bargain of any kind, proposes to do this: Give me that which I want, and you shall have this which you want, is the meaning of every such offer and it is in this manner that we obtain from one another the far greater part of those good offices which we stand in need of. It is not from the benevolence of the butcher, the brewer, or the baker, that we expect our dinner, but from their regard to their own interest. We address ourselves, not to their humanity but to their self-love, and never talk to them of our own necessities but of their advantages.   (1776: 14)

The message of this passage cannot be clearer. One cannot rely on good will or moral dedication on the part of suppliers to ensure that wants will be met. Only if it is clear to those suppliers that their own interests will be served by meeting those wants can one be confident that the task will be carried out: 'It is not from the benevolence of the butcher, the brewer, or the baker that we expect our dinner, but from their regard to their own interest.' Moreover, it is pointless to do otherwise: 'it is in vain for him to expect it from their benevolence only'.[4]

The placement of this discussion at the very opening of the book,[5] together with the fact that the same discussion with the same example[6] appears in both reports of Smith's Glasgow lectures of the previous decade (Anon. 1978, report of Smith's 1762–3 lectures: 347–8; report of 1766: 493) suggests strongly that this was a matter of fundamental importance to him; that it, along with the division of labour, was a matter crucial for the understanding of the sources of the wealth of nations.

Moreover, careful rereading of the invisible-hand passage confirms that the same notion is clearly being repeated there, and that it is, indeed, a central part of the message.

> [The individual] generally, indeed, neither intends to promote the public interest, nor knows how much he is promoting it. . . . By pursuing his own interest he frequently promotes that of the society more effectually than when he really intends to promote it. I have never known much good done by those who affected to trade for the public good. It is an affectation, indeed, not very common among merchants, and very few words need be employed in dissuading them from it.   (1776: 423)

Smith tells us also, on similar grounds, that where rewards are divorced from performance, society is apt to be short-changed. It will be recalled that Smith uses university professors as a prime example:

> In every profession, the exertion of the greater part of those who exercise it, is always in proportion to the necessity they are under of making that exertion. This necessity is greatest with those to whom the emoluments of their profession are the only source from which they expect their fortune, or even their ordinary revenue and subsistence . . .
>
> In [some] universities the teacher is prohibited from receiving any honorary or fee from his pupils, and his salary constitutes the whole of the revenue which he derives from his office. His interest is, in this case, set as directly in opposition to his duty as it is possible to set it. It is the interest of every man to live as much at his ease as he can; and if his emoluments are to be precisely the same, whether he does, or does not perform some very laborious duty, it is certainly his interest, at least as interest is vulgarly understood, either to neglect it altogether, or, if he is subject to some authority which will not suffer him to do this, to perform it in as careless and slovenly a manner as that authority will permit. . . . In the university of Oxford, the greater part of the public professors have, for these many years, given up altogether even the pretence of teaching.[7] (1776: 423)

I conclude that Smithian welfare economics is, above all, an analysis of the way in which the market mechanism harnesses selfishness in the service of the general welfare, about the constant danger that this beneficent mechanism will be undermined by those who find themselves severely constrained by it, and about the unavailability of any effective alternative, most notably the futility of appeals to voluntary exercise of the precepts of morality as a substitute for pursuit of self-interest as a means to contribute to economic welfare.

This viewpoint has, of course, been inherited by those who belong to the mainstream of today's economic analysis. Economists are displaying just this heritage when they argue for rules to make the polluters pay as the most effective means for protection of the environment, and express scepticism about the romantic environmentalists' appeal to the conscience of the public and to 'the responsibilities of business'.

The same heritage of Smith's doctrine comes to the fore in discussions of the aspirations of the economies of Eastern Europe, as they announce their intention to turn to the market, hoping thereby to achieve the prosperity of the free-market economies. Smith's analysis might also appropriately be cited by observers when they opine that this hope of the East Europeans is foredoomed if they persist in the intention of preventing successful entrepreneurs from accumulating substantial wealth, for in doing so they will preclude the effective pursuit of self-interest without which the market mechanism cannot carry out the purposes of the invisible hand.

CONCLUDING COMMENT

We have seen that the invisible-hand doctrine, and with it the entire welfare analysis of *The Wealth of Nations*, is in a number of very basic respects quite different from what most non-specialists believe it to be. Its theological roots will, no doubt, be the side of the matter that is most surprising to modern readers. But perhaps more fundamental for modern economic application is the doctrine's lack of concern with the niceties of resource allocation and its focus upon the importance of the role of self-interest for economic efficiency. This has nothing to do with elimination of an economic role for the public sector, for even here the doctrine's primary lesson is about how government can most effectively adapt the workings of the economy to its purposes. To protect the environment effectively, the doctrine implies, one must make it *unprofitable* for firms to act otherwise, and appeals to conscience are predestined to fail. It is then that the invisible hand can be relied upon to guide the economy.

NOTES

1. Curiously, in this invisible-hand passage, too, part of the theme is the unintentional benefits that 'providence' has arranged to derive from pursuit of wealth by self-interested individuals. Only, this time, the social benefit is justice in real income distribution(!). The argument is that the wealthy can consume only limited amounts of food and clothing themselves and so, instead, they spend the bulk of their income on servants and other employees, thereby creating income for the less affluent:

   > the rich . . . consume little more than the poor, and in spite of their natural selfishness and rapacity, though . . . the sole end which they propose from the labours of all the thousands whom they employ, be the gratification of their own vain and insatiable desires, they divide with the poor the produce of all their improvements. They are led by an invisible hand to make nearly the same distribution of the necessaries of life, which would have been made, had the earth been divided into equal portions among all its inhabitants; and thus, *without intending it, without knowing it*, advance the interest of the society, and afford means to the multiplication of the species. When providence divided the earth among a few lordly masters, it neither forgot nor abandoned those who seemed to have been left out in the partition. (my italics)

2. One may well surmise that in Smith's view it is because the *competitive* market is so severe a taskmaster that 'merchants and manufacturers' seek constantly to find ways to undermine its restraints. That is why they 'rarely meet together, even for meriment and diversion, but the conversation ends in a conspiracy against the public, or in some contrivance to raise prices' (1776: 128). How else can one make sense of Smith's repeated and acidly denigrating remarks on the motives and behaviour of business persons (as in the last two sentences of the invisible-hand passage)? After all, according to his biographers, Glasgow merchants were among Smith's closest friends.

3. Smith adds immediately:

   > Society, however, cannot subsist among those who are at all times ready to hurt and injure one another. . . . If there is any society among robbers and murderers, they must at least, according to the trite observation, abstain from robbing and murdering one another. Beneficence, therefore, is less essential to the existence of society than justice.

   This judgement helps to account for Smith's emphasis of the importance of government's role in the administration of justice, relative to any benefits to be expected from direct economic activity by the state.

4. Smith's focus on the social role of self-interest has for a long time puzzled the specialists because of the difficulty of reconciling this position with the central subject of Smith's other work. For *The Theory of Moral Sentiments*, as its name implies, has as its subject the role of human morality and empathy with the feeling of others, and their contribution to the welfare of other persons. There is an extensive literature discussing the reconcilability of the two writings, a subject which in the German writings was accorded a title of its own: 'the Adam Smith problem'. And there *is* some reason, despite the preceding quotation from the *Moral Sentiments* to conclude that Smith of *The Wealth of Nations* does differ somewhat with the Smith of *The Theory of Moral Sentiments*, where he writes, 'Man, say [those who are fond of deducing all our sentiments from certain refinements of self-love], conscious of . . . the need which he has for the assistance of others, rejoices whenever he observes that they adopt his own passions, because he is then assured of that assistance' (Part I, Section 1, Chapter II, first page).

5. To a modern reader, for whom value theory is the centrepiece of economic analysis, concern with the efficacy of voluntarism and with the value of the pursuit of self-interest may appear a secondary matter. But one may well believe that to Smith, with his focus on the nature and sources of the wealth of nations, the priorities were reversed. Thus, it may hardly be accidental that the value theory discussion only occurs much later in the book.

6. 'When you apply to a brewer or butcher [for] beer or for bread, you do not explain to him how much you stand in need of these, but how much it would be [to his] interest to allow you to have them for a certain price. You do not address his humanity, but his self love' (p. 348).

7. Smith does note that his friend, David Hume, cited the clergy as an egregious exception:

   > if we consider the matter more closely, we shall find, that [the self-]interested diligence of the clergy is

what every wise legislator will study to prevent; because, in every religion except the true, it is highly pernicious, and it has even a natural tendency to pervert the true, by infusing into it a strong mixture of superstition, folly, and delusion. Each ghostly practitioner, in order to render himself more precious and sacred in the eyes of his retainers, will inspire them with the most violent abhorrence of all other sects, and continually endeavour, by some novelty, to excite the languid devotion of his audience. No regard will be paid to truth, morals, or decency in the doctrines inculcated. Every tenet will be adopted that best suits the disorderly affections of the human frame. Customers will be drawn to each conventicle by new industry and address in practising on the passions and credulity of the populace. And in the end, the civil magistrate will find, that he has dearly paid for his pretended frugality, in saving a fixed establishment for the priests; and that in reality the most decent and advantageous composition, which he can make with the spiritual guides, is to bribe their indolence, by assigning stated salaries to their profession.   (Hume, quoted by Smith, p. 743)

4.   The Direction of Economic Research

George J. Stigler

This paper addresses the direction of economic research in two senses of 'direction': what forces influence ('direct') the choices of subjects on which economists write, and how have these forces – and the corresponding subjects or directions of inquiry – changed over time? The development of economic literature in Great Britain will be the primary focus of study, but some attention will be paid to American and continental economics.

THE PRE-ACADEMIC ERA

In the centuries which preceded the decline of mercantilist doctrine, if not its practice, under the attacks of Hume and Smith, economics was a wholly non-academic subject, cultivated primarily by people with a strong stake in the public policies governing international trade and finance. As Viner (1937) observes:

> The mercantilist literature . . . consisted in the main of writings by or on behalf of 'merchants' or businessmen, who had the usual capacity for identifying their own with the national welfare. Disinterested exposition of trade doctrine was by no means totally absent from the mercantilist literature, and in the eighteenth century many of the tracts were written to serve party rather than self. But the great bulk of the mercantilist literature consisted of tracts which were partly or wholly, frankly or disguisedly, special pleas for special economic interests. Freedom for themselves, restrictions for others, such was the essence of the usual program of legislation of the mercantilist tracts of merchant authorship.

Viner's generalization is confirmed by a study of the main writers he surveyed in his famous essay on mercantilism: merchants and businessmen dominate the literature of that period (see Appendix A).

We commonly, and I think properly, date the establishment of economics as a science – as an enterprise sustained by interactive economists – from the appearance of *The Wealth of Nations*. Yet in the century following that treatise, the major writings in England continued to come from non-academic economists. The exceptions are quickly enumerated. Malthus was a professor for much of his life – beginning seven years after he wrote the *Essay on Population* – and McCulloch, Longfield, Senior, Whately and a few others held short-term professorships. Adam Smith left academic life in 1763 and *The Wealth of Nations* was written during a decade in which he was an annuitant of the Duke of Buccleuch. But that concludes the main list of academicians: Hume, Ricardo, James Mill, John Stuart Mill, Torrens, Bailey, Thornton, de Quincy, Wakefield and a large number of other economists had no academic post.

We may measure the diversity of economic writers in the early nineteenth century from the studies of the periodical literature by Frank W. Fetter (1953, 1958a, 1958b, 1960, 1962 and 1965). The *Edinburgh Review* 'was the closest approach that Great Britain had to an economic journal', and we tabulate the authorship (sometimes probable authorship in that age of anonymity) of its economic articles between 1802 and 1847 in Table 4.1. Even with the hyperactive pen of McCulloch, who accounted for almost 30 per cent of all the articles, the economists accounted for less than half of the articles, and for less

Table 4.1:   Economic articles in the Edinburgh Review, *1802–47*

Economists	Number of articles[a]	
Horner	8	
Buchanan	3.5	
Malthus	6	
J. Mill	3	
Chalmers	4	
McCulloch	78	
Torrens	1	
Senior	9	
J. S. Mill	1	
Merivale	4	
	—	117.5
Non-economists		
Brougham	27.5	
39 others	86	
	—	113.5
Unidentified authors		31
Total		262

Source: Fetter 1953

Note:
[a] Counting jointly-written articles as one-half for each author

than one-fourth of the writers, on economic subjects. The authorship of an article was much more likely to be identified if it was written by an economist, so most of the unknown authors of the 31 articles should be reckoned among the non-economists. The role of economists in the three other major journals of the period (presented in Table 4.2) was even less conspicuous. No journal required a period of protracted study of economics from its writers on the subject.

How did the economists of the period support themselves and what incentive system did they face? A few economists were wealthy and wrote out of the desire to mould public policy and/or to achieve personal fame – two goals that are probably analytically indistinguishable. Ricardo, who as a speculator in government bonds amassed a fortune estimated to be £700,000 at his death, and roughly $15 million in modern terms, is the prototype of this group, but the group probably includes also Senior, an extremely

Table 4.2: *Economic articles in British journals*

Journal	Period covered	Writers		Articles[a]			
		Economists	Other	Economists	Other	Unknown	Total
Westminster Review	1824–51	8	22	76[b]	35	143	254
Quarterly Review	1809–52	5	73	20[c]	198	32	250
Blackwood's	1817–53	2	46	59[d]	227	47	333
Edinburgh Review	1802–47	10	40	117.5[e]	113.5	31	262
Totals		25	181	272.5	573.5	253	1 099

Sources: Fetter 1953, 1958a, 1958b, 1960, 1962

Notes:
[a] Counting jointly-written articles as one-half
[b] 45.5 by T. P. Thompson
[c] 12 by Scrope
[d] 48 by Sir A. Alison
[e] 78 by McCulloch

successful lawyer, Scrope, who married an heiress and adopted her name, the Earl of Lauderdale and a few others.

The larger number of economists derived their livelihood directly or indirectly from their economic writings. Those who contributed to the journals of the day were well paid: the *Edinburgh Review* paid at least 30 shillings on average per page to its contributors.[1] (For a modern dollar equivalent, one should multiply this rate (£1.5) by about 14 – to get £21 or about $30 per page.) It is possible that this mode of payment led to their practice of writing 'I cannot do better than to use the author's words', and follow with a two-page quotation. Recall that the articles were published anonymously, a practice to which we shall return.

The financial rewards for successful writing were sometimes sumptuous. Ruskin played a double role in Victorian literature: he was both a major art critic and historian and a prolific and violently aggressive opponent of the private enterprise system. His royalties for many years were of the order of £4,000 per year, which if accumulated and converted to modern currency but kept at 1860 levels of taxation was enough to ransom at least one king. That measure of success was of course unusual, but there were numerous economists who parlayed their economic and other writings into lucrative civil service positions, including McCulloch, Richard Jones and the senior and junior Mills.

The economic articles published in the *Edinburgh Review* were chiefly devoted to the policy problems of the times: emigration, inflation, taxation, protection, poor laws and the like (Table 4.3). This journal was at first published by young members of the Scottish intellectual renaissance and only gradually became the explicit and authoritative organ of the Whig Party. The *Quarterly* was instituted by the Tories as a response; *Blackwood's* highest task was long the defence of all things Scottish; and the *Westminster Review*, founded by Bentham and James Mill, sought to advance utilitarianism (Fetter 1965). It would be wrong to describe any of these journals as rigidly doctrinaire by modern standards, but each sought to promote a general philosophy and a set of economic policies. The anonymity of the writers reinforced the dominant role of the editors of these journals.

Table 4.3:   Economic articles in the Edinburgh Review, *1802–47, by subject*

Subject area	Number of articles
General treatises	24
Population:	
Emigration	4
Other	7
Money and banking	22
Taxation and debt, state of the economy	26
Corn laws	8
Agriculture	10
International trade	31
Foreign economic systems	13
Ireland	18
Industry studies, except manufacturing	9
Manufacturing	10
Colonies	30
Labour:	
Unions	2
Poor laws	17
Other	5
Church, tithes	7
Entails, absenteeism, tenancy	3
Other	16
Total	262

Economists have long believed that workers distribute themselves in various callings in such a way that workers of equal skill secure equal net advantages in each of the callings in which they work. We speak of net advantages to take account of the differences in costs of special training or equipment or probability of unemployment and other conditions of employment in each calling. The net advantages of barbers should be nearly equal on average in cities A and B even if people go shaggy in B. The net advantages of professors of law and practising attorneys of equal ability should approach equality, giving due allowance for hours and intensity of work, vacations and the like. This line of argument says that the distribution of labour among callings is governed primarily by the demands for the various callings. The Americans will have relatively more hockey players, the Spaniards relatively more bullfighters.

The argument should apply equally to intellectual callings. The net advantages of a skilful propagandist should be about equal, whichever party he supports. The average earnings of protectionists, such as Malthus, should have approximated those of free traders, such as McCulloch. We can hardly test this prediction of earnings for the economists writing on economic policy in the first half of the nineteenth century, but a theory that works for modern labour markets ought to have worked at least roughly for defenders and critics of the Corn Laws or the Factory Acts in an earlier period.

The demands of editors and readers governed the selection of problems in this pre-academic period. The Goldsmith Library's *Catalogue of Economic Literature* (1981) offers striking illustrations of the responsiveness of the literature (here books and pamphlets) to the interests of the moment. The numbers of items reported on the Corn Laws in the first controversy at the end of the Napoleonic Wars were

1813	0
1814	39
1815	42
1816	2

with a great revival of the subject in the late 1830s and early 1840s.

Beginning about 1830, the subject of colonies entered a period of intense interest. Later topics included the Factory Acts, the attempts to alleviate the plight of the handloom weavers, the crisis of the Irish famine leading to the repeal of the Corn Laws, and the concern with absentee ownership in Ireland.

One can discuss any issue of public policy with negligible analytical apparatus, and journalists and legislators demonstrate this fact in all ages. Without that apparatus it is often difficult or impossible to sort out all the issues and forces and deal with them consistently: the recent discussions of governmental deficits and trade deficits is proof enough of that. This fact sharpens the query: why did the literature of economics, even in the pre-academic age, give a significant amount of attention to abstract or formal theory, unlike the other social sciences?

Frank Knight gave a good answer (in his lectures): the explanation of the interest in systematic theory was related to the *laissez-faire* philosophy. When one seeks the removal of governmental policies calculated to control and direct the economy, there is an obligation to show how the unregulated economy will perform. If a mercantilist state ceases to nurture the nation's supply of gold, what will govern the international distribution of gold? – a question brilliantly answered by Hume. When workers and wage rates are left free to seek their own occupations and wage levels, in contrast to the controls of a guild or caste system, how will the allocation of labour be determined? – a question brilliantly answered by Smith. If international trade is free, is it possible that one trading nation loses from trade what the other gains? – a question Ricardo answered in the negative by developing the theory of comparative costs. On this view the economic analysis of the workings of free markets was required of supporters of a private enterprise system.

An alternative hypothesis is that the utilitarian theory, especially in its Benthamite version of a calculus of utility maximization, was the origin of systematic and increasingly more formal theorizing. This *could* have happened – Jevons based his utility theory explicitly on Bentham – but it did not take place. The proposed explanation has difficulty, moreover, in explaining the absence of a comparable development of theory in political science. When James Mill wrote his famous *Britannica* article on government, it was rigid and axiomatic in exposition but it did not explain how governments work. Macaulay's powerful rebuttal could, indeed, play upon Mill's lack of logical rigour and absence of inductive support.

The German economics of the period indirectly supports our hypothesis on the role of *laissez-faire*. Although there were fine theorists such as von Thünen and Mangoldt, they exerted no influence upon the main Historical School, which patterned its methodology after the historical jurisprudence of the Savigny school. The German Historical School was strongly socialistic in its policy views, and the *Verein für Sozialpolitik* was devoted to bringing about governmental solutions of economic problems. During the flowering of the physical sciences in Germany in the generations before the First World War, not a single major contribution to economics, location theory excepted, came from a German economist. During the same period the classically liberal Austrian School had a significant influence on the development of economics in the United States.

ECONOMICS BECOMES AN ACADEMIC CALLING

Let us begin with a brief look at the statistical record of the changing occupations of economists. We have not attempted even a sample census of economists in earlier periods, but we have examined some lists of well-known economists. For Britain we combine the list I once compiled in 'Statistical Studies in the History of Economic Thought' with names from Mark Blaug's and Paul Sturges's *Who's Who in Economics* (1983). For Germany we use the authoritative encyclopaedia, *Handwörterbuch der Staatswissenschaften* (1923 and 1956 editions).

We tabulate the British data by birth-year of economists, to which 33 years should be added on average for the publication of the person's first economic work (see Table 4.4). The birth period 1841–60, when the number of future academicians began to grow rapidly, includes Ashley, Cunningham, Edgeworth, Foxwell, Marshall, Nicholson, Smart and Toynbee, as well as Wicksteed who was not primarily an academician. The prominent economists from after 1860 were increasingly academic – and after 1900 well-nigh exclusively academic.

Table 4.4:   *England: primary occupations of 129 mentionable economists born 1701 to 1900*

| Birth year | Number | Academic occupation | | Non-academic occupation | | | | |
		Economics	Other	Business & finance	Independent wealth	Civil Service	Journalism	Other[a]
1701–20	5	–	–	1	1	1	1	1
1721–40	5	–	2	–	1	–	–	2
1741–60	8	1	–	2	3	1	1	–
1761–80	16	1	1	6	1	1	5	1
1781–1800	22	3	3	6	3	2	3	2
Total 1701–1800	56	5	6	15	9	5	10	6
1801–20	12	1	–	2	–	3	5[b]	1
1821–40	14	5	3	4	–	1	1	–
1841–60	17	8	2	–	–	1	5	1
1861–80	18	10	2	–	–	6	–	–
1881–1900	12	10	1	–	–	1	–	–
Total 1801–1900	73	34	8	6	0	12	11	2

Primary sources: Blaug and Sturges 1983; Stigler 1964.

Notes:
[a] Usually clergy; 2 law, 1 medicine, 1 engineer
[b] Includes Marx, Engels

The German data differ in at least two important respects from the British pattern (see Table 4.5).[2] First, the field is less sharply defined: it includes Cameralism, the study of the economic and regulatory functions of the state, and political science and parts of sociology. Secondly, the academic period began at least half a century earlier. A third probable difference is that the criteria for inclusion in our selection from the *Handwörterbücher* are less demanding.

Table 4.5: Germany[a]: primary occupations of 160 mentionable economists born 1701 to 1900

Birth year	Number	Academic occupation		Non-academic occupation				
		Economics	Other	Business & finance	Independent wealth	Civil Service	Journalism	Other[b]
1701–20	8	1	3	–	–	3	–	1
1721–40	3	1	–	–	–	1	–	1
1741–60	9	6	2	–	–	1	–	–
1761–80	6	2	2	–	–	2	–	–
1781–1800	9	3	2	–	–	2	1	1
Total 1701–1800	35	13	9	0	0	9	1	3
1801–20	9	6	–	1	–	1	1[c]	1
1821–40	30	18	1	2	–	5	3	1
1841–60	23	17	1	1	–	2	1	1
1861–80	35	26	4	1	–	3	1	–
1881–1900	28	22	2	1	–	2	–	1
Total 1801–1900	125	89	8	6	0	13	6	3

Primary source: Handwörterbuch der Staatswissenschaften (1923 and 1956).

Notes:
[a] Includes Austrian and Swiss economists
[b] Clergy, law, education, agriculture
[c] Excludes Marx and Engels (included in Table 4.4)

The American experience is similar to the British, and apparently was uninfluenced by the fact that in the last two decades of the nineteenth century, a large number of American economists studied in German universities.[3]

Britain had few professorships in political economy. Oxford's Drummond Professor held only a five-year tenure (with possible re-election), but Edgeworth held the chair from 1891 to 1922. Cambridge's professorship had similar tenure from 1828 until 1863, when a professorship of political economy carrying £300 per year was given to Henry Fawcett. Manchester's chair in political economy was established in 1898, although Jevons was appointed to a joint chair in economics and mental and moral science in 1866. Adam Smith's university, Glasgow, did not have a professorship of political economy until 1896.[4]

Presumably the economists who were not publishing any research in this later period were even more predominantly in academic institutions because in England and the

United States, at least, they were seldom in government or business. Judging from the histories of the teaching of economics in the United States, however, the early teachers of political economy were almost never specialists in economics. We may safely conclude that in the English-speaking world economics became an academic calling by the latter third of the nineteenth century.

Although economics reached its full academic status by the First World War, it has not remained primarily academic so far as the employment of economists is concerned. A substantial growth of economists in government began in the 1920s[5] and in business somewhat later. The National Science Foundation enumerates economists by accepting self-designation (*US Scientists and Engineers, 1982*), and has the American profession composed of

> 103,100 individuals, of whom
> 21,800 were in education
> 53,300 were in business and industry
> 22,900 were in governments

and about 14 per cent held PhDs. Large numbers of these economists were in management and research and in business research and consulting, with only 16,000 being teachers. In 1984 the American Economic Association had 7,660 academic members (or 56.2 per cent of its individual American members).

Important research is conducted in government and noteworthy research has come from business,[6] but most fundamental and direction-setting research comes from the academic sector, and I shall confine the subsequent discussion to that sector. The number of influential economic scholars is a matter difficult to enumerate, and even then no doubt may be disputed, but it probably numbers fewer than 200.

THE PROFESSIONALIZATION OF ECONOMICS

As academic institutions became the main employers of economists, the organization of the research level of the profession altered in important ways. To begin with, economics was accepted into the universities because it was becoming systematic and rigorous and because it dealt with social problems of undisputed importance. The theoretical system of economics in turn became *more* formal, either because in academia the methods and achievements of sciences such as physics were held up as the model for other sciences or because the subject matter invited such methods.

The increasing rigour and abstraction of the premier economic literature meant that the general public, and even the members of other disciplines, became unqualified to judge the quality of economists and the desirability of various kinds of research. The only people able to understand and appraise economics became the economists themselves.

The immediate demanders of economists' services, in short, are a self-selected and self-perpetuating group of specialists in the subject. A group can achieve this measure of independence only if it achieves a substantial consensus on the quality of research and researchers. The consensus is not achieved by a plebiscite of the members of the profession but by an élite group within the profession, and this group is self-chosen on the basis of quality of work.

This system could not emerge or prevail for any important period unless there were forces that induced the substantial consensus. There are societies in which the consensus is achieved or assisted by coercion: by the centralization of control over the research market. In our profession the consensus has come primarily from agreement on the nature of high-quality research.

This agreement does not represent literal acceptances of particular theories by the élite. During the 1930s Edward Chamberlin proposed a theory of monopolistic competition and Joan Robinson proposed a theory of imperfect competition. The profession had no difficulty in treating these as major pieces of work. I thought at the time that Chamberlin's theory represented an unsuccessful departure from the prevailing theory of competition, but I had no reservations on the distinction of his performance: the freshness of the view and the ingenuity of the theoretical development. In Joan Robinson's case, the powerful lucidity of her mind was undeniable even though it was applied to problems that had a much higher content of geometry than of economics.

The consensus has fuzzy borders. The economists who admire Leontief's work on input–output structures only moderately overlap the group that admires the empirical work of Simon Kuznets or the group that admires the work on rational expectations. The point is that some important economists like most of these performances and few important economists are outraged by any of them. A deep cleavage in which two large groups each believed the other's work was worthless would destroy the consensus.

To say that there is a general consensus of the nature of high-quality work does not mean that the profession cannot sometimes be wrong. What was once interesting and fashionable can pass out of the discipline – examples are linear programming (soon given to operations research) and workable competition (given to obscurity).

The élite members of the profession of economics are the senior faculties of a dozen or score of the major universities. The composition of these élite schools is not immutable: Chicago elbowed its way in before the First World War, Yale was off the list in the decade of the 1930s, MIT joined the group after the Second World War, and so on. Nevertheless, there is a good deal of persistence of the same schools in the list. These universities recruit their faculties primarily from the graduates of this same set of universities, and the vast majority of the best graduate students presumably attend these schools. The appointments of new assistant professors at the élite schools come largely from these same élite schools, and lower-ranked departments recruit in lesser proportions from those schools.[7] The élite schools also specialize substantially more in theoretical than in empirical economists (see Appendix B).

So it is the demands of the major economic departments that determine which scholars deserve promotion, appointments to select schools, and grants from private foundations or the National Science Foundation. To predict the most popular new subjects in economics one should look at the work being done by the new appointments and promotions of economists at the major schools.

On a day-to-day basis, the individual professor enjoys large freedom, including the freedom to do nothing. But how does he reach the position of even a promising young scholar, let alone the tenured professor, still less the professor well endowed with research grants? Not by self-designation, but by impressing established scholars in his field. How does he succeed in having his research results published in the professional journals? The answer is by writing papers that please editors and referees.

In effect, the control over a profession is given less to powerful ministers of education and powerful heads of research institutes than to the leaders of the research field, and admittedly this represents a partial decentralization. It is true that in the United States we have a large enough set of employers of research scholars and enough variety of interests to allow scholars of diverse abilities and viewpoints to rise to eminence.[8] Still, there is a measure of conformity demanded by the professional establishment. I believe the potentialities for central control over economic research are growing because of the increasing concentration of research funds in foundations and the federal government.

Although the profession governs the allocation of resources within the discipline, of course it does not determine the total amount of resources devoted to economics. If scholars had this power we know that the remainder of the population would soon perish from starvation. In the longer run a science is not self-perpetuating in its composition and problems. Sooner or later those in power will ask for results or better results. The results need not be simply utilitarian (cure disease X or depression Y), but they must satisfy a significant element of the society that they are worth their cost. I conjecture that even here competition plays a large role: competition among disciplines to solve important problems (illustrated by the absorption of zoology and botany by biology), and competition of rival national sciences. German and French economics were dominated for several generations by non-theoretical traditions (historical analysis in Germany, sociological analysis in France), and both have been giving way to the more successful English-American economics.

Economists have been remarkably successful in selling their product in this century. Every large business has at least one economist, and the largest business of all has a Council of Economic Advisors, which on suitable occasions is allowed within the White House. The only addition to the list of Nobel prizes since their founding has been economics. Economics is often the most popular undergraduate major in our colleges. All the tedious (to us) humour about the differences of opinion among economists (five economists will have six opinions – two from Keynes), or our infatuation with abstract thinking ('It's all right in practice but it won't work in theory'), are really envious gibes. Denunciation of America is almost the only bond that unifies European intellectuals, and criticism of economics is the chief bond joining the other social sciences. How much sweeter is envy than pity.

APPENDIX A: ECONOMIC WRITERS IN THE MERCANTILIST PERIOD

	Dates	*Occupation*
I. **Businessmen and bankers**		
Barbon, Nicholas	1640–98	Banker, physician
Cantillon, Richard	1697–1734	Banker
Child, Josiah	1630–99	Merchant
Davanzati, Bernardo	1529–1606	Merchant
Decker, Matthew	1679–1749	Merchant
Fortrey, Samuel	1622–81	Merchant
Gervaise, Isaac	18th century[a]	Merchant
Law, John	1671–1729	Banker, merchant, statesman
Malynes, Gerard de	1586–1641	Merchant, Assay Master
Manley, Thomas	1628–90	Merchant, King's Council
Misselden, Edward	1608–54	Merchant

	Dates	*Occupation*
Mun, Thomas	1571–1641	Merchant
North, Dudley	1641–1691	Merchant, civil servant
Patterson, William	1658–1719	Merchant, banker
Postlethwayt, Malachy	1707–1767	Businessman

II. **Professionals**

Berkeley, George	1685–1753	Clergyman
Hobbes, Thomas	1588–1679	Philosopher
Hume, David	1711–1776	Philosopher, historian
Locke, John	1632–1704	Philosopher, statesman
Mandeville, Bernard	1670–1733	Physician, writer
Petty, William	1623–1687	Physician, professor, independently wealthy
Vaughan, Rice	17th century[b]	Barrister
Wallace, Robert	1697–1771	Clergyman

III. **Statesmen and civil servants**

Bacon, Francis	1561–1626	Attorney General, Lord Chancellor
Davenant, Charles	1656–1714	Commissioner of Excise, Inspector General of Exports and Imports
Hales, John	died 1571	Exchequer posts
Harris, Joseph	1702–1764	Assay Master
More, Thomas	1477–1535	Lord Chancellor, diplomat
Temple, William	1628–1699	Statesman, diplomat
Walpole, Robert	1676–1745	Prime Minister

IV. **Other writers**

Bellers, John	1654–1725	Social reformer
Coke, Roger	1626–1696	Writer
Defoe, Daniel	1659–1731	Novelist, reformer
Gee, Joshua	1700–1750	Pamphleteer
Massie, Joseph	died 1784	Writer
Vanderlint, Jacob	died 1740	Pamphleteer

Sources: These writers, all taken from Viner (1937), are those for whom biographical data are given in selected sources: Blaug and Sturges (1986); *Dictionary of National Biography* (1908–09); *Encyclopedia of the Social Sciences* (1930–5); Mai (1975); McConnell (1943).

Notes:
[a] Principal work, 1720
[b] Principal work, 1675

APPENDIX B: SOURCES OF ASSISTANT PROFESSORS IN ECONOMICS DEPARTMENTS

The assistant professors appointed in four major graduate centres during 1968–84, and the appointments in 1973 and 1978 in a random sample of upper- and lower-middle-graded schools were examined for the schools in which they received their PhDs (see Table 4.A6).[9] The composition of the three sets of universities was as follows:

(a)   Four highest rated schools with 1980 grades:
      Chicago   72
      Harvard   72
      MIT   73
      Stanford   72

(b)   The upper-middle-ranked schools (all graded between 50 and 56):
      Boston University
      Duke
      Iowa State
      North Carolina
      Purdue
      U. of Southern California
      Virginia

(c)   The lower-middle-ranked schools (all graded between 41 and 46):
      Boston College
      Colorado
      Colorado State
      Kentucky
      Missouri
      New School
      SUNY–Binghamton
      Utah
      Wisconsin–Milwaukee

The recruitment of assistant professors from doctoral graduates of the highest-ranked schools (those with scores of 70 or more – they include Princeton and Yale as well as the four listed in (a)) varied as follows:

Economics departments	*Number*	*Per cent of asst. profs*[10]
Four highest-rated programmes	78	64.5
Upper-middle ranks	34	30.6
Lower-middle ranks	16[11]	18.2

The recruitments from schools ranking in the 60s were:[12]

Four highest-rated programmes	35	28.9
Upper-middle ranks	41	36.9
Lower-middle ranks	24	27.3

Table 4.A6: *Assistant professors by source of doctorate*

School of Assistant Professorship	School of Doctorate			
	Six top schools (rated in 70s)	Next tier (rated in 60s)	All other	Total US schools
Highest rated schools:[a]				
Chicago	12	7	0	19
Harvard	40	8	3	51
MIT	12	8	1	21
Stanford	14	12	4	30
Group total	78	35	8	121
Berkeley[a]	20	5	3	28
Upper-middle-rated schools:[b]				
Boston University	9	2	2	13
Duke	2	6	3	11
Iowa State	3	6	10	19
North Carolina	3	10	9	22
Purdue	4	6	5	15
U. of Southern California	4	5	2	11
Virginia	9	6	5	20
Group total	34	41	36	111
Lower-middle rated schools:[b]				
Boston College	10	4	0	14
Colorado	0	2	5	7
Colorado State	1	5	9	15
Kentucky	0	4	8	12
Missouri	0	1	9	10
New School	1	1	0	2
SUNY–Binghamton	2	1	4	7
Utah	0	4	4	8
Wisconsin–Milwaukee	2	2	9	13
Group total	16	24	48	88

Notes:
[a] Faculties of 1968–9, 1973–4, 1977–8, 1980–1 and 1984–5; source: correspondence with the individual institutions, supplemented by source in b below. Berkeley was added to our sample to provide information on a highly-rated public institution (score = 65).
[b] Faculties of 1973–4 and 1978–9; source: Economics Institute (1975, 1979); separate agricultural economics departments excluded.

APPENDIX C: THESIS TOPICS IN ECONOMICS

We have surveyed the thesis titles for all economic doctoral degrees conferred by three groups of schools during 1963–4, 1973–5 and 1983–4.

(a)   Highly-rated schools:
       Berkeley
       Chicago
       Harvard
       MIT
       Stanford
(b)   Upper-middle-rated schools:
       Boston University
       Duke
       Iowa State
       North Carolina
       Purdue
       U. of Southern California
       Virginia
(c)   Lower-middle-rated schools:
       Boston College
       Colorado
       Colorado State
       Kentucky
       Missouri
       New School
       SUNY–Binghamton
       Utah
       Wisconsin–Milwaukee

The thesis titles were classified as theoretical or empirical, and in the frequent cases of ambiguity, the abstract of the thesis was examined if available. Of course the classifications (which were made chiefly by graduate students in economics) involved judgement, but the broad pattern revealed by Table 4.A7 is trustworthy. In recent decades the higher the ranking of a school, the larger the fraction of theses that were theoretical. Of course, one would expect that result because the leading theorists are usually on the faculties of higher-ranked schools and are the major reason these schools are ranked high.

The subject matters of the theses at these schools are selectively summarized in Table 4.A8. Classification becomes increasingly more difficult and only two generalizations seem supportable:

(a)   Microeconomic subjects (including industrial organization and labour) have at least regained parity with macroeconomics in the 1980s.
(b)   In general there are no marked differences in area choices in the two classes of schools. The most fashionable recent theoretical fields (information and uncertainty, game theory and the more empirical economics of the family) are more frequently found in the top-ranked schools.

Table 4.A7: Theses classified by theoretical vs empirical

	Number of dissertations		
	Leading schools	Upper-middle- rated	Lower-middle- rated
1963–4			
Theoretical	50	16	6
Empirical	40	8	5
1973–5			
Theoretical	139	54	44
Empirical	111	55	68
1983–4			
Theoretical	86	25	14
Empirical	37	24	31
Percentage of theoretical theses:			
1963–4	55.6	66.7	54.5
1973–5	55.6	49.5	39.3
1983–4	69.9	51.0	31.1

Table 4.A8: Selected thesis subject areas

	Number of dissertations					
	5 leading schools			Middle 16 schools		
Subject	1963–4	1973–5	1983–4	1963–4	1973–5	1983–4
Broad areas: Theory						
Microeconomics	7	27	15	5	11	3
Welfare economics	0	4	2	1	1	1
Industrial organization	2	3	6	4	6	2
Labour	2	8	4	2	3	3
(Empirical Labour)	12	16	4	2	13	6
Macroeconomic theory	5	10	9	0	5	4
Monetary & fiscal theory	6	24	8	2	21	5
(Empirical monetary & fiscal theory)	5	6	5	1	7	8
International economic theory	5	12	5	1	3	6
(Empirical international)	3	7	7	1	15	7
Specific topics						
Uncertainty, information	1	4	5	1	4	2
Game theory	0	0	3	1	0	0
Rational expectations	0	1	2	0	0	3
Human capital	1	1	0	0	0	0
Economics of the family	0	2	2	0	1	0

NOTES

1. See Greig (1948: 62).
2. On the evolution of economic instruction in Germany, see Hennings (1988).
3. See Parish (1967) and Herbst (1965). See also Seligman (1925) and Dorfman (1946–59).
4. See Checkland (1951) and Hayek (1946).
5. See Coats *et al.* (1981) in the issue of *History and Political Economy* devoted to 'Economists in Government'.
6. See Roos (1934) and Court (1939).
7. Harvard appointed 24 of its 52 new assistant professors during this period from its own PhDs – a practice not followed by the other élite schools. Harvard's appointments are primarily to provide teaching services, not future members of the department.
8. Ben-David, Joseph (1968–9) emphasized the difference between the United States and Europe in the decentralization and competitiveness of our university system.
9. The grading of the schools for 1980 is from Jones *et al.* (1982). The ratings are based on a survey of economics faculty members and are mean ratings of 'the scholarly quality of [graduate economics] program faculty', standardized scores: mean = 50, standard deviation = 10.
10. Percentage of those assistant professors with PhD information and with PhDs from US institutions. In addition MIT recruited three Oxford and one Cambridge PhD, Harvard recruited one Oxford PhD and Duke recruited one from Australia. The numbers of assistant professors with no doctoral information available are as follows: four highest = 7 (5.3% of all assistant professors); upper-middle = 17 (13.2%); lower-middle = 9 (9.3%).
11. Ten by Boston College.
12. We also investigated Berkeley (ranked 65 and a major producer of PhDs) assistant professors. As of 1968–84: 71.4% were recruited from schools ranked in the 70s and 17.9% from schools ranked in the 60s.

5. The Underworld of Economics: Heresy and Heterodoxy in Economic Thought

Meghnad Desai

In the *General Theory*, Keynes started many hares but none so fleet of foot as the one concerning the underworld of economics. As early as Chapter 3 he attributes the disappearance of the question of effective demand to the triumph of Ricardian economics. Recall his words (1936: 32) (since in any case he writes so well, he is always worth recalling):

> [Ricardo] conquered England as completely as the Holy Inquisition conquered Spain. Not only was his theory accepted by the city, by statesmen and by the academic world. But controversy ceased; the other point of view completely disappeared; it ceased to be discussed. The great puzzle of effective demand with which Malthus had wrestled vanished from economic literature. You will not find it mentioned even once in the whole works of Marshall, Edgeworth and Professor Pigou from whose hands the classical theory has received its most mature embodiment. It could only live furtively, below the surface, in the underworlds of Karl Marx, Silvio Gesell or Major Douglas.

Further on in the *General Theory*, in Chapter 23, Keynes returns to some of the themes which have passed under the surface. Here while there is only a passing and unflattering reference to Marx, there is much space devoted to the heterodoxies of the Mercantilists: Mandeville, Gesell and of course Major Douglas as well as Hobson.

Do these authors constitute an underworld of economics? How would one decide who is above and who is under? Keynes gives no criterion and of course his selection of authors in his Chapter 23 is notoriously selective. I should like in this essay to map this terrain – the underworld of economics. It will not, I am afraid, be an A-to-Z of the underworld: more like those mediaeval maps of the world, suggestive of the general shape of things but hopelessly vague about the details. In any case, Mark Blaug knows he can do it much better and if nothing else this will flatter his conceit.

WHAT IS HETERODOXY, WHAT IS HERESY?

Let us begin with such hints as Keynes provides. At the very end of Chapter 23 he comes to Major Douglas and succinctly describes what makes one a citizen of the underworld. Thus, Douglas's strength was that the 'orthodoxy [had] no valid reply to much of his destructive criticism'. But then (1936: 370–1),

> On the other hand, the detail of his diagnosis, in particular the so-called A + B theorem, includes

much mere mystification. But while the details of his derivation are wrong he deserves some recognition. Major Douglas is entitled to claim, as against some of his orthodox adversaries, that he at least has not been wholly oblivious of the outstanding problem of our economic system. Yet he has scarcely established an equal claim to rank – a private perhaps, but not a major in the brave army of heretics – with Mandeville, Malthus, Gesell and Hobson, who following their intuitions, have preferred to see the truth obscurely and imperfectly rather than maintain error, reached indeed with clearness and consistency and by easy logic but on hypotheses inappropriate to the facts.

The criteria according to Keynes are therefore: (a) critique of orthodoxy; (b) ability to focus on the outstanding problem of our economic system; (c) ability to see the truth obscurely but imperfectly; (d) inability to achieve or deliberate avoidance of clarity, consistency, easy logic or the ability to propose hypotheses inappropriate to facts. But that only defines the officers. What about the many of us who are only likely to be privates in the great army of heretics? Here Keynes spots an unfailing trait of the heretic. This is in the claim to have devised a formula or a theorem which is at one and the same time simple, mystifying and muddled. Indeed the great mark of many heretics is the profound belief that they have in their possession a simple, of course mathematical, formula – a mantra – which solves all the basic problems of economics. If only the academic monopolists of economic truth will listen!

Who are the heretics 54 years later? Keynes of course made the underground respectable. He gave many the feeling that being in the opposition, being derided by the official journals, was a sure mark of truth. Indeed, some of the members of the 'circus' never became comfortable with being in the position in which they found themselves at the heyday of Keynesian orthodoxy. They were for ever yearning to be against the establishment – the bastard Keynesianism and rushing off to foment yet another revolution.

I think however that Cambridge Keynesians (Joan Robinson, Richard Kahn, Nicholas Kaldor) or the neo-Ricardians (Pierro Sraffa and his associates) should not count as heretics. They were incisive logicians and their battles were within the 'church'; they were battling for a claim to truth, not rejecting the faith. I would similarly not include Marx as a heretic but as a dissident branch of the church. Marx accepted much of classical theory; indeed, some would say that all that is good in him comes from Ricardo as much as others (including here myself), that all that is worth preserving in Marx is due to his deviation from Ricardo. In either case, Marx would claim as his ancestor Adam Smith and that ought to be the litmus test.

If boundaries are to be drawn, they must be drawn so as not to include the merely unpopular or the self-consciously unfashionable in the category of the economics of the heretical. Much of post-Keynesian economics, neo-Austrian economics, Institutional economics and radical/neo-Marxian economics partakes of the ordinary discourse of economics. The practitioners of these fashions use bits of price theory (Marshallian rather than Walrasian; imperfectly competitive rather than competitive); they use macroeconomic concepts: income, capital, money, wages; they use diagrams and less mathematics (though not the Sraffians, who use a lot of matrix algebra). Indeed, they are economists perhaps out of the inner sanctum of orthodoxy but in no way underground.

Lest I be thought arbitrary, let me draw up an ascending hierarchy of heterodoxy. The principle I shall use is the same as Dante used in his journey to Hell. There are, as you will recall, concentric circles by which he descends from the outer periphery to the very bottom where at the centre is the Devil himself. Our journey with no Virgil to guide us will be in reverse.

At the bottom will be the abode of deepest orthodoxy; from there we shall climb layer by layer to the outward light of heresy. The process is reversible as are definitions; most people will consider that the light is with the orthodoxy and the darkness outside. This, in any case, is a 'heretic-friendly' essay.

Hell for Dante is divided into the upper Hell and the nether Hell. In classifying the kinds of souls that reside in each of the nine layers of Hell, Dante uses the criteria of Aristotle as to what constitutes wrong behaviour. The least-bad reason for wrong behaviour is incontinence, a failure to control the appetite. The lustful, the gluttonous, the hoarders, the spendthrift and the wrathful occupy four circles in the upper Hell. The other category of wrongful behaviour is due to perverted appetite or bestiality. It is the violent who occupy this circle which is the second from the top in the nether Hell. Lastly we have fraud or malice as the most serious ground since it involves 'an abuse of the specifically human faculty of reason'. (This quote as well as all other information on Dante's Hell is from the notes attached to her translation by Dorothy Sayers (yes, that Dorothy Sayers); Dante/Sayers (1949).)

To this three-part list of wrong behaviour Dante added two extra categories. These were due to wrong belief. The first was unbelieving people born in the pre-Christian era or in some other way with a credible excuse for being heathens. The other category was for misbelief: Christians who had gone astray – despite the opportunity to know better had chosen to disbelieve. It is the misbelievers who occupy the City of Dis, the entrance to nether Hell. The unbelievers live in a limbo right at the entrance of the upper Hell; theirs is probably the least intolerable situation in Dante's Hell.

The nine circles of Hell thus comprise one of unbelievers, four of the incontinent, one of the heretics in the City of Dis, one of the violent and two for the malicious and fraudulent. Above all these is the Vestibule of the Futile, 'who have neither faith nor works'; not being a circle, the Vestibule bears no number.

Let us then reverse the course that Dante took and go, not from the top to the bottom, but from the very bottom at the core of economic orthodoxy. There is no way one can define heresy or heterodoxy before one has defined the 'true' faith.

What then is the true faith of an economist? We must beware here of many arcane internecine battles going on where as many are eager to wear the mantle of the true believers as to flaunt their variant of belief as heresy. Thus we cannot be delayed by battles such as those between salt-water and sweet-water American economists, nor by those who think that discrete rather than continuous isoquants draw a boundary between belief and misbelief. As economists, we know that price adjustments and quantity adjustments are symmetric by duality, just as there is no difference between tariffs and quotas in theory. General equilibrium is no more than a method of analysis and partial equilibrium has no special virtue except that sometimes you can draw diagrams to illustrate it. Nor can we take the view that the use of mathematics marks the virtuous (or by the symmetry of our argument, the suspect). Let the older economists lament that somehow economics has gone astray in using the methods of natural sciences; we recall that to follow in the footsteps of the great Doctor Newton was the ambition of the Scottish philosophers of the eighteenth century among whom our founder Adam Smith was the best.

Let me try to list what I believe constitutes the true faith of economists. The constituent elements are: equilibrium; rationality; autonomy.

The holy trinity of economic theory that I have outlined above may look rather idiosyncratic but let me explain its role. Take the last first. Autonomy stands for the proposition that economic relationships/actions can be understood in relative isolation from other subject areas. This is the core belief; those who disagree (rightly or wrongly is not at issue) and would like to bring in history, sociology, ethics, politics, psychology and so on, are regarded with indulgence at best (especially if these people have proved their credentials as true believers previously, for example, Herbert Simon or Joseph Schumpeter) or contempt at worst. (The reaction to the new left/radical attempt at introducing their concerns into the agenda of economics met with this reaction.)

The economist's belief in autonomy is a multi-layered one. Thus within economics allocation and distribution can be studied separately according to the strict neoclassical sect of the true religion, or real and monetary/financial variables can (should?) be studied separately. This is not a matter of specialization or division of labour but of a methodological stance. Economics is independent of other areas; indeed, the true believer from Robbins to Gary Becker would like to reduce all human behaviour to the economic one; not just autonomy or hegemony but totality is the true believer's dream.

Rationality is broader than individual rationality. As purpose-directed action at the individual level or as systemic behaviour in larger collectivities (class, economy), it characterizes classical as well as neoclassical economics. The famous theorem about the Invisible Hand asserts that individual or local rationality leads to agreeable systemic behaviour. As I shall argue below, Marx as well as Keynes accepted local/individual rationality but doubted that the outcome would be benevolent at the system level. Thus, local rationality led to global irrationality. Ricardo, for example, would admit none of this distinction. Even without a specifically individualist assumption, the system rationality leaves no scope for any deviation from rational behaviour in his system. It is enough that classes behave in certain logical fashion.

Optimization is then a special kind of rationality that neoclassical economics, especially in the postwar period, has come more and more to emphasize. Methodological individualism is also more explicitly displayed in twentieth-century economics as compared to that of the early nineteenth century. This is a matter of taste; Marx would no more entertain the study of irrational behaviour than would Mill, Walras or Samuelson. Whether one maximizes utility or something else is beside the point; satisficing is rational and in terms of computational costs may even be more 'rational' than optimizing. Ask an economist about drug-taking behaviour or altruism, the immediate reaction is to reach for a rational behaviour model.

By implication, the same argument extends to expectations. Rational expectations are just one strong version of rationality. Adaptive expectations are not irrational. Keynes's game of musical chairs is played with local rationality by the players involved, given their information structure and their objectives. If they happen to cut their throats by bad judgement, that is merely a logical outcome of locally rational behaviour, not of irrational behaviour. The elementary Prisoners' Dilemma game exploits this peculiarity of local rationality.

Lastly we come to equilibrium. More ink has been wasted on this term in the internecine disputes than any other. Again, whether fixed–price or flex-price, partial or general, static or dynamic, equilibrium remains equilibrium. Keynes has as much equilibrium as the economists he battles with in the *General Theory*. Often when someone asserts that s/he does not believe in equilibrium – someone who is not residing in the Vestibule of the Futile with no faith and no works – what they mean is that they prefer dynamic to static equilibrium. The neo-Ricardians are as much equilibrium theorists as are their opponent neoclassicals. Post-Keynesians use the methods of partial equilibrium inherited from Marshall, Pigou, Joan Robinson and Kalecki. Marx in his Scheme of Expanded Reproduction proposed a 'super-equilibrium' dynamic model for capitalism, one that caused a lot of debate among Marxists in the half century after his death (see Desai (1979), Morishima (1973)).

Equilibrium thus broadly interpreted is the standard theorizing tool for economists. The trouble with equilibrium is, to use an expression of Aldous Huxley when he set up his paradox about fiction, is that it makes too much sense; reality hardly ever makes sense, to the naked eye at least. Economists pride themselves therefore on not being distracted by reality but concentrating on their prior theory to arrive at their results. The dispute between the Cambridge campuses across the Atlantic was not about facts but about rival *a priori* constructs: my equilibrium against yours.

A classic divide occurs in terms of short-run and long-run equilibrium. Can monetary injections increase real output? The Humean Milton Friedman will say yes in the short run but not in the long run. The Ricardian Robert Lucas would say neither in the short nor in the long run. All appearance of real output gain is noise or misperception. Most fixed-price equilibrium theorists will say that their picture is a short-run one; in the long run we are all in the same boat. There is, of course, disequilibrium dynamics; bubbles, bifurcations, chaos. But most disequilibrium stories are short-run ones. Bubbles eventually burst. Limit cycles reproduce themselves with predictable regularity. Only rarely, as in Goodwin's model of the class struggle, do you get an economy in perpetual disequilibrium; attractive though this is, it is a fragile result coming from a structurally unstable model (Goodwin 1967; Goodwin, Kruger and Vercelli 1984).

The basic trinity of our faith is then established: autonomy, rationality, equilibrium. Can we then define misbelief and unbelief in this framework? We have to choose, to begin with, the representatives of the true faith, those economists who never flinch from adhering to these three tenets. At the head of this select band, I should put a favourite of Mark Blaug's – David Ricardo. Ricardo is the first economist for whom no subsequent development of economics could have come as a surprise. He avoids any historical or institutional discussion ruthlessly. The contrast between the styles of Smith and Ricardo is quite marked. Smith writes in the style of an eighteenth-century *philosophe*, encompassing all knowledge, unifying, synthesizing, ever eager to refer back to the Romans or to Tartary. On the tenet of autonomy, Smith fails miserably. He may have made it possible for the rest of us to be narrow but it would not have been if we had followed his example. Ricardo it is who dwells in the world of rational economic man, with the equilibrium tendency working inexorably and pitilessly (one reason why Marx liked him so much). History, political institutions, moral philosophy play no part in his discourse.

Ricardo is also an extreme rationalist. Recall that when Malthus objected that some of his assumptions were not true in practice he replied to the effect that questions of fact were separate from questions of science; he, Ricardo, was concerned with questions of science. Thus it was that he could invent economists' time so different from historical or real time. Profit rates equalize across industries remorselessly. Adam Smith could be suspected of a residual fondness for agriculture as being more important than other activities, but not so Ricardo.

Equilibrium in the sense of systemic order is, of course, also much more a Ricardian device than a Smithian one. The formalization of Smith's system of natural liberty into an inexorable machine to solve all problems of public policy, establishing the science of political economy is Ricardo's achievement. This is seen nowhere more than in his Theory of Comparative Advantage; here is a deliberately unrealistic, powerfully counter-intuitive argument that won the world of affairs by its sheer logical force.

In my inverted Dantesque scheme, at the very bottom of this Hell, at the earth's centre stands Ricardo. As Dante says on seeing Dis,

> The Emperor of the sorrowful realm was there,
> Out of the girding ice he stood breast high,
> And to his arm alone the giants were
> Less comparable than to a giant I;
> Judge then how huge the stature of the whole
> That so huge a part bears symmetry.
>   Canto XXXIV, 28–33

In the subsequent 175 years since Ricardo wrote, it is not until we get to the new classical economics that anything of comparative intensity to the three principles appears. It was Wicksell who invented the notion of the Natural Rate of Interest in trying to reconcile Ricardian theory to disagreeable facts that Tooke had collected. As an unobservable magnitude which could only be determined by the theory but not independently of it, Wicksell's device added to the Ricardian system a technique which for ever made economics immune from empirical attacks. The New Classical economists took this notion and gave it rigorous Ricardian *a priorist* foundations. No proposition, no data that contradicted the Natural Rate Hypothesis could be possibly rational. All that the salt-water New Keynesian could say was that maybe in the long run the economy could not deviate from the Natural Rate but there could be short-run deviations from it. In this they are at one with the Humean position of Milton Friedman, who also admits the possibility of a real output increase from a monetary injection in the short run. The Lucas–Sargent–Barro–Wallace school closes off all these options as deviations from rational behaviour.

Allied to these are some Marxists and some neo-Ricardians. There are Marxists who deny that government spending can do any good since surplus value is created in production and total profits are determined by that total of surplus value. No manipulation of nominal spending can help capitalists. Neo-Ricardians embrace the long run as the only terrain on which serious theorizing is possible. Steady states are their favourite equilibrium devices. It is no wonder that Garegnani (1978) is dissatisfied with Keynes's theory in much the same way as Lucas is; it lacks a long-run theory of output/microfoundations.

Theorizing for Ricardo is then the supreme value. It is the logical elegance and completeness of the argument, the willingness to follow the argument where it would lead regardless of facts, regardless of the urgency of any practical problem to be solved – that is what characterizes the Ricardian and indeed the holder of the true faith. From here on the rest of us deviate in one way or another. We fail on autonomy as Adam Smith or John Stuart Mill does. We may not hold to full rationality and allow for deviations to persist even for an instant from what theory would allow. We may be enticed by the delusion that in the short run there would be some remission from the juggernaut, that the long run may come but, pray to God, not yet.

Mild deviations like these are not, however, heresy, but they do lead to fierce sectarian battles. One particular battle that Mark Blaug surveyed with relish was the Cambridge–Cambridge debate. With the hindsight of a quarter of a century we can see a curious inversion. It was Marshall who, feigning to follow Ricardo, started the fashion of theory as a tool for solving practical problems. He was willing to live with a patchwork quilt;

Ricardian in his trade theory, an eclectic combination of utility and cost of production in his value theory, dynamic in his theory of the representative firm, static in his demand theory, utilitarian in his welfare economics and so on, Marshall could be said to treat theories like a box of tissues; pick up a new one each time you need to blow your nose/solve a problem. There need be no overall architectonic unity about one's theory; not consistency but usefulness was the criterion. It was the Massachusetts Cambridge economists who were the Marshallians. They were willing to have an aggregate two-factor Cobb Douglas production function to explain income shares at the macro level, be Walrasians if they had to teach advanced theory where the notion of aggregate capital stock was unnecessary or be Marshallian in discussing industrial structures. To them, the aggregate production function was a useful device, not a life's philosophy. To the English Cambridge theorists, this was vulgar economics; they were all Ricardians. In 1926, when Sraffa had first pointed out the inconsistency in Marshall's thought, he had been ignored if not grossly misunderstood by Joan Robinson. In 1960 he won the battle to save Cambridge from the Marshallians, except that now they were called neoclassicals and were mainly Americans. Much ink was spilt on the issues under debate. The American Marshallians admitted their errors and went merrily along as before, aware of no great sin. To the Cambridge Ricardians this was in no way enough; they wanted a surrender signed, a *mea culpa* which would lead to excommunication, withdrawal of the licence to practise economics. Foul they cried, but the world took no notice. The church was in one of its tolerant moods and no action was taken.

One must, of course, not be dogmatic; over his or rarely her career, an economist can move in and out of the ambit of the earth's centre of orthodoxy. Lord Kaldor started impeccably as an orthodox neoclassical economist, a darling of Hayek and Robbins and later became a Keynesian, an avowed enemy of Monetarism (Desai 1979b; 1991). Joan Robinson was at one time or another a Pigouvian neoclassical price theorist, a Keynesian and a Ricardian. Of course, in each of these roles she was a pioneer; but as Geoff Harcourt (1990) has told us, towards the end of her life she wondered whether her late conversion to Ricardianism had been wise – all those steady states are after all so utterly devoid of any empirical content.

It would be a fascinating exercise to place economists, living and dead, in the various circles of Hell commensurate with the degree of their divergence from the trinity of beliefs. Apart from the laws of libel, there are also space considerations which prevent me from pursuing that path. We must however try to pin down what heresy is in this context. Who can we place in the City of Dis, at the entrance to the nether Hell?

Heresy is not unbelief, it is misbelief. A heretic needs to have been taught the true doctrine, believed once but then set up in opposition to the true doctrine. The Oxford English Dictionary defines heresy thus:

> Theological or religious opinion or doctrine maintained in opposition, or held to be contrary, to the 'catholic' or orthodox doctrine of the Christian Church, or by extension to that of any church, creed or religious system, considered as orthodox.

To this definition, the *OED* adds an illustrative quotation from John Locke on the nature of heresy:

> Use, which is the Supreme Law, has determined that Heresie relates to Errors in Faith, and Schism to those in Worship or Discipline.   (First Letter on Toleration, 61)

It is thus very important not to classify as heretics those who could not have known any better, that is, those who are not properly trained economists. Those who hold opinions merely in opposition to the received doctrine may comprise a motley crowd – those who never did have instruction in the true faith, those who subscribe to other religions: heathens, atheists and so on. The *OED* defines heterodoxy much more mildly than it does heresy:

> Of doctrines, opinions etc. – Not in accordance with established doctrines or opinions or those generally recognised as right or 'orthodox'.

> Of persons – Holding opinions not in accord with some acknowledged standard.

WHO ARE THE HERETICS?

Keynes clearly qualifies. He had the benefit of Marshall and Pigou. He taught in the seat of one of the major sects, Cambridge, which contested for domination with Lausanne, as well as a minor sect in Vienna. Each sect had its text in which the followers thought all truth was contained. (It is all in Marshall.) But as a leading light of the Cambridge neoclassical tendency, Keynes knew better. He had subscribed to the basic tenets of Marshallian economics. He then defected. In doing so, like many a heretic before him, he split his own church even more than the rivals. Also typically he mislabelled the tendency he was opposing, calling them classical instead of neoclassical, grouping the nineteenth-century classicals with the Marshallians. At the same time he never openly denounced Marshall and even used the old doctrine as far as value theory was concerned. He left the Austrians and the Walrasians alone who none the less attacked him from the Swedish and London redoubts that they had established.

The still-faithful have fought ever since with the schismatics to claim Keynes on one side or another, eliding his differences with orthodoxy or highlighting them. The many attempts even now being made to find out what Keynes really meant testify to the living heresy in Keynes. Keynes has also to be given credit for directly identifying Ricardo as the arch-enemy, in disputing the relevance as well as the existence of a long-run equilibrium for a decentralized, capitalist economy. Although committed to autonomy, he was distinctly wobbly on rationality, especially in his remarks about the stock markets, as Irving Fisher, a true orthodox in most matters, could have told him.

Marx is a different matter. He may have been an autodidact in economics, but he had a German doctorate in philosophy – in those days it would have been demeaning for him, even had it been possible, to go to a university to learn economics, a fledgling subject. He did what he was taught to do. Using the method of immanent criticism, he mastered classical political economy to the extent that at times he was more Ricardian than Ricardo. But his real intent was to subvert classical political economy from within, as it were, exactly as the method of immanent criticism dictates. Unfortunately for him, the orthodox bits are better worked out in *Capital* I than the critical bits. So Marx appears at times to belong to the bottom along with the new classicals and the neo-Ricardians. If, however, we take his pronounced intentions into account as well as the subsequent, unfinished volumes of *Capital*, he would like to be among the heretics if not even further out still. Marx in our context has to be regarded as a split soul wandering between the nethermost Ricardian region and the City of Dis with Keynes.

But we must nail down the nature of his heresy. He did not and could not accept autonomy, although many think that he made the economic element determinant 'in the final analysis' in his theory of historical materialism. (Others think it was technology/forces of production.) It is necessary, however, to remember that what was economic for Marx was much broader than how we or even Ricardo defined it. On rationality Marx could be said to accept individual rationality while predicting that the system was irrational precisely because individuals behaved rationally. The Invisible Hand worked merely to pick the pockets, if not throttle the workers. On equilibrium he played fast and loose; the Schemes for reproduction are super-equilibrium exercises, while elsewhere there are cycles and crises. One has to conclude that Marx would be happy neither in the City of Dis (he and Keynes would be bound to loathe each other) nor at the bottom of Hell with Ricardo. A wandering soul traversing all the levels of Hell, surely.

Heresy is something with which orthodoxy is willing to engage in battle, though many who pretend to be heretics are merely schismatic (refer to Locke above who contrasts errors in faith with errors in worship or discipline). The empirical attack on price theory of a P. W. S. Andrews is beyond heresy, whereas a Kalecki or Sraffa is seen indulgently as starting but a family quarrel.

Marxist economists – Lenin, Bukharin or Rosa Luxemburg – fare much better because they talk the language of economists, about prices and values, profits and crises, accumulation and labour markets.

BEYOND HERESY: WHO DWELLS IN THE UPPER HELL?

Heresy is however not the same as heterodoxy; misbelief is less of a transgression than unbelief. The unbeliever may be a heathen, never having had the chance to subscribe to the true religion. Alternatively, s/he may have unconverted, or chosen not to believe despite every opportunity to do so. I would like to argue that it is this transgression – unbelief – or heterodoxy, as I will call it, which is 'beyond the pale' for economists. We can be rude about the heretics or we may challenge them; but the unbelievers are embarrassing. One can only denounce them at worst or ignore them at best. Marshall went to a meeting that Henry George was holding in Cambridge precisely with the intention of denouncing him. He had to be exposed as a false prophet. In this sense Veblen is at worst a heretic, but Henry George is an enemy.

Subsequent generations ignore the unbelievers, but their contemporaries feel a need to excoriate them. The best example of such a dweller in the upper Hell is in my view John Ruskin. The unbeliever attacks economics root and branch, from Adam Smith downwards. Ruskin did so at a time when he had already become the favourite 'coffee-table' author of the Victorian bourgeoisie; he also did so eloquently. The reaction to *Unto This Last* (1860) was horrendous. Thackeray, having commissioned these articles, had to cut Ruskin short. In its book form, *Unto This Last* languished for 20 years. Economists did not reply to the attacks of Ruskin (as far as I know, no prominent economist of the time answered him). But Ruskin was a far more powerful voice of the underworld of economics than the monetary cranks that Keynes immortalized. William Morris and many of the early English Socialists were influenced by Ruskin. The first batch of elected Labour Party MPs cited Ruskin as the strongest influence through his *Unto This Last*. Gandhi took him to India.

Ruskin's power is that he denies every proposition of economics, from the benefits of division of labour to the definition of wealth and the conception of *homo economicus* even as an abstraction. He may be absurd when he argues for equal wages regardless of productivity differences. But if we examine the long-run impact of his thought on actual economic life rather than economic thought, he comes out ahead. In the preface to *Unto This Last*, he argues the benefits of state provision of free primary and secondary education and the economic benefits of industrial training; elsewhere he values health and longevity as more important than monetary accumulation as a measure of wealth. He abhors the pollution caused by much industrial activity. While we have come to appreciate the validity of this way of looking at the economy (see, for example, the recent Human Development Report of the United Nations Development Programme), his contemporaries thought this was economic madness, analytically unsound, if not palpable nonsense. He lives on better in the modern welfare state than do the heroes of the economists from those days. Who outside academic economics cares about Jevons? What did he contribute to human welfare, except perhaps a theory of index numbers? Could it be that heresy is more policy-effective than truth, and heterodoxy even more so?

The heterodox does not trust the economist's wisdom nor his goodwill, He has no analysis to match the economist's. He does not make the textbooks. Assigned for ever outside the nether Hell, the unbeliever is beyond the pale, to be forever ignored. But out there in the real world the people hungry for a solution to their problems, almost any solution, listen easily to the unbeliever since economists do not speak to them. Our presumption that we are correct because we have theory neither pleases them nor reassures them. They are moved more by the passionate urgency of the unbeliever, his sense of realism (the upper Hell is closer to the earth even in Dante's geography) than they are by our confidence in our science.

It is this world that the monetary cranks once occupied and it is these people that Keynes quite wrongly labelled as heretics. When unemployment and depression were the most severe problems, it was these people – Gesell, Major Douglas, Foster and Catchings, Ezra Pound in his economic outings – who were seized of the urgency of the problems and impatient at the economists' smugness. At that time someone from within – Keynes – heard their message but came to a solution which the economists could not ignore even had they disagreed with it. This was because Keynes was previously a believer, a fully paid-up member of the club. Economics was saved perhaps by that happy accident. In denouncing the Keynesian heresy rather than ignoring it as heterodoxy, economics permanently expanded its ability to face up to practical problems.

It may be that with the global ecological debate we are again at a similar juncture; the troops outside the walled town of economics are impatient and proposing a variety of radical solutions. Economists take the view that they have the tools to tackle all these problems; that their equilibrium theorizing and reliance on rationality are enough to get us out of the ecological challenge.

Above the nether Hell this confidence is derided. All those years ago Ruskin threw fundamental doubts on the economists system of valuation – their value theory. Classical or neoclassical, the economists value theory is commodity fetishistic. Ruskin and William Morris as much as the young naïve Marx of 1844 (before he read the classics and digested them) all reject the division of labour and the utility of material gratification Their Utopianism was anti-progressive; only Marx changed his Utopianism the other way around. Only by speeding up the juggernaut will liberation come, he said.

It is in the total rejection of the value theory of all economics that the ecological movement stamps itself with a heterodoxical face; there is and can be no dialogue. This is no heresy; this is way beyond all that. There is little one can do to test the rival systems; the facts that may vindicate one side may come too late for all of us. In the depression, the fear was of social and political anarchy, a destruction of capitalism. Now the stakes are higher. Only another heretic can bridge the gulf that so totally separates the economists from the ecologists. Heresy is, after all, a device to tame the concerns of heterodoxy in as much as they may affect the life and death of the faithful.

6. The Macroeconomics of Thomas Joplin*

Denis O'Brien

INTRODUCTION

Thomas Joplin was born probably about 1790 in Newcastle – although this belief is based upon the age claimed by Joplin in late life; an extensive search of the records in both Durham and Newcastle has failed to reveal any record of his birth.[1] The family were timber merchants, hailing originally from a village called Satley, 15 miles south-west of Newcastle upon Tyne. Perhaps because the timber in the area of Satley was becoming exhausted, the Joplins seem to have transferred their business to Newcastle where both Thomas Joplin and his father were timber merchants.[2] A call upon him to act as a guarantor for a bank in financial difficulties turned his attention to the subject of banking, and the result was his essay 'On the General Principles and Present Practice of Banking' which first appeared in 1822. This work, which went through many subsequent editions, acted as the flagship for Joplin's campaign to break the monopoly of joint-stock banking enjoyed by the Bank of England, so as to permit the establishment of such banks in England and Wales. (The Scots already enjoyed the advantages of this form of banking organization, and Joplin repeatedly extolled the virtues of their system.)

Joplin's attention having become fully engaged by the question of banking, it was natural that he should have broadened his enquiry to more general economic matters, and especially to the regulation of the money supply. The initial outcome of this was his *Outlines of a System of Political Economy* which appeared in 1823. It was at this very early stage, several years before the idea became general, that Joplin put forward the basic principle that a mixed currency of metal and paper should fluctuate in amount exactly as an identically circumstanced fully metallic currency would have done. This idea was to become the cornerstone of the Currency School position in the 1830s.[3] However Joplin – throughout his life very much an outsider – was to find himself in sharp disagreement with the Currency School. For whereas the Currency School believed that the Bank of England note issue was central to the money supply and the country banks merely a disequilibrating force, Joplin developed a macroeconomic model designed to show how disequilibrium would occur constantly if the national money supply had *two* unco-ordinated sources, as he believed it had.

The remainder of Joplin's career involved battling on both these fronts. On the one hand he fought long and hard, and ultimately successfully, to establish joint-stock banking. The British commercial bank system that exists today is, to a quite extraordinary extent, the legacy of his efforts.[4] Secondly, he put forward a plan for reform of the British monetary system so as to make it *unicentral*, so that the principle of 'metallic fluctuation' could safely be applied to the regulation of the *national* money supply. In this latter effort he was largely unsuccessful. The Currency School recommendations framed the Bank Charter Act of 1844, which focused almost entirely upon the note issue of the Bank of England, and did nothing to regulate the issues of the country banks beyond placing an overall ceiling on the issues of each bank and aiming at the ultimate extinction of those issues. In the short term such an approach, as Joplin correctly foresaw, could produce only financial crisis.[5]

In the course of his efforts to establish joint-stock banks, Joplin succeeded in establishing not one but two important banks, and was involved with a number of minor ones. In 1824 he established the Provincial Bank of Ireland, a joint-stock bank operating with branches; and in 1833, after prolonged efforts, and with the help of his cousin George Fife Angas, the pioneer of South Australia, he established the National Provincial Bank of England.[6]

But Joplin seems to have been incapable of sustaining a working relàtionship for any length of time. He was, it is evident from his writings, an extremely abrasive individual. In addition to this he was, as a North-Easterner, very much an outsider in the City of London circles. For reasons that are not entirely clear, he left the Provincial Bank of Ireland, of which he was the Secretary, within two years of its foundation; and, after a prolonged – and exceedingly public – row over the question of whether branches should have local shareholders, he left the National Provincial Bank of England, again within two years of foundation.

Possibly as a result of these conflicts, his health broke down and he seems to have been a sick man from at least the mid-1830s until his death in 1847. Moreover his prolonged conflicts with banks with which he was associated, including the London and County Bank, resulted in his being driven from these organizations with little or no financial compensation. He was in fact, especially after various unsuccessful business ventures in the late 1830s, living in some poverty in Gravesend in Kent. None the less, apparently undaunted by life's rebuffs, he continued to write on macroeconomics, fiercely resisting the proposals which became the Bank Act of 1844, and he also engaged in a campaign to attack the organization of prostitution, seeking as an ally in this the somewhat unlikely figure of Henry Brougham.[7]

It is clear from a rather pathetic appeal for money which appeared in the *Banker's Magazine* of 1846,[8] that Joplin was in considerable financial and personal difficulties and felt, not unreasonably, that the joint-stock banks, by now prosperous organizations, owed him some recognition. This he did not receive – indeed they seem to have been determined to forget about Joplin as quickly as possible, for there is no mention of him at all in the six volumes of Gilbart's works. This is highly significant given Gilbart's position both as a leading joint-stock banker (and one-time associate of Joplin's in the Irish enterprise) and as a leading writer on banking. Joplin died while making a second attempt to secure a remedy for his health problems at a continental spa in April 1847.[9]

Joplin's work has received extraordinarily little attention, which is all the more surprising given the sheer quantity which he wrote and also the intellectual vigour of his contribution. In the limited space available here, all that can be done is to attempt to outline the macroeconomic model to which Joplin adhered consistently, and which turns out to be, at least in some respects, significantly superior to what was on offer from the famous names in the Currency and Banking Schools.

OUTPUT AND EXPENDITURE

The starting-point for Joplin's approach to macroeconomic problems was the annual income of a country. The equality of expenditure with income was the basic equilibrium condition which Joplin called the 'Fulcrum of the Argument'.[10] This equilibrium condition is indeed a key factor in understanding Joplin's macroeconomics. In terms of later classifications, the approach which he based upon this is closer to Keynes than to Wicksell.

Income received from productive activity was expended on consumption and investment or (a quantitatively insignificant possibility) it was hoarded. Demand for loans included not only investment in productive capacity and in stocks but also consumption borrowing. If the capital market were allowed to clear through variation in the rate of interest, consumption borrowing plus investment borrowing should equal savings.[11]

In an open economy expenditure equalled output plus net imports. A balance of payments surplus resulted in aggregate demand being greater than aggregate supply at the existing price level. This excess aggregate demand raised producer incomes, output and the price level.[12]

A balance of payments surplus raised aggregate demand by raising the money supply. The level of aggregate demand depended upon the money supply and its velocity. Velocity of circulation was not, however, fixed. The demand for money could vary. It was a function of the level of income and of the rate of interest. Joplin viewed the demand for balances as being negatively related to the rate of interest. He calculated that the interest elasticity of demand for consumption balances was slightly greater than minus one. He gives no calculation for the interest elasticity of financial balances but is clear that a fall in the rate of interest, and the concomitant rise in property values, would involve the holding of greater balances for transactions in property.

At equilibrium levels of income the demand for balances was proportional to the level of income. However, out of equilibrium it was possible for balances to fall, and velocity to rise, with an upsurge in activity.[13]

JOPLIN'S MACROECONOMIC MODEL

Joplin's macroeconomic model is framed in terms of the concept of a circular flow of income around the system. It thus rests upon the 'Fulcrum of the Argument':

> The demand for labour in money determines the amount of money which the labouring class have to give for corn, and what they have to give the farmer gets. It moves in a circle, consumption is promoted at the price which the corn produces, and the corn produces the price at which its consumption is promoted.   (Joplin 1828: 76)

It is upon this basis that Joplin was to explore the way in which monetary arrangements could dislocate the circular flow, resulting in a fall in national income and the emergence of unemployment.

Aggregate demand depends upon the money supply.[14] Changes in the level of aggregate demand, produced by changes in the money supply, will have multiple effects on the level of income. Joplin provided possibly the earliest clear statement of the existence of a multiplier:

> Income, however, once generated, will multiply itself in its progress, and pass through many hands before it is finally expended in a demand for that produce which gave it birth.   (Joplin 1828: 71)

The price level depended upon the demand for tradeables – what Joplin called the 'consumptive circulation' in contrast to the 'abstract circulation' which was employed in financial transactions. An increase in the money supply increased aggregate demand. Merchants would then increase the size of their stocks, and the transmission of this demand to producers would increase employment. Increased employment would result in increased consumption. Since supply was less than perfectly elastic, increased output implied increased prices. (There are clear similarities here with the work of Hawtrey, and with some of that of Keynes.) Thus a rise in money income involved a rise in real income *and* a rise in prices.[15]

The money supply, and thus aggregate demand, were necessarily linked to the balance of payments. There was an equilibrium level of national prices at which payments would balance. A rise in the price level above that national equilibrium level would lower exports, and increase imports, with the resulting balance of payments deficit lowering the money supply again.[16]

While a rise in the money supply produced a rise in money income, a contraction in the money supply would result in a movement in the opposite direction. Wages and working hours would fall, labour income and profits would decline, and the consequent reduction in the desired level of merchants' stocks would feed back to producers as reduced demand for output, resulting in the emergence of unemployment. Reductions in the money supply, if accompanied by a rise in the rate of interest, also raised the cost of stock holding, thus further reducing the desired level of stocks. Stocks were thus an extremely important part of the mechanism by which monetary disturbance was transmitted.[17]

Even more important, however, was the role of the labour market. An increase in the demand for labour increased the demand for commodities, especially food, with a consequent rise in prices. In Joplin's view expenditure *on* labour was itself the determinant of the expenditure *by* labour which in turn determined the price of foodstuffs.[18]

The direct conclusion from this model – in strong contrast to most classical writing – was that if depression existed this was due to a lack of aggregate demand. In the early 1820s Joplin pointed both to monetary causes and to reductions in government expenditure as responsible for the reduction in aggregate demand which produced unemployment and depression. He was not talking about aggregate demand failure of the capital-stock adjustment kind associated with Lauderdale and Malthus, but with aggregate demand failure which was a result of monetary, and to some extent fiscal, mismanagement.[19]

If aggregate demand fell, the first output market to be affected was that of agriculture. Agricultural prices fell. Since farmers faced fixed charges this resulted in, at best, depression of agricultural profits and, at worst, bankruptcy. Joplin laid particular stress upon the importance of fixed charges in agriculture and was a life-long defender of the Corn Laws, considering that a 60-shilling price of corn was a desirable target, given the level of agricultural fixed charges.[20]

In all this it is striking to note that Joplin considered the possibility that the circular flow of income and expenditure could be equilibrated at various levels. In other words, monetary contraction could result in an income level which was stable but with unemployment existing. To move from a lower to a higher level, 'pump priming' was necessary. Changes in aggregate demand altered not only the price level, but also national income and employment. It was also true that changes in national income affected the balance of payments; a fall in national income, with a rise in unemployment, would reduce expenditure and thus the demand for imports. However it was possible for the lower level of national income to be an equilibrium one in relation to the balance of payments, because a reduction in British imports would affect the foreign level of money income and thus the demand for British exports.[21]

A model of this kind clearly involves a positively sloped aggregate supply schedule. This seems to have been exactly what Joplin envisaged. An increase in aggregate demand would initially result in an increase in employment at the old wage rate. However the expenditure of the extra wages thus earned would lead to a rise in prices, which would lead in turn to increased agricultural output, profits and investment. Wages were sticky, and would move upwards after the rise in food prices.[22]

Thus an increase in aggregate demand, as a result of an increase in the money supply, would produce an expansion of aggregate supply. Joplin expected that this would occur not only because of a higher participation rate but also because of an increased supply of labour from the existing labour force. (Joplin refers to few other economists, and those mostly in a negative way, but in this context he acknowledged the work of Hume.[23])

However, the effects of an increase in the money supply in increasing aggregate demand were lagged. Joplin believed that the lag between an increase in the money supply and an increase in aggregate demand was as much as twelve months. But through its effects on aggregate demand, a change in the money supply affected stocks, employment, imports and exports, the exchange rate and the price level.[24]

In all this, perhaps the most striking thing is the extent to which Joplin emphasized the importance of unemployment. Amongst his contemporaries, perhaps only Thomas Attwood paid so much attention to this. The essential point which Joplin emphasized was that a defective paper currency, leading either directly or through a balance of payments deficit to monetary contraction, would result in unemployment.[25]

PROBLEMS OF A PAPER CURRENCY

Such monetary changes would arise if a currency which was wholly, or partly, a paper currency did not behave as an identically circumstanced metallic currency would have done. But this general principle extended far beyond the familiar Currency School prescription that it should do so in relation to the balance of payments. Joplin's view was much more comprehensive. He argued that, while a metallic currency would maintain the circular flow which was necessary for macroeconomic equilibrium, the creation and destruction of paper money broke the circular flow. Most critically, a paper currency allowed a banker to lend money which had not first been saved, thus breaking the link between savings and investment.[26] As Joplin put it:

> [I]t may easily be conceived, that without the aid of a proper currency, to assist in keeping the income and expenditure upon a par with each other, the expenditure must at all times have a tendency either to exceed or fall short of the income. (1844a: 27)

Because of the fundamentally faulty mechanisms governing the supply of paper currency (which will be explored further below) the country experienced constant monetary disequilibrium. The changes in the money supply, both directly and through their effect upon flows across the exchanges, resulted in constant changes in aggregate demand and thus in real income.[27]

Joplin's concerns over the mechanisms for varying the supply of money involved several considerations. First, there was the fundamental problem that there were two sources for the money supply, that these were unco-ordinated, and that the most important source (the country banks) was largely unresponsive to the balance of payments. Secondly, there was the problem that what links there were between the country money supply and the London money supply were actually disequilibrating. Thirdly, the nature of the market for loanable funds in the country produced random changes in the money supply.

However, before turning to these problems it is necessary to address one very fundamental distinction concerning the nature of the money supply which Joplin made. This distinction was between the 'abstract circulation' and the 'consumptive circulation', which has been touched on already. The abstract circulation was employed in the exchange of property and financial assets. Such exchange took place, for the most part, in London, and employed the very large denomination Bank of England notes as well as bank deposits. Joplin estimated that half of Bank of England notes were used in this way.

The 'consumptive circulation' was that money employed for expenditure upon consumption goods – principally tradeables. Joplin identified this with the country bank-notes, nine tenths of which were for denominations of less than £20. Although the *total* of Bank of England notes was approximately the same as that of country bank-notes, their velocity was, he estimated, only a quarter of that of the country bank-notes, and so aggregate demand, and hence the national price level, were mainly dependent upon the country bank-note supply. The country bank-note issue was thus the key to monetary equilibrium.[28]

Joplin supported this line of argument not only by reference to population distribution, roughly adjusted for higher consumption per head in London (and Lancashire) – this was the basis of his velocity estimate – but also on the basis of price series for wheat (as representing the general price level) and changes in the supply of bank-notes from London and the country.[29]

Such an approach is in dramatic contrast to the main nineteenth-century monetary writings which placed the issues of the Bank of England at centre stage. For Joplin it was the country banks and their notes which mattered. But if, in turn, there were problems over the determination of the supply of these notes, this had serious implications for the national money supply.

COUNTRY BANKS AND THEIR NOTES

While Joplin recognized that the issues of country bank-notes could be constrained both by relative inter-regional prices and by reserve losses, he concentrated his attention upon the effects of variations in the demand for, and supply of, loanable funds on these issues. The argument was this. The country banks, operating under a paper currency issued at will by bankers, could not know what the equilibrium rate of interest was. In such a state of ignorance, the country banks found it necessary to hold their minimum lending rate at around 5 per cent and to allow the loan market to clear by varying the supply of bank-notes rather than by allowing the rate of interest to clear it. An increased demand for loans would result in the country in an increase in lending. It was the money supply, rather than the rate of interest, which fluctuated in order to clear the market for loanable funds.[30]

What Joplin had in mind is shown in Figure 6.1. In this particular case a shift in the demand for loanable funds, with a given supply of savings, produces a change in the money supply; but equally, a shift in the savings function with a given demand for loans would have a similar effect.[31]

The basic problem, as already indicated, was that without a metallic currency, *or a paper currency which exactly simulated a metallic currency*, there was no way that the country banks could know the equilibrium rate of interest and so, from considerations of safety, they kept their lending rate at the maximum of 5 per cent allowed by the Usury Laws.[32]

> But with a paper currency, issued at pleasure by a great many bankers, all ignorant of the amount of each others issues, the savings of income can never be distinguished. . . . a banker can never know whether his own notes on hand, represent income which has been saved or not; he, consequently, can never know the real value of capital [the market clearing rate of interest], and is compelled to deal with his customers at one fixed rate of interest.   (1826: 38–9)

Figure 6.1

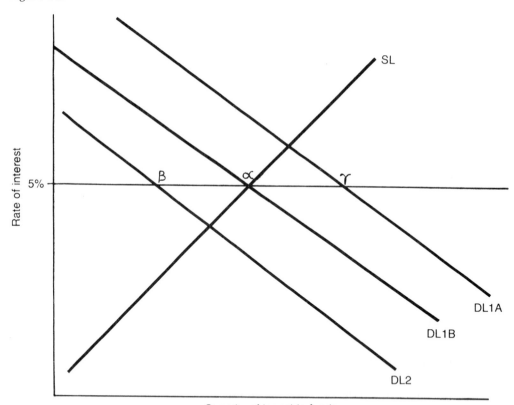

Suppose that, at α, the 5 per cent maximum interest allowed under the Usury Laws clears the loan market at the intersection of SL and DL1B. A shift of DL to DL2, with the rate of interest *fixed* at 5 per cent will result in net money destruction of α − β, the amount by which money saved at 5 per cent exceeds money invested. If the initial demand for loans had been DL1A, there would have been net money creation per period of γ − α. A shift from DL1A to DL2 would thus involve a switch from monetary expansion to monetary contraction.

The contrast with a metallic currency was fundamental.

With a metallic currency, on the contrary, the Banker would always know the state of the market. In the first place, he could not lend money until it had been saved and placed in his hands, and he would have a particular amount to lend. On the other hand, he would have more or fewer persons wanting to borrow, and in proportion as the demand would exceed, or fall short of the amount he had to lend, he would raise or lower his terms. (1832: 109)

It was true that, *within* the domestic banking system, over-issue by an individual bank, or even by banks in a region acting together, would encounter clearing pressures in the form of a demand for bills on London. But if there were expansion by *all* the country banks – which could easily happen if the country as a whole experienced similar variations in the demand for funds – then significant changes in the money supply and aggregate demand would take place, and any correction resulting from an adverse balance of payments (or from a balance of payments surplus if there had been monetary contraction) would be long delayed.[33]

The reason for the delay was two-fold. First, there was a significant lag between expansion of the money supply and a change in the national level of prices and output – Joplin put this at about 12 months. Secondly and most fundamentally, Joplin held that the country bank-note issue would in any case fail to respond in the way in which it ought to have done (if equilibrium were to be achieved) to monetary flows over the balance of payments. He was quite clear that the data showed that the country bank-note supply did not move in the same direction as metallic flows across the exchanges. Rather, it acted independently and not infrequently moved in the opposite direction. In particular he pointed out that exportation of gold in 1824–5 was accompanied by an increase in the supply of country bank-notes, which he attributed to increased demand for loans. Conversely, the assets of the country banks in London increased by more than £10 million in 1818 to 1822 (which, as we shall see, indicated that there had been a significant gold inflow); yet over the same period the country bank-note issue *fell* by £10 million.[34]

To some extent, this perverse behaviour was inbuilt. Thus, when harvest failure led to corn imports and a balance of payments deficit, the money supply should have contracted. But because of increased demand for bank lending *resulting from* the harvest failure, the money supply increased instead.[35]

Although Joplin was, as we shall see, prepared to afford considerable importance to the role of deposits in the *London* money market, the focus of his attention in the country was on notes rather than deposits. The reasoning here was that the prices of commodities were influenced by the expenditure of notes rather than by that of deposits subject to cheque. But in the London money market things were different.[36]

THE LONDON MONEY MARKET

In contrast to the loan market in which the country banks operated, the rate of interest in London fluctuated with alterations in the supply of, and demand for, loans, and thus cleared the market. Even the Bank of England, as the sole supplier of paper currency in London, effectively varied its rate of interest, through altering the terms on which it would buy exchequer bills, even though it appeared to be holding Bank Rate fixed.[37]

But this market was disturbed by the fact that it bore the brunt of all flows across the exchanges initiated by changes in the money supply produced by the behaviour of the country banks. In Joplin's view, the London money market, as essentially a market for savings, should not be affected by flows across the exchanges which related to national income rather than to capital transactions. But the existing monetary system diverted flows of national income across the exchanges to flow through the London money market.[38]

The source of the problem was essentially that international balances were settled in precious metals but that, within the domestic monetary system, there were parallel, and competing, sources of metal substitutes.

There were three aspects to this. First, there was the problem that all imported gold ended up in London. Secondly, there was the related fact that the country bank reserves were held in London. Thirdly – and for Joplin this was the most crucial matter of all – one importation of gold produced a *double* effect upon the money supply, adding an equal amount of country bank-notes and of money in London.

The gold ultimately ended in London because a country banker would buy it with his own notes and then send it to London either for purchasing gilt-edged securities or as a deposit at call. Alternatively, a merchant receiving gold would dispose of the gold in London, receiving in exchange a bill on the London agent which would be sold to the country banks in exchange for their notes. In strong contrast to the case of a metallic currency which would simply pass through London, the gold was detained there.[39]

The practice of the country banks in holding reserves as interest-bearing deposits in London, rather than holding gold, was central to this argument. It in turn led to the process by which a gold inflow not only affected the country bank-note supply, in the ways already seen, but also increased the availability of funds in London. This was the 'doubling' argument. Joplin put forward this line of reasoning from the 1820s. As the debates leading to the Bank Act of 1844 intensified, Joplin restated the argument with increased emphasis:[40]

> In short, on an importation and exportation of the precious metals, a double issue and double contraction takes place: one in the country and one in London; and the issue and contraction in London being illegitimate and unnatural, and such as would not take place with a metallic currency, produces those evils under which we have so long suffered. (1841: 13)

Three years later, as the Act loomed, Joplin wrote:

> The bullion received from abroad, being purchased up by the country bankers, is not only put into circulation in London where it has no business to be at all, but this is done by its being lent out at interest, as if it were money saved out of income. (1844a: 35)

It is important to appreciate that Joplin's argument here did not rely upon deposit multiplication within the London money market. He was simply arguing that an inflow of funds produced, in that market, extra deposits directly. This was buttressed by the idea that a London bank holding the country bank reserves would present the gold to the Bank of England which would issue notes, thus producing extra liquidity in the London market. But at a late stage in the argument Joplin added – probably under the influence of Torrens's supplement to his *Letter to Lord Melbourne* – an explanation of the mechanism of the deposit multiplier. He presented, in fact, what is now the standard explanation in textbooks (probably derived by Torrens himself from Pennington) of the geometric series resulting from the practice of lending on the basis of a fractional reserve system, and estimated that the deposit multiplier was around 6·7.[41]

But this was an important further development because Joplin was quite clear that most transactions in London were by cheque so that 'a transferable deposit and a bank note are equally money' (1844a: 39) – indeed cheques on deposits were 'the chief mode of payment in commercial transactions' (1841: 10).

But the fact that London transactions were conducted to a considerable extent by cheque meant that the Bank of England notes in the 'abstract circulation' were, in truth, the till money of the London banks and, unless they had excess precautionary reserves, could not be drawn down without causing severe difficulties in the London money market. Contraction in fact produced 'sudden and violent' panics (1844b: 40). These were the inevitable outcome of the existing monetary system and occurred in London whenever an outflow of gold was accompanied by a reduction in Bank of England notes, as recommended by the Bank's Currency School critics.[42]

For two reasons Joplin held that the correct response of the Bank to such a panic was to *increase* its note issue, by providing extra financial accommodation to the London money market. First, the circulation of the Bank of England was largely irrelevant to the national price level, and thus to the balance of payments, since it was mainly employed in the 'abstract circulation'. Secondly, the demand for money depended not only on the volume of transactions and the rate of interest, but also on a precautionary motive. In panic, the precautionary demand for funds increased dramatically, and the Bank could safely lend extra funds without the money lent getting into circulation. Notes issued to meet such a precautionary demand would automatically return to the Bank after the panic was over.[43]

Joplin in fact urged this course of action on the Bank in a newspaper article published on a fateful evening in 1825 and later claimed, repeatedly and with some considerable justification, to have stopped the panic of that year.[44]

THE DEMAND FOR AND SUPPLY OF LOANABLE FUNDS

Joplin was not concerned with hoarding, which he regarded as quantitatively insignificant.[45] Nor was he concerned with the kind of capital-stock adjustment problem which seems to have been at the centre of the argument of Lauderdale and Malthus.[46] His concern about savings related directly to its impact, through the market for loanable funds, upon the money supply.

The supply of savings was interest-elastic although the function itself would shift around with variations in the level of income. The demand for funds was also interest-elastic. It represented a demand for borrowing for productive expenditure, to finance losses in trade and commerce, for consumption expenditure and for government expenditure. Just as the savings function could shift with changes in the level of income so the loan demand function could also shift with changes in the general level of prosperity. However, Joplin also stressed the possibility that there might be *exogenous* shifts in the demand for funds. The two he stressed were, first, borrowing by government – sharply reduced after 1815 – and, secondly, harvest failure which increased the demand for loans from the agricultural sector.[47]

With a rigid interest rate, an inequality between savings and investment would produce a change in the money supply along the lines already indicated.[48] (Additionally, such an inequality could produce a change in the velocity of the money supply and thus alter aggregate demand in that way as well.[49]) An excess of borrowing over savings could, by placing command over resources in the hands of borrowers, impose forced saving upon the earners of income at the previous price level.[50]

In his writings in the 1820s Joplin laid particular stress upon changes in government expenditure as producing such inequalities. The majority of his attention, in dealing with government expenditure, is thus concentrated upon the monetary implications – with a fall in government expenditure, savings would be greater than the demand for borrowing, leading to a contraction of the money supply. It was this contraction of the money supply which he blamed for the agricultural depression of the early 1820s.[51] The reason that Joplin concentrated mainly upon the monetary effects is that he regarded government as having the power to crowd out private expenditure to a considerable extent.[52] Private borrowers could not pay more than the maximum of 5 per cent permitted by the Usury Laws, but the price of gilt-edged showed that government pushed the rate of interest higher than this. However, Joplin was prepared to concede that the private sector had recourse to trade credit at such times, trade credit being available when aggregate demand was at a high level because of government expenditure and the economy was buoyant. Government could thus, to some extent, make a net addition to the level of aggregate demand; and reductions in government expenditure, correspondingly, could produce a reduction in the level of aggregate demand quite apart from the effect of such a reduction upon the money supply.[53] Joplin did not think that reform of government expenditure was necessarily going to be of benefit to those sensitive to the level of aggregate demand:

> Now the abolition of sinecures, the reduction of salaries, and the consequent repeal of taxes, are, in themselves, most desirable, more especially to those by whom the taxes are paid; but they can hardly be beneficial to the working and productive classes, the demand for whose labour and industry may be increased by extravagance, but can hardly be so by economy. (1823: 6)

MONETARY CONTROL AND THE BANK OF ENGLAND

But it was the monetary problem which remained paramount for Joplin. In the light of this it is hardly surprising that he directed both his considerable powers of analysis and his considerable powers of invective at the Bank of England and its monetary management.[54] His basic position was that the Bank had managed to apply bad management to a defective monetary system. First, it had, even after the crisis of 1825, failed to learn to distinguish between internal and external sources of pressure upon its resources, and was thus forever in danger of causing panic.[55] Secondly, it was, in the 1830s, moving towards a system of matching gold outflows with note reductions which, because of the 'doubling' effect, could be disastrous if carried through. It was following this policy because it believed that it was able to control the exchanges, the general price level and the inflows and outflows of gold. Joplin was entirely convinced that this was not the case; from that point of view the critical part of the money supply derived from the country banks and these were almost entirely outside the control of the Bank of England. He cited data to show that the country bank-notes and the Bank of England notes moved in *opposite* directions. Thus a contraction by the Bank of England did not affect the amount of those notes which controlled aggregate demand and the price level.[56]

But in any case, even if the Bank had been in such a position, it would have had very limited freedom of manoeuvre. This was partly because it was the government's bank and in this position might – and Joplin pointed to an episode in 1824 when this had very nearly happened – find itself in the position of having to create extra money because of a shortfall in government borrowing.[57] But the main problem was simply that an attempt by the Bank to contract its note issue was likely to precipitate the collapse of the London money market. Indeed, given the irrelevance of the Bank of England note issue to the balance of payments, Joplin believed that the correct course for the Bank was to attempt to *neutralize* the effects of precious-metal flows across the exchanges. It could do this by failing to cancel notes which it received in exchange for gold, using those notes to buy gilt-edged securities and thus returning the notes to the market. Conversely, it could dampen the effect of a gold inflow by selling gilt-edged securities to mop up the extra notes which it issued in exchange for gold.[58] Although the Bank's room for manoeuvre here was limited (partly by its own belief about its power to influence the exchanges and partly by a reluctance to part with gilt-edged securities when gold flowed in, reducing the average yield on the asset side of its balance sheet) Joplin believed such neutralization was extremely important if financial crises were to be avoided. For the Bank was in a very difficult position. In Joplin's view, based upon the experience of 20 years, the maximum reduction in its notes that could be made without causing financial collapse was only of the order of £1.5–2 million even though gold flows could be of the order of £10 million. [59]

But if the Bank did neutralize the effects of monetary flows in this way, the side effects of doing so would be serious. For while it would protect the London money market, and thus the trade of that part of the country which was affected by the London money market, notably Lancashire, it would at the same time *prevent* correction of disequilibrating changes in the money supply, originating in the country banks, by flows across the exchanges. There was thus the prospect of perpetual disequilibria and a continuing threat hanging over the London money market.[60]

The difficulties of the Bank were also considerably increased by the activities of its critics who, under the influence of the Bullion Committee of 1810 and the Ricardian Definition of Excess, impressed upon the Bank the idea that it was necessary to match gold inflows and outflows exactly with changes in the Bank of England note issue, believing this to be the monetary base which controlled aggregate monetary demand for the economy as a whole. If the Bank ignored this opinion it appeared to be ignoring the best professional opinion; but if it followed it, it was in danger of producing financial collapse.[61]

Its most serious attempt to follow it was the so-called Palmer Rule, under which, starting from a position just before the onset of a balance of payments deficit, it aimed to have bullion equal to one-third of its combined liabilities of notes and deposits. The Bank then matched gold flows against note and deposit variations on a one-for-one basis. Joplin found this to be peculiarly inept. Given the fragile state of the London money market, the appropriate reserve against deposits was not bullion at all, but notes. The Palmer Rule not only confused London with England – like the Bank's critics – but confused note circulation with deposits. Moreover, with a given gold reserve, accidental variations in deposits would constrain the Bank to make unnecessary variations in the note issue in order to follow its balance sheet rule.[62]

JOPLIN'S PLAN

The remedy for all these difficulties was clearly to abolish competing and unco-ordinated centres of money supply, and to replace these with a single *national* money supply which would vary exactly as an identically circumstanced metallic currency would have done.[63] It was not necessary to have either a metallic currency, or a 100 per cent reserve which would in any case not cover commercial payments in London, which were made by cheque.[64] A currency organized in this way, because it would behave exactly like a metallic currency, would also have the advantage of allowing the loan market to clear since the bankers would now know the state of that market.[65] A change in conditions in the loan market would change the rate of interest, not the money supply.

Joplin originally proposed a plan which would involve allocating the national equilibrium note issue, to be estimated from past data, between newly established joint-stock banks.[66] Government would guarantee the note issue and the banks would pay government a seignorage for this privilege. Bullion dealings would be in the hands of a Board of Commissioners – Joplin's proposals predate Ricardo's here. Incoming bullion would be purchased by the Commissioners who would issue bullion receipts. Such bullion receipts could be presented at any of the participating banks, and the bank would be obliged to purchase it for *new* notes. The bank would then return the receipt to the Commissioners, acquiring a credit with the Commissioners as a result. In the case of a gold outflow the banks would buy back their own notes by drafts drawn against their balances with the Commission, *cancelling those notes*, and such drafts could then be used to obtain bullion for export. Such flows could also take place between different regions of the country, with drafts on the Bullion Commissioners being used in place of bullion. However, to avoid unnecessary use of such drafts, the Commissioners would charge an amount equal to the cost of transmitting bullion between regions, thus encouraging the use of commercial bills to settle inter-regional balances. Such a system would have the advantage not only of producing a unitary national money supply, linked directly to the balance of payments; it would also ensure that that national money supply was distributed between regions in the correct proportions.

With a unified money supply, a scarcity of funds in London could be matched by flows from the country; the London money market would no longer have a special disruptive role, and there would be no panics.[67]

Perhaps most importantly of all, changes in aggregate demand would be very limited. It would be possible for the country to maintain macroeconomic equilibrium. No longer would the stickiness of wages, and to a lesser extent prices, be reflected in the emergence of unemployment in the train of rapidly fluctuating levels of aggregate demand.[68]

With this in mind, Joplin made the daring proposal that in the event of a significant exogenous change – principally a harvest failure – the country should *temporarily abandon convertibility*. The exchange rate would be allowed to float freely until such time as, first, corn imports had met the immediate emergency and, secondly, harvests had resumed their normal level.[69]

Hardly surprisingly, such a suggestion was anathema to both the Currency and Banking Schools – convertibility was not an issue between them. Once again, Joplin emerges as the outsider. He was in fact a considerable distance intellectually from both groups. A firm belief in the idea that causality ran from the money supply to the price level excluded him from the Banking School. But he was an almost equal distance from the Currency School, with which he has sometimes been associated in the secondary literature, because he believed that to adopt metallic fluctuation for Bank of England notes alone would be disastrous, and that the proposal for the Separation of Departments which was designed to achieve this would achieve nothing but a repetition of crises like that of 1825[70] – a belief which was vindicated by the crises of 1847 and 1857, occurring after Joplin's death.

Joplin made a number of changes in his plan over the years in an attempt to placate the Bank of England and the private banks. By 1839 he was prepared to include the private banks in his scheme as note issuers, alongside the joint-stock banks which by then had been established; and he was even prepared to hand over the management of the currency to the Bank of England, leaving the Commissioners in a supervisory role, which included the possibility of suspending convertibility envisaged above.[71] But the basic plan remained firmly grounded upon the necessity of having a national money supply under firm control, to produce macroeconomic stability and full employment.

CONCLUSION

Joplin presented a macroeconomic model in which an open economy, with two competing sources of money supply, suffered from fluctuations in aggregate demand, unemployment and depression. He showed how changes in savings, investment and government expenditure with a fixed rate of interest would destabilize the level of economic activity. He then used this analysis to show that the Bank of England, under a mistaken belief that it was in a position to control the money supply and to rectify the balance of payments, was responsible, through its mismanagement, for repeated distress and recurrent panics.

Joplin's performance, despite the rough-hewn nature of much that he wrote because of the pressures upon him, deserves to be ranked with, and in some respects above, the well-known contributions from the members of the Currency and Banking Schools. But Joplin, partly through circumstances, and partly through unfortunate personal characteristics, was, and remained throughout his life, an outsider. Had the programme which he first put forward in 1823 been adopted, it is likely that the monetary history of the 1840s and 1850s would have been a good deal less turbulent.

NOTES

* The author is engaged on a full-length study of Joplin.
1. I am grateful to Patricia O'Doherty of Gravesend Public Library for a copy of the 1841 Census Return. See also Crick and Wadsworth 1936.
2. Phillips 1894: 104.
3. O'Brien 1971: 70–144.
4. Gregory 1926.
5. For a Bank of England's eye view of the crises of 1847 and 1857, see Clapham 1944: II. 199–211, 226–38.
6. Hodder 1891: 85–9; Withers 1933: 29–43; Gregory 1936: 16–17, 335–53, 360.
7. Letters of 9 March 1843, 26 February 1844, Brougham MSS, University College, London. See also Phillips 1894: 107.
8. [Joplin] 1846.
9. Crick and Wadsworth 1936: 325–6: *Gentleman's Magazine*, xxix (March 1848), 320–1.
10. Joplin 1823: 32–3.
11. Ibid.: 44–5; 1825: 24–5; 1839: 14; 1844a: 2–3.
12. Joplin 1823: 171.
13. Ibid.: 176–8, 226; 1825: 46–51, 65, 70–1; 1832: 56–7.
14. Joplin 1825: 60; 1828: 242; 1831a: 6; 1844a: 6, 14, 76.
15. Joplin 1823: xiii, 174, 186, 226; 1833: 97; 1833–4: 26–8; 1838: 107.
16. Joplin 1823: 19, 171–3; 1825: 30–3; 1826: 34–5; 1844a: 13–16.
17. Joplin 1823: 195; 1832: 116, 167–8; 1833–4: 27; 1839: 43; 1841: 12.
18. Joplin 1832: 86, 91; 1844b: 73.
19. Joplin 1823: xv; 1825: xx.
20. Joplin 1825: 60; 1844a: 1, 7, 14–15.
21. Joplin 1825: 60; 1844a: 6; 1844b: 73–9.
22. Joplin 1825: xxi; 1828: 66.
23. Joplin 1832: 142–5, 224–7 (dating from 1825).

24. Joplin 1828: 175–6; 1832: 224–7.
25. Joplin 1825: 60; 1826: 79; 1828: 7, 41, 51, 66, 94–5, 239–41; 1831a: 6–7; 1832: 162; 1833: 97; 1838: 2–5; 1844a: 1, 4, 35–6, 45, 85–7; 1844b: 1.
26. Joplin 1826: 15–16, 34, 38, 54–7; 1832: 101, 107–9; 1844a: 19, 24–5, 27, 29–30, 77–8.
27. Joplin 1823: 192; 1825: 11, 12, 37; 1826: 54; 1844a: 18–19.
28. Joplin 1823: 156–7; 1825: xxv, 23–6; 1826: 48; 1828: 28–32; 1831b: 8; 1832: 89–98.
29. Joplin 1825: 48; 1826: 48–52; 1827: xiii; 1831b: 8; 1832: 87–9, 113–14.
30. Joplin 1822: 572; 1825: 4, 11–12, 25, 53; 1826: 35–6; 1827: 193, 195; 1828: 34, 163–4.
31. It was a pleasure to discover Tom Wilson's priority here (1948: 11).
32. Joplin 1825: 37–8; 1826: 38–9; 1828: 161–2; 1831b: 8–9; 1832: 109, 111; 1839: 15; 1841: 70–1; 1844a: 25, 33.
33. Joplin 1823: 201–14; 1825: 12, 35–7; 1826: 44–5; 1828: 155–8; 1839: 20–1; 1841: 76–7; 1844a: 20.
34. Joplin 1825: 35–8, 40, 82–3; 1826: 41–3; 1828: 139–41, 148–50, 163–6; 1832: 224–7; 1833: 55–6; 1833–4: 25, 28–31; 1841: 14–15; 1844a: 23–4, 28–30, 57; 1844b: 9–10.
35. Joplin 1825: 43–4.
36. Joplin 1828: 187; 1832: 276–7; 1841: 18, 70–1.
37. Joplin 1828: 150–3; 1832: 111–13.
38. Joplin 1839: 38–41; 1844a: 19, 21, 31.
39. Joplin 1823: 211–13; 1825: 84–6; 1833: 90–1; 1844a: 19–20, 35, 46; 1844b: 33; 1845b: 7.
40. Joplin 1823: 206–9; 1825: xxix–xxx, 38, 83–6; 1826: 42, 67–8; 1828: 142–5, 148–54, 159; 1832: 162–8, 273–4; 1841: 13, 23–52; 1844a: 19–20, 34–6, 57; 1844b: 33–5; 1845a (suppt): 7.
41. Joplin 1841: 32–4; 1844a: 41, 43, 49, 53; 1844b: 36–8.
42. Joplin 1839: 36–7; 1841: 9–10, 29–30, 48; 1844b: 35–8.
43. Joplin 1828: 175–6; 1832: 219–20, 227–32; 1833: 55–62; 1833–4: 21–2, 27–8; 1841: 42–5, 51–2; 1844b: 56–7.
44. Joplin 1832: 219, 227–30; 1833–4: 21–2.
45. Joplin 1823: 58; 1826: 15–16; 1828: 52–3; 1832: 102; 1839: 17; 1844a: 2.
46. Joplin 1823: 38. But see 1832: 126, and 1841: 47.
47. Joplin 1823: 57–8, 61–2, 251; 1828: 165; 1832: 105–6.
48. Joplin 1828: 158–64; 1832: 101, 108, 113, 120–1; 1839: 14–15; 1844a: 25–7, 77.
49. Joplin 1823: 64; 1845a (suppt): 7.
50. Joplin 1825: 28; 1826: 35–6; 1828: 146–7.
51. Joplin 1823: xv, 65, 224; 1825: 53; 1831a: 6.
52. Joplin 1823: 66–8; 1825: xix–xx.
53. Joplin 1823: 65; 1828: 165.
54. Joplin 1832: 324–30; 1833: 87–96; 1833–4: 40–4; 1838: 107.
55. Joplin 1833–4: 3–26; 1837: 113–22; 1841: 37–8, 60–1; 1844b: 20–4.
56. Joplin 1823: 259; 1825: xxvi–xxviii, 6–7, 45; 1826: 46–8; 1828: 28–32; 1832: 119–20, 217–19.
57. Joplin 1833: 47–55.
58. Joplin 1825: 86–7; 1832: 168–72; 1839: 45–6; 1841: 13–14, 37–8; 1844a: 46–9, 55; 1844b: 4–5.
59. Joplin 1841: 60–1; 1844a: 50–1; 1844b: 18–24.
60. Joplin 1832: 170–1; 1841: 14.
61. Joplin 1833: 90–100, 112–18; 1844a: 47.
62. Joplin 1828: 148; 1833: 37–47, 76; 1838: 12–13.
63. Joplin 1837: 57–8; 1838: 17–18; 1839: 2, 18–23; 1844b: 50–1, 86; 1845a (suppt): 3–4.
64. Joplin 1841: 28–9.
65. Joplin 1825: 15–16; 1839: 15, 23; 1841: 74.
66. Joplin 1823: 262–77; 1825: 16–17; 1826: 63–70, 78; 1832: 152–6, 172–3; 1839: 22–3, 54–5; 1840; 1841: 74.
67. Joplin 1839: 36, 47–50; 1841: 7, 10, 17–18, 42–4, 50; 1844: 55–6; 1844b: 24, 42–3; 1845b: 9.
68. Joplin 1832: 156–7.
69. Joplin 1826: 76–7; 1828: 243–4.
70. Joplin 1841: 20–1, 56; 1844b: 6–7.
71. Joplin 1839: 56–7; 1841: 15–20, 41–2, 52, 72–6; 1844a: 62–7; 1844b: 44–52.

Part II

7. How Inflation Undermines Economic Performance

Walter Eltis*

INTRODUCTION

It is still widely believed, and especially by academic economists who follow the Keynesian tradition, that the control of inflation matters far less than output and employment. Their approach is at first sight compatible with the compensation test that is commonly applied to estimate whether an economic change is beneficial to welfare. Can the gainers compensate the losers and still remain better off after they have done so? Anything that raises an economy's aggregate output should pass that test, because if an economy produces more and the extra is correctly measured, those who benefit must by definition have enough extra GNP to compensate the losers and still gain themselves. The deflationary policies that are often needed to bring inflation down are liable to reduce GNP in the first instance, and many economists have been unwilling to recommend this temporary sacrifice of output, employment and growth, which must produce more losers than gainers until output recovers. For the same reason economists who follow the Keynesian tradition have been especially ready to recommend reflationary policies, even when these are likely to raise the inflation rate, because they believe that such increases in inflation will be of minor significance in comparison with the benefits from extra output, which are bound to produce more gainers than losers.

But if inflationary economies perform less well in the medium and long term, they will produce more losers than gainers if a long enough time horizon is considered and the future is not unduly discounted. It will be suggested in this chapter that there are several reasons why inflationary economies will eventually underperform those which achieve near-price stability and in that event the compensation test applied with a sufficiently long time horizon will not favour an acquiescence in inflation.

HISTORICAL ASPECTS

The high point of economists' growth-mindedness and indifference to inflation came in the period of high Keynesianism that followed the adoption of *The General Theory of Employment, Interest and Money* as the theoretical foundation for policy advice in all English-speaking countries in the decade after the Second World War. This is no accident. In the *General Theory* there is the statement (1936: 300), 'in general, supply price will increase as output from a given equipment is increased. Thus increasing output will be associated with rising prices, apart from any change in the wage unit.' So, disregarding any changes in wages, Keynes says that if output is raised from a given capital stock, prices will also tend to rise. If wages rise as well, the inflationary effect will be that much greater.

81

In the conditions of the 1930s when Keynes wrote, it was widely believed that it was a world-wide problem that prices had become too low in the slump and that it would be a beneficial consequence of reflationary policies if these restored 'adequate' prices. It is a central proposition in *The General Theory* that the application of Keynesian boosts to demand will raise, or rather restore, prices to more appropriate and higher levels. Some post-Keynesians have preferred to describe supply curves as horizontal and claim that modern industry will generally supply more at an unchanged selling price, but discount sales below list-prices are prevalent where demand is depressed, so *de facto* prices as against list-prices will certainly tend to be higher, the greater the level of demand in relation to productive capacity as Keynes himself insisted.

Keynesians initially welcomed the inflationary tendency of demand expansionary policies. The United Kingdom Treasury was gradually converted to a Keynesian approach during the Second World War, and in 1943 a Steering Group, contemplating postwar policy argued the advantages of moderate inflation:

> A rise in prices and incomes sufficiently slow to avoid a violent disturbance of the expectations of the recipients of fixed income, yet sufficiently perceptible gradually to unloose the dead hand of debt, has much to be said in its favour.   (Booth 1983: 113)

The Treasury evidently believed at this time that the inflation rate could be increased without a corresponding need to raise interest rates and without bond-holders noticing that the real value of their capital was diminishing. This belief had some plausibility until 1955 when Professor Sir Dennis Robertson remarked on hearing that the Church of England was switching from government bonds to equity shares, 'if you can't fool the Church of England, there is no one left you can fool any more'. After just 12 years the policy of running an inflationary economy in order gradually to eliminate government debt was played out.

But in the 1950s Keynesians discovered a new argument in favour of inflation, that it would have a favourable impact on long-term growth. Nicholas Kaldor (later Lord Kaldor), a senior adviser to United Kingdom Labour governments in 1964–70 and again from 1974–9 provided a foretaste of this approach in the advice (published in 1960) which he offered to the Radcliffe Committee on the Working of the Monetary System. His memorandum has a section headed 'The Dangers of a Regime of Stable Prices', and he goes on to say (Kaldor 1960: 149):

> it is dangerous for a weakly progressive economy to aim at a regime of stable prices . . . since when the rate of growth of production is low . . . stable prices are only consisent with low rates of profit which may be insufficient to maintain the inducement to invest. . . . in the United Kingdom the rate of growth of the 'real' gross national product in the period 1950–57 was three per cent a year. If inflation had been entirely avoided, the average rate of profit on new investment would have been . . . 6 per cent.

Kaldor regarded a 6 per cent nominal rate of return on capital as inadequate because with nominal interest rates in the plausible United Kingdom range of 4 to 7 per cent there would be too little incentive to invest. His calculations for the Radcliffe Committee were based on his recently discovered formula (Kaldor 1960: 148) for the determination of the rate of profit (r) that, 'as a first approximation' this can be taken 'as being equal to the rate of growth in the money value of the gross national product (g) divided by the proportion of profits saved (s_p)'. That is, $r = g/s_p$. He offers examples of 0.4 and 0.5 for s_p, the proportion of profits saved, and assumes for the quoted calculations he presents that half of profits are saved, so that $s_p = 0.5$ and $r = 2g$. This produces the remarkably simple result that industry's rate of return on capital can be expected to be twice the rate of growth of nominal GNP. So, if the inflation rate could be raised by 1 per cent which would raise g (the rate of growth of nominal GNP) 1 per cent, then r, the rate of profit on capital, would be raised by 2 percentage points. In the early Keynesian manner Kaldor made no reference to the possibility that nominal interest rates might rise as inflation increased. Hence each 1 per cent advance in inflation would raise the rate of profit 2 percentage points without any tendency to increase the rate of interest. It is no wonder that he went on to recommend that Britain's inflation rate which was no more than 1 per cent in 1959 should be raised to 4½ per cent because this together with the economy's underlying real growth of 3 per cent would produce a rate of growth of nominal GNP of 7½ per cent and a rate of return on capital of 15 per cent. United Kingdom inflation rose sharply after 1959 and it peaked at 27 per cent in 1975, a year in which company profitability virtually disappeared. Nobody today would wish to resurrect Kaldor's proposition that each 1 per cent addition to inflation raises the nominal rate of return on capital by 2 percentage points. Nor do economists believe any longer that the rate of interest can be held down when inflation rises.

During the 1960s and the 1970s there was a growing realization that if inflation raises the rate of profit it will also raise the rate of interest so inflation will not boost profit rates relative to interest rates and so stimulate the inducement to invest. The world's inflationary economies began to devalue regularly, and the United Kingdom with 7 per cent more inflation than West Germany in 1978 and 1979 had developed long- and short-term interest rates that were 6 per cent above Germany's. The market expectation was presumably that since the United Kingdom had 7 per cent more inflation than Germany it would have to devalue by something like 7 per cent per annum averaged over the years in relation to Germany's currency, and holders of sterling assets would need to be compensated for this regular tendency towards devaluation with extra interest of around 7 per cent per annum. The Keynesian policy of inflating to stimulate profits and growth was therefore played out by 1979 because the United Kingdom's extra inflation had raised the rate of interest as much as the rate of profit. In 1898 Knut Wicksell (1898: 3–4) had predicted that this would be the outcome of using inflation to generate an apparent increase in profitability:

> It is . . . widely believed that what is most desirable of all is a state of affairs in which prices are rising slowly but steadily, . . . if a gradual rise in prices, in accordance with an approximately known schedule, could be reckoned on with certainty, it would be taken into account in all current business contracts; with the result that its supposed beneficial influence would necessarily be reduced to a minimum. Those people who prefer a continually upward moving to a stationary price level forcibly remind one of those who purposely keep their watches a little fast so as to be more certain of catching their trains. But to achieve their purpose they must not be conscious or remain conscious of the fact that their watches are fast; otherwise they become accustomed to take the extra few minutes into account and so after all, in spite of their artfulness, arrive too late. . . . (Wicksell 1898)

By 1979 the attempts to set the inflationary clocks of United Kingdom business ahead of the interest rate had failed and British industrialists were missing as many trains as in the 1920s and the 1930s when price stability had been the norm. This became increasingly understood in the late 1970s when there was also a growing concern whether, because of supply–side weaknesses and rigidities which were tending to produce near-vertical aggregate supply curves, United Kingdom industry would actually produce more in response to extra demand. Wage-setting behaviour appeared to be absorbing most injections of demand into higher pay with the result that the impact of higher demand was felt mainly in higher prices. In 1976 Mr James Callaghan, the Labour Prime Minister, launched a celebrated attack on the previous Keynesian orthodoxy which had recommended policies to raise employment whenever this was judged to be less than 'full', whatever the inflationary consequences:

> We used to think that you could spend your way out of a recession and increase employment by cutting taxes and boosting government spending. I tell you in all candour that the option no longer exists, and that in so far as it ever did exist, it only worked on each occasion since the war by injecting a bigger dose of inflation into the economy, followed by a higher level of unemployment as the next step. Higher inflation followed by higher unemployment. We have just escaped from the highest rate of inflation this country has known; we have not yet escaped from the consequences: high unemployment. That is the history of the last twenty years.

Mr Callaghan's government adopted monetary targets in 1976 and increased the priority attached to reducing inflation. The Conservative government, led by Mrs Margaret Thatcher which was elected in 1979, pushed the priority attached to reducing inflation still further and by 1981 her government's tight monetary and fiscal policies had more than doubled unemployment. At about this time economists developed the concept of 'hysteresis', which suggested that temporary sacrifices of employment and production could easily become long-term ones as unemployed workers lost skills and work-attitudes so that they become unemployable and formed part of a permanently larger pool of unemployment. The rise in unemployment from 1979 to 1981 and the growing belief that a good deal of this might become near-permanent caused great distress to the British economics profession, and many academic economists could not understand why it was right to sacrifice so much output and employment in order to reduce inflation.

POLITICAL CONSEQUENCES

In contrast, a number of politicians in several countries had become aware that there is considerable political mileage in reducing inflation. Two stylized political facts can be mentioned. In the United Kingdom since the Second World War no government which has significantly raised the rate of inflation has been re-elected, while four governments which reduced inflation, or stabilized it, have been re-elected. In the United States since the Second World War, no President where inflation rose significantly during his first term has been re-elected, while several Presidents who held or reduced inflation have been re-elected. Why is there this conflict between the apparent political appreciation of the damage that inflation causes and the belief of many economists that overriding priority should be attached to short-term output employment and growth? What is the damage to economies that politicians perceive which fails to enter into the calculus of many economists in English-speaking countries? Frank Hahn, who became a Professor of Economics in Cambridge University shortly before Lord Kaldor's retirement, is a notable recent example. In lectures he gave in Birmingham in 1981 he said (1982: 106), 'inflation as such is not an outstanding evil, nor do I believe it to be costly in the sense that economists use that term'. He also said, 'I am after all this left with the outstanding problem in inflation theory: why do people seem to hate it? Why does it drive politicians to destructive frenzy?' (101), and he cannot 'explain the election of governments whose top priority is the reduction of inflation whatever the consequence' (103).

So what is the economic damage that inflation causes which Hahn was unable to see but which must be quite widely discernible in the political community at large? One obvious cost of inflation is that if the general price level has a continual tendency to rise, prices in general will alter more frequently and by larger amounts. This will make it more difficult for producers and consumers to take efficient decisions because it will be harder for them to distinguish changes in relative prices which ought to elicit changes in resource allocation from changes in the general price level, which should, according to Hahn, be compatible with neutral behaviour.

ECONOMIC EFFECTS

Hahn did not, of course, replicate Kaldor's error of supposing that inflation will be good for business because it raises the rate of profit without increasing the rate of interest. He relied instead on the proposition that two economies in steady growth with different rates of inflation are in essence the same real economy. Under steady growth with inflation perfectly anticipated, each percentage point addition to the rate of inflation will raise both the nominal rate of return on capital and the rate of interest 1 percentage point. If it is supposed that in a typical OECD economy in the late 1980s the real rate of return on capital was 10 per cent and the real rate of interest 5 per cent, then with zero inflation the nominal rate of return on capital would also be 10 per cent and the nominal interest rate 5 per cent. With 10 per cent inflation, the nominal return on capital and the nominal interest rate would both become 10 percentage points higher, so the rate of profit would become 21 per cent instead of 10 per cent (allowing for compounding) while the nominal rate of interest would be 15½ per cent instead of 5 per cent. At first sight the incentive to invest should be the same in the inflationary economy with a nominal rate of profit of 21 per cent and an interest rate of 15½ per cent as it is in the economy enjoying the advantages of price stability with a profit rate of 10 per cent and an interest rate of 5 per cent, for the profit rate is 5 percentage points above the interest rate in both economies. In real terms they appear to be the same economy.

If the government of the inflationary economy decided to reduce inflation to zero, the rate of profit would gradually fall from 21 per cent to 10 per cent, and the interest rate from 15½ to 5 per cent, and it is not obvious at first sight what significant real advantages would be attained, but a very high economic price in terms of transitional unemployment would have to be incurred while inflationary expectations were squeezed out of the economy. This price is liable to be especially great if, as appears to be the case in the United Kingdom, prices and wages are 'sticky' downwards which will prolong the recessionary conditions which prevail while the inflation rate is being brought down. Hahn and others who use this line of argument insist that it is not worth this temporary sacrifice of real production and employment to move from 10 per cent to zero inflation when the real benefits that price stability would confer are unclear.

But the proposition that economies with 10 per cent and zero inflation are essentially the same economy omits to bring out that the ratio of interest payments to profits is considerably higher in the inflationary economy. This is illustrated in Table 7.1, where some of the detailed differences between these two hypothetical economies are brought out. The share of profits will not in general be higher in the inflationary economy, because inflation does not normally allow companies to widen profit margins. Prices rise faster but so do wages and other costs. The aggregate interest bill will in contrast be a higher ratio

Table 7.1:   *The general impact of inflation on companies in steady 3 per cent growth*

	Company output	Capital stock	Company profits	Company debt	Interest payments	Profits net of interest
Zero inflation		K	P	D	i × D	P − i × D
5% interest rate						
Year 1	100.0	200.0	20.0	60.0	3.00	17.00
Year 2	103.0	206.0	20.6	61.8	3.09	17.51
10 per cent inflation						
15.5% interest rate						
Year 1	100.0	200.0	20.0	60.0	9.30	10.70
Year 2	113.3	226.6	22.66	67.98	10.54	12.12

It is assumed in this example that the real rate of growth is 3 per cent, and the real rate of interest 5 per cent. Where inflation is 10 per cent the growth of money output is therefore 13.3 per cent and the nominal rate of interest is 15.5 per cent. Physical company capital is assumed to be twice the value of output, and companies borrow amounts each year which maintain debt at three-tenths of the nominal value of their capital stock on which they pay 5 per cent when there is zero inflation and 15.5 per cent when there is 10 per cent inflation. Profits net of capital consumption are one-tenth of the value of physical capital. These are typical OECD ratios.

of the national income in the inflationary economy. In the illustrations in Table 7.1, where the ratio of company debt to the capital stock is assumed to be 30 per cent whether inflation is zero or 10 per cent, net profits are 20 per cent of output in both economies, but interest is 3 per cent of output in the economy with price stability and 9 per cent of output in the economy with 10 per cent inflation. Hence interest costs absorb 3/20 of profits in the economy with price stability and 9/20 of profits where there is 10 per cent price inflation. It is therefore far from true that the two economies are essentially the same, because nominal interest payments are a far higher ratio of GNP in the inflationary economy, even in the steady-state conditions so far assumed where inflation is perfectly anticipated.

If interest costs are a higher ratio of output and profits in a steady state when inflation is faster, then as soon as there is a departure from steady-state conditions companies will be far more vulnerable to financial destabilization in the inflationary economy. Shock events that disturb the smooth growth of profitability will therefore leave companies less able to finance the payment of interest on debt.

Some would question whether it is realistic to suppose as in Table 7.1 that companies in inflationary economies carry as much debt as they have to bear where there is price stability. It is widely supposed, as the United Kingdom Treasury assumed in 1943, that inflation wipes out debt. Would it not be discovered in the inflationary economy that as inflation rises company debt gradually disappears? Sadly for the businessmen, in such economies this does not actually occur. Inflation does not improve companies' cash flow in relation to the costs they must incur. Wage and raw material costs generally rise at least as rapidly as final prices so, as in Table 7.1, net profit margins become no wider and companies' requirements for outside finance rise as fast as prices. In the United Kingdom recent inflationary episodes have greatly increased the need for companies to borrow. The assumption in Table 7.1 that companies borrow an amount each year which holds their ratio of debt to real capital stable is therefore a closer statement of their true financial needs in inflationary conditions, than the naïve belief that inflation assists them by wiping out their past debt.

If none the less companies preferred to respond to inflation by holding down their total interest payments to the proportion of profits that they regarded as appropriate in non-inflationary conditions, then in the example set out in Table 7.1, the ratio of debt to capital would have to be reduced from 30 per cent to approximately 10 per cent. With a third as much debt companies could pay the three-times-higher interest rate that prevailed with 10 per cent inflation and still maintain the same ratio of interest payments to profits. Companies can therefore choose either to maintain their ratio of debt to capital, in which case they will have to pay far more interest as in Table 7.1, or to greatly reduce the level of their debt if they wish to keep their interest outgoings down. This brings out starkly how the impact of inflation upon company finance cannot be neutral. Companies cannot maintain the same level of debt to capital *and* the same ratio of nominal interest to profits as equivalent companies in a non-inflationary economy. One or other of these must give.

Table 7.2: Impact of inflation on investment

| | | Present values | | | | | |
| | | With zero inflation and 5% nominal interest rate | | | With 10% inflation and 15.5% nominal interest rate | | |
Year	Cost	Gross profits	Discount factor 5% PA	Net present values of future profits	Gross profits	Discount factor 15.5% PA	Net present values of future profits
0	100						
1		16.27	0.95	15.50	17.90	0.87	15.50
2		16.27	0.91	14.76	19.69	0.75	14.76
3		16.27	0.86	14.06	21.66	0.65	14.06
4		16.27	0.82	13.39	23.83	0.56	13.39
5		16.27	0.78	12.75	26.21	0.49	12.75
6		16.27	0.75	12.14	28.83	0.42	12.14
7		16.27	0.71	11.57	31.71	0.36	11.57
8		16.27	0.68	11.02	34.89	0.32	11.02
9		16.27	0.64	10.49	38.37	0.27	10.49
10		16.27	0.61	9.99	42.21	0.24	9.99

		Present value returns:	125.67		Present value returns:	125.67
		Cost:	100.00		Cost:	100.00
		Net present value:	25.67		Net present value:	25.67

The example shown in these tables compares projects with identical constant real rates of return of 10 per cent (and neglects all tax questions). It shows the impact of an increase in inflation from zero (on the left-hand side) to 10 per cent per annum (on the right-hand side) which leaves the real rate of interest unchanged at 5 per cent. When inflation is 10 per cent the nominal interest rate rises from 5 per cent on the left to 15.5 per cent (allowing for compounding) on the right. The 10 per cent inflation which is assumed to influence wages and prices similarly is assumed to boost money profits (on the right) by a cumulative 10 per cent per annum. The discounted present value of aggregate future returns is exactly the same in the left- and right-hand tables. The extra inflation which raises nominal interest rates equally has no effect on the discounted present value of expected future profits, and it has no impact on the net present value of the projects. This is 25.67 both where inflation is zero and where it is 10 per cent.

The example set out in Table 7.1 is concerned with the way in which inflation puts pressure on the finances of companies in the aggregate. The precise way in which a particular investment project may be influenced is set out in Table 7.2 which is drawn up with assumptions parallel to those in Table 7.1. This shows in detail how an increase in inflation from zero to 10 per cent reduces company liquidity and puts financial pressure on to corporations. The same real capital investment project is compared in the two hypothetical economies so far considered. On the left there is no inflation and nominal interest rates are assumed to be 5 per cent, while on the right, there is 10 per cent inflation and nominal interest rates are 15½ per cent, so as in Table 7.1 the real rate of interest, net of inflation is 5 per cent in both cases. The investments each have a real yield of 10 per cent and they are identical investments, so on a Net Present Value basis they provide identical real returns and identical present value returns. But the effect of 10 per cent inflation is that, on the right, every year's profits rise at a cumulative 10 per cent a year, because it is assumed that wages and prices rise at a cumulative 10 per cent a year.

What is the difference for companies between the positions on the left and on the right? The main difference is that on the right where there is 10 per cent inflation they have to pay 15½ interest on an investment of 100, so the first year's cash flow, the first year's profit of 17.9, is almost entirely absorbed by interest. On the left, where there is no inflation, they have much the same profit, 16.27, but interest of only 5 because the rate of interest is only 5 per cent so profits are three-times interest. Where there is inflation, profits rise in the later years and come to much exceed interest, but at the beginning, having to pay 15½ per cent interest and receiving almost the same profits means that a company is in a difficult cash-flow position.

Suppose the occurrence of one of the things that commonly happens to interrupt the smooth working of an investment in the early years of its life. One possibility is that new technology does not work as efficiently as expected, so there is difficulty in making machinery work properly at the beginning of its life. A second possibility is that there is a recession in the first two years which temporarily weakens markets, so that what a machine can produce cannot all be sold. A third possibility is that there may be strikes which disrupt the early cash flows. In these cases a company that is paying 15½ per cent interest will find that its liquidity is severely damaged. A company that is paying only 5 per cent can far more readily survive such setbacks in the early years.

The result is that statistically (as Sushil Wadhwani (1985) has shown) there is a linkage between inflation and bankruptcies. Wadhwani estimates that each 1 per cent on the inflation rate adds 5.8 per cent to the number of bankruptcies. That is on the assumption that each 1 per cent addition to inflation raises the rate of interest by a full 1 per cent (as in Tables 7.1 and 7.2), so that the real rate of interest is unaffected. Wadhwani also considers the case where, when the rate of inflation rises 1 per cent, the interest rate rises by only one-half a percent. In that event, there is still a 3.4 per cent increase in the number of bankruptcies. Now, because raising inflation adds to the number of bankruptcies it also makes investments appear riskier, and because of this the Stock Exchange places them in a higher-risk class. So there is the undoubted technical effect that, as soon as risk and uncertainty are introduced into the economic argument to create the possibility that investments may go badly in their early years, inflation creates a possible inhibition against investment. This arises because when inflation increases, company profits rise far less than the rate of interest, so interest costs increase enormously more than profits in the early years of investments. Later, of course, companies get all this back, so there is no difference if perfect foresight or rational expectations are assumed, or if an investment can actually perform as expected right through its life.

Wadhwani also finds that because investments are in a higher-risk class, each 1 per cent addition to inflation cuts Stock Exchange prices by 8 per cent. This has the effect (allowing for compounding) that where inflation is 7 percentage points faster, a company's equity share price can be expected to be more than 40 per cent lower in relation to its earnings than in an economy with price stability (since $0.92^7 = 0.56$). It will also be that much lower in relation to the replacement cost of its physical assets. A foreign company that wishes to break into a market has the option of setting up its own plant or buying an existing company. If a company's shares are half as expensive in relation to the replacement cost of its physical assets, takeovers will often become the cheaper option. Extra inflation which damages the level of Stock Exchange prices will also therefore render companies more vulnerable to domestic and international takeover, a phenomenon from which the United Kingdom has suffered in its inflationary periods.

One reason why production is riskier in an inflationary economy with adverse pressures on company cash flows and liquidity arises because the 10 per cent inflationary element of a 15½ per cent interest rate is in essence a capital repayment. With 10 per cent inflation, the real debt owed on money previously borrowed will be 10 per cent less after a year, and what appears to be 10 per cent extra interest is actually compensation to creditors for the reduction in the real value of their outstanding loans. The 10 per cent higher interest rate therefore has the same kind of impact as a compulsory 10 per cent capital repayment would have in a stable price economy. A correctly anticipated 10 per cent inflation which raises the interest rate 10 percentage points has the effect of making such debt repayments compulsory. With 10 per cent inflation, approximately half the real value of a loan will be eroded and have to be repaid via higher nominal interest payments within seven years, and two-thirds in 10 years (since $0.90^7 = 0.48$ and $0.90^{10} = 0.35$). If a company wishes to borrow for 20 or 25 years, inflation renders this difficult, because the forced repayments it imposes mean that loans have to be repaid rather fast. With 100 per cent inflation, half the real value of a loan is eroded in one year, so the average period of a loan cannot exceed around two years.

In principle, companies can maintain the real value of their debt as in the assumed example in Table 7.1 by taking out further loans each year. With 100 per cent inflation a company which had an original debt of £1 million and wished to maintain its real value could increase its debt to £2 million after one year, £4 million after two years and so on. It could thus maintain the real value of its debt and so continue to owe the same true amount if it borrowed a further £1 million after one year, and a further £2 million after two years. It could ease its liquidity problems if it could continually add to its outstanding nominal debt with regular extra borrowing of this kind. By such means companies could in effect borrow long-term and avoid the tendency for inflation to continually force them to repay debt more quickly than ideal commercial considerations call for.

But there are two reasons why the effect of inflation on debt and interest cannot be so easily compensated through continual extra borrowing. It might not actually be practical to borrow these extra sums each year. Lenders would have to judge all the time whether the borrowing companies were still creditworthy. In addition the extra loans would involve transaction costs – at a minimum in the form of extra time and trouble – so companies would not be indifferent between borrowing £1 million in a stable price environment and borrowing an original £1 million and having to borrow further sums each year to maintain the real period of debt in an inflationary environment.

THE IMPACT ON THE HOUSING MARKET

So far the argument has been concerned with the impact of inflation on companies, but there are similar adverse effects when families borrow money to finance home ownership. The market for housing has a pervasive influence in modern economies on both the economic condition of families and the efficiency with which the labour market functions. People commonly borrow to buy houses which cost between three and four times their annual salary, and aim to repay their loans over a period such as 20, 25 or 30 years. If there is 10 per cent inflation and a worker has to pay 15½ per cent interest, then if he buys a house for between 300 and 400 when his salary is 100 he will have to pay between 46½ and 62 or 46½ and 62 per cent of his income as interest when he first buys the house. With 10 per cent inflation, 30 or 40 of this 'interest' is in effect a capital repayment: inflation at 10 per cent is obliging the worker to repay the loan in little more than 10 years, when he would actually wish to pay for the house over 20, 25 or 30 years. But he cannot easily take out an extra loan each year. Transaction costs would stand in the way of this, even if his creditworthiness remained adequate for a regular schedule of extra borrowing. So when there is inflation it is more difficult for the workers and the middle classes to buy houses. If, on the other hand, there is no inflation and interest rates are only 5 per cent, then when the worker's salary is 100 and the house costs between 300 and 400, only 15 to 20 per cent of the worker's salary is needed to pay interest for the house, which he can finance without complications.

The greatest damage from inflation arises when workers buy houses when the interest rate is low, and then inflation increases and the interest rate rises and suddenly they have to pay far more interest than they had expected, which puts enormous pressure on them and which therefore makes this aspect of higher inflation extremely unpopular with workers and salary-earners. For those who are house buyers, if the interest rate they pay is adjusted upwards with inflation, they end up after a few years paying far more interest than they expected when they first bought their homes. The extra sums of money that workers caught in this situation have to pay are potentially very high fractions of a worker's income. If an employee still owes three times his income when inflation and interest rates rise by 5 percentage points, the extra interest he will have to pay will amount to approximately 15 per cent of his income, and this will very significantly reduce his standard of living. This is one of the aspects of an acceleration of inflation that may help to explain why this is so unpopular with electorates. Those who receive 5 per cent extra interest on their deposits are merely being compensated for faster inflation, while borrowers for home ownership see their family cash-flows devastated, although they will subsequently find that the real value of their debt falls far faster.

There is a further impact of inflation on the housing market that is equally significant. Local governments who build houses for poorer workers face the same inflation arithmetic; namely, that when they borrow from central government at 15½ per cent, they will have to pay interest of between 46½ and 62 per cent of the incomes of the workers who rent their new houses. As they can charge as rent no more than 25 per cent of a low-paid worker's income, building such houses will involve very large financial deficits. Faced by these, local governments mostly stop building houses for rent when interest rates rise to 15 per cent or more with the result that government-funded housing becomes scarce. Like workers and companies, most local authorities are not prepared to undertake a programme of continual extra borrowing at nominal interest rates of 15 per cent or more in order to finance a housing programme. The result of a slow-down of local authority housing is then that the low-paid who cannot afford to buy houses become immobile, because they are unable to obtain housing in a new district if they wish to move to take a job that happens to be available there, so they stay in their current houses where they enjoy security of tenure. This then impedes the free movement of labour, with the result that it becomes scarce in areas where there are growing employment opportunities, and where there is at the same time insufficient housing for extra workers, which accentuates inflation.

This difficulty does not arise in conditions of price stability because local governments which build when interest rates are 5 per cent need charge no more than 15 to 20 per cent of a low-paid worker's wage to recover their interest, so they can build without incurring huge financial deficits when they let their houses at reasonable rents. The greater availability of low-cost housing to rent goes on to improve the mobility of labour and it also raises the welfare of low-income families which are less likely to suffer from inadequate housing in addition to their other difficulties.

SOCIAL EFFECTS

In addition to this damage to the housing market, inflation adds to the pressures that trade unions have to deal with, as Sir John Hicks explained in his account of *The Crisis in Keynesian Economics* (1974). If prices are stable, workers' standards of living remain intact. Even if they do not get pay increases, what they are accustomed to buy can still be purchased, so they do not need tough bargaining with the underlying sanction of strike action in order to protect living standards. But if there is 10 per cent inflation, then, if they do not get pay increases, they will lose 10 per cent of their standard of living each year, so they will need the protection of trade unions powerful enough to achieve results. If any attempt is made to give workers less than 10 per cent or to delay the 10 per cent, each group of workers will need effective trade unions to represent them in order to put pressure on the rest of the community for their annual 10 per cent. And some studies have suggested that statistically there is a relationship in the United Kingdom which suggests that the faster the rate of inflation, the greater the amount of strike activity and industrial action.

Strike activity by trade unions has, in the language of economics, a massive negative external effect. So far as the participants to a dispute are concerned, the position is internalized. A union will call strike action if it judges that its members will gain more by a strike than they will lose. But, added to the effect on the welfare of the trade unionists, there is an impact on everyone else in the community that is negative, because there will be disruption to many others whenever any group of workers strikes. If it is arguable that the faster the rate of inflation, the greater the degree of disruption due to strike action, it follows again that there is a possible explanation of why the people of a country who vote at elections appear to be hostile to inflation. They may be reacting as much to consequences such as a greater prevalence of strikes as to the faster price rises themselves for which they may well be adequately compensated via faster rises in their money incomes. Voters are also bound to react adversely to the impression that a government does not appear to be in control if there are large numbers of strikes which cause extensive personal inconvenience.

In addition to their effect on the lives of families, strikes seriously interrupt the smooth flow of production and the ability of companies to meet orders on time. Markets lost through delayed deliveries may go permanently to the producers of other countries. Multinational companies are likely to respond by gradually shifting their manufacturing sites away from countries where production becomes unreliable.

An increased risk of interruptions to production also damages productivity by denying companies the use of 'just in time' ordering and stock-control systems which can produce very significant reductions in the cost of working capital and its integration into the production process. Inflation-prone economies will suffer industrially if they at the same time become strike-prone and it must be remembered that strikes in only a small fraction of companies can devastate production in a great many. Each manufacturing company typically buys components from several hundred others and the absence of any one of these can hold up the potential to produce and deliver.

The industrial relations costs of inflation are only partly captured by strike statistics. There is a plethora of evidence to demonstrate that bargaining becomes a much more complex and time-consuming activity in inflationary periods, and concern about general inflation distorts consideration of the 'real' issues associated with the need to raise productivity in order to improve international competitiveness. This feeds through to worker attitudes and behaviour in many adverse ways. Strikes are only the tip of this iceberg.

There is a further way in which inflation damages a society and economy which is more difficult to clarify, and that is its influence upon the relative rewards of those who create value-added in industry and those who carry out financial transactions. If prices are stable and industrialists develop new products which create high value-added per worker then they will make money, but rarely more than 10 to 20 per cent of the costs they have to incur. If there is an inflationary situation with high interest rates and a good deal of uncertainty, it is possible for industrialists to create products with high value-added, and then to have to sell them in the wrong currency, to pay the wrong interest rates, to suffer all kinds of changes in money prices and wages which mean that the potential profit margins of 10 to 20 per cent that their high value-added production generates can very easily be eliminated. Because technically successful industrialists may be wiped out by the financial vicissitudes that accompany inflation, manufacturing companies will be placed in a higher-risk class than in economies where prices are stable, and as more capital investment has to be committed which is product-specific than in the financial sector the relative attraction of committing resources to production is diminished. There will be a corresponding relative incentive for clever, intelligent and well-educated people to go into banking, insurance and finance and not into production, because the rewards from correct financial decisions and the purchase and sale of well-selected pieces of paper are raised relative to the rewards from the creation of value-added in the form of physical commodities. And so there is a tendency, with inflation, for a society's most talented and ambitious people to move away from industry and into the financial sector. This is one of the most insidious impacts of inflation.

THE IMPACT OF GOVERNMENT COUNTER-INFLATIONARY POLICY

Because of the extent of these various kinds of damage which politicians and electorates are becoming very much aware of, governments realize that inflation has to be stopped. This adds to the uncertainty of business because it is not clear whether governments will seek to halt inflation mainly by cutting public exenditure or by raising taxation and in the latter case, which actual taxes are increased will matter a good deal to companies. Alternatively, it may be that counter-inflation strategy will mainly take the form of higher interest rates and a consequent rise in the exchange rate. When inflation is unacceptably high the knowledge that one or more of these is in the offing will interfere with the long-term planning of investment in capital equipment, research and development and innovation which can take decades to bear fruit. Such business uncertainties lead to a short-termism which is absent in Germany, Japan and now France where, because inflation is under control, companies have no reason to fear a major adverse shift in government policy and its consequences.

Everyone in an inflationary economy is aware that at some point in the future deflation will follow, but because the Phillips curve is non-linear (since increases in demand have a far greater tendency to raise wages and prices than have reductions in demand to reduce them), the damage to the national income when the government tries to reduce inflation will be far greater than the gain when it acquiesces in an increase. So if there is a cycle which takes the form 'Keynes on, Keynes off, Keynes on, Keynes off' – expansion followed by contraction, expansion followed by contraction – its net effect will be very damaging to production and efficiency, because the loss of GNP will be greater in the downside than the gains on the upside.

CONCLUSION

One reason why inflation is damaging that has not been emphasized is the one that Milton Friedman has set out and which has become very familiar, namely, that the faster the rate of inflation, the less use a society will make of money balances, because everybody economizes in money balances when inflation destroys their real value. It is widely argued that this is statistically a modest effect at inflation rates of 10 per cent or less and the adverse impacts to which most importance should be attached are those associated with the squeeze on company liquidity; the effect that workers acting defensively to protect their standards of living disrupt the rest of the community; and the effect that the young and the educated find that there are greater rewards in the financial sector than in production. These will all have a substantial adverse impact on the growth of output and living standards in the medium and the long term.

Some economists accept this but believe that the way to deal with any damage caused by inflation is simply to index: that with indexing there is no need to worry about inflation, because most of the difficulties referred to will disappear. If the companies illustrated in Table 7.1 could sell indexed bonds, they could maintain their debt-to-capital ratio without raising interest payments relative to profits. But if the experience of the countries which actually index is examined, they usually have indexes that are not entirely accurate; there are often four or five indexes that matter, and people can exercise arbitrage advantages by jumping from index to index. Indexing can also involve massive administrative costs, and even the best systems fail to avoid time-lags in adjustment. There is at present no country where indexing deals satisfactorily with the difficulties that have been outlined.

Because in practice indexing has failed to protect the wealth and living standards of those who draw the short straws in inflationary periods, inflation inevitably redistributes wealth and it does so in an arbitrary manner. Those who are slow to react and adjust lose wealth, while others are rewarded because they are quick to see opportunities. There is a consequent sense of injustice if it appears that it is the industrious and productive who are losing their wealth to those who are merely alert and manipulative. The perceptions of injustice that result from these arbitrary redistributions of wealth can have severe social effects as the losers feel that they have been let down by society. That may be inflation's most significant social effect, but there are also the several ways in which it damages economic and industrial efficiency. It is therefore worth considerable sacrifices to get it down towards the 3 per cent level which was achieved in 1990 by France, Germany, Belgium and Holland, the core economies in the European Exchange Rate Mechanism which the United Kingdom has now joined.

NOTE

* This article is developed with the benefit of comments and criticisms from Alex Bowen, Milton Friedman, Robin Matthews, Ken Mayhew, Martha Prevezer, Martin Ricketts and Howard White from the 1990 Bateman Memorial Lecture, 'How Inflation Undermines Industrial Success', a shortened version of which appeared in the *National Westminster Bank Quarterly Review* in February 1991.

8. The Methodology of Scientific Research Programmes in Economics: Criticisms and Conjectures

Bruce J. Caldwell

Methodological writings in economics are not all of a piece; they exhibit considerable diversity. There are the pronouncements of practitioners about how economics is done and these often include, explicitly or implicitly, warnings about how not to do it. Not philosophically self-conscious, such accounts typically look to examples of best practice from within the discipline. Two good examples of this type of work are the articles by Milton Freidman (1953) and Melvin Reder (1982).

Methodological argumentation is also used, this time as a weapon, by critics of 'mainstream economic theory'. Sometimes critics provide philosophical arguments in their attacks. For example, Ludwig von Mises (1949) and Martin Hollis and E. J. Nell (1975) both decry the alleged positivist underpinnings of neoclassical economics and propose a rationalist foundation in its place. Other opponents ignore philosophy and focus instead on the realism of assumptions of economic theory, or its limited predictive ability, or its heavy use of mathematical formalism.

A third approach to methodology is much more explicit in the importance it accords to philosophy, and particularly to arguments from the philosophy of science. Practitioners of this approach include both philosophers of science who are interested in economics as an example of a science and economists who look towards the philosophy of science for insights about how science works. Our focus will be on members of the latter group.

Some famous economists have drawn on the philosophy of science to buttress their methodological arguments. Paul Samuelson is one example, though he also looked towards other sciences (particularly physics) for his exemplars of good practice. Fritz Machlup is another, though his borrowings from the philosophy of science were often eclectic.[1] T. W. Hutchison is probably the best example. His famous (1938) book introduced empiricist philosophy of science to English-speaking economists, and later he became a cautious but consistent advocate of Popperian thought. Mark Blaug who, like Hutchison, borrows heavily from Popper, should also be included. Indeed, he is arguably the leading modern representative among economists of the third tradition.

Though it is arbitrary to fix a date to it, I like to think of 1976 as marking the beginning of the modern era in economic methodology. Two books published that year were seminal. *Microeconomic Laws* by philosopher Alexander Rosenberg was the first extended attempt by a philosopher of science to analyse the structure of economic theory. *Method and Appraisal in Economics*, edited by Spiro Latsis, was a collection of papers, written by economists, whose purpose was to examine whether philosopher Imre Lakatos's methodological framework (the 'Methodology of Scientific Research Programmes', or MSRP) could be applied within their discipline (Lakatos 1970).

In the last decade or so, work within the third tradition has grown dramatically. Mark Blaug played an important role in the expansion by providing the first text-length survey of the field, *The Methodology of Economics* (1980a), the first third of which was devoted to the philosophy of science. In 1985 the journal *Economics and Philosophy* began publication under the editorship of a philosopher (Daniel Hausman) and an economist (Michael McPherson). The ranks both of philosophers studying economics and of economists interested in philosophy have increased steadily. A recent bibliography of the field contains over 2 000 entries, and most of these were published within the last fifteen years (Redman 1989).

Though the third tradition includes both philosophers and economists, it is important to emphasize that each group typically has a different research agenda. In particular, economists have usually been most interested in questions of theory appraisal and have looked to the philosophy of science for separate, independent standards against which to compare economic theories. This certainly has been the approach taken by Mark Blaug, who gradually came to view Lakatos's MSRP as providing the requisite standards for economics. Given his prominence in the field, it is worthwhile briefly to reconstruct how Mark Blaug might come to hold this position.

BLAUG AND THE MSRP: A SITUATIONAL ANALYSIS

There are three good reasons why Mark Blaug might turn towards Lakatos. All of them have to do with Karl Popper's philosophy of science.

Mark Blaug has long been an advocate of Popperian thought and has used his falsificationist framework effectively to assess the development of economic doctrines in the various editions of his text, *Economic Theory in Retrospect*. Popper offers a number of prescriptions for proper scientific procedure. The most important of these is that scientists should test theories – the more severely the better – in an attempt to refute them. The best theories are those which have survived frequent and strenuous attempts at falsification. Popper insists further that falsifications be taken seriously. In particular, he warns against 'immunizing stratagems', or changes in a theory which are undertaken solely to keep it from being refuted. He notes that it is always easy to save a theory from a refutation by simply altering it so that the new modified theory accounts for the anomalous outcome. Popper explicitly prohibits such *ad hoc* theory adjustments.

Popper's pronouncements about proper scientific procedure cause a number of problems for Blaug the historian of science and methodologist.

(a)   Falsificationism is a normative doctrine, its goal is to provide criteria for demarcating the scientific from the non-scientific, and for eliminating false theories from science. As such, it cannot be faulted for failing to describe scientific practice, though one could hope that it would be descriptive of certain paradigmatic episodes of 'good science', however they might be determined. The problem for economics is that a review of its history reveals precious little evidence of any falsificationist practice. As Blaug put it in his book on methodology (1980: 128): 'Modern economists frequently preach falsificationism, as we have seen, but they rarely practice it: their working philosophy of science is aptly described as "innocuous falsificationism".'

It turns out that economics was not unique in this respect, nor, for that matter, was falsificationism. By the 1960s there was a growing awareness among philosophers of science that a number of prescriptivist empiricist doctrines (for example, operationalism, logical positivism, logical empiricism) seemed inadequate for describing actual scientific practice, including the so-called paradigmatic episodes. The reaction of some scholars was to reject normative philosophy altogether and to embrace instead the more descriptively adequate models of science being developed within the history and sociology of science. Thomas Kuhn's *The Structure of Scientific Revolutions* (1962) is the most famous example of such an alternative. Though the gains in descriptive adequacy were evident, the problem with such analyses was that they lacked normative punch: they did not provide criteria for judging good science from bad, they were relativistic when it came to matters of appraisal. It should finally be mentioned that, from the present perspective, the tendency towards relativism has if anything gained strength in the intervening years, as deconstructionist and anti-foundationalist elements have worked their way into discourse about the sciences.

As an historian of thought interested in appraising the theories of economists, Mark Blaug faced a dilemma. Popper's normative philosophy of science was too strict, but Kuhn's relativism was too lax. By providing a methodological programme which claimed to be at once prescriptively robust and descriptively adequate, Lakatos's MSRP appeared to save the day.

Even better, Lakatos's promises seemed plausible. The MSRP clearly contained prescriptive content: Lakatos provided explicit criteria for appraising research programmes as either progressive or degenerating. And Lakatos also intended that the MSRP be able to make sense of both the best instances of current practice as well as past episodes of successful scientific achievements. Indeed, he even claimed (Lakatos 1971) that the MSRP could itself be tested against the history of a science by seeing how well it rationalizes the best gambits of scientific progress, as determined by the scientific élite. Given the limitations of Popper and Kuhn, it was natural for Blaug to urge economists to look more closely at the Lakatosian framework. This is just what he did in his contribution to the Latsis volume (Blaug 1976b).

(b) As first noted in Hands (1985a), there exists a tension between Popper's writings on the methodology of the natural sciences and his writings on the methodology of the social sciences. Hands distinguishes between two different Poppers. Popper$_n$ (for natural sciences) is the falsificationist Popper whom we have just met. Popper$_s$ (for social sciences) is an advocate of situational analysis. A social science explanation which utilizes situational analysis proceeds as follows. The explanandum (or event to be explained) is deduced from an explanans, which contains three elements: a description of the situation, an analysis of what action is reasonable in the situation, and a rationality postulate stating that agents will always act reasonably or appropriately. Explaining an agent's action or some other social phenomenon using situational analysis reduces to showing that whatever occurred was reasonable, or understandable, or appropriate, given the agent(s) and the situational constraints.

What happens when the actual outcome does not conform with the prediction of the situational analysis? In such instances, Popper$_s$ advises the social scientist to revise either the description of the situation or the analysis of what a reasonable agent would do. Such revisions occur until one obtains a prediction of what actually took place. Most important,

Popper$_s$ specifically prohibits the social scientist from ever rejecting the rationality postulate.

The source of the tension between Popper$_n$ and Popper$_s$ should now be clear. By manipulating the description of the situation until the 'right' result is obtained, by making sure never to reject the rationality postulate, the social scientist is engaging in an immunizing stratagem of the most egregious kind. Such behaviour flies in the face of Popper$_n$'s prescription against *ad hoc* theory adjustments, but it is precisely the behaviour that Popper$_s$ recommends. How is one to respond to this apparent inconsistency in Popper's thought?

As noted earlier, Mark Blaug likes falsificationism (though he feels it is too little practised by economists). He also (1985b) tends to discount Popper's specific account of situational logic. If I understand his position correctly, Blaug's solution to Popper's apparent inconsistency is to reconstruct situational analysis along Lakatosian lines. Following Latsis (1972), the rationality postulate is viewed as a part of the hard core of neoclassical theory. Its use is justified only to the extent that neoclassical theory continues to progress as a research programme. How progressive has it been? Blaug's assessment of the programme in radical economics sheds some light on the question. Though he remains an 'unconverted neoclassical', he concludes that 'a study of radical economics leaves one ultimately almost as unhappy with orthodox economics as with radical economics' (Blaug 1983: 238). From Blaug's vantage point, the neoclassical research programme needs a lot more work, but at present it still looks like the best game in town.

(c)   So far I have argued that it was natural for a Popperian like Mark Blaug to be enthusiastic about Lakatos, because Lakatos improves on Popper in just those areas where an historian of thought and a methodologist might judge Popper to be weakest. None of this would matter, however, if it turned out that the MSRP did not apply to economics.

But happily, it seemed that the MSRP fits economics remarkably well. The Lakatosian categories of hard cores, protective belts and positive and negative heuristics made sense to economists, especially neoclassical economists, when they thought about their discipline. Though economists might differ as to its exact content, the neoclassical programme appears to have certain hard-core elements, irrefutable parts which are specifically insulated from criticism. Though these hard-core elements are protected, there is also obviously a tremendous amount of empirical work within economics, and it is natural to characterize such work as lying in a protective belt around the hard-core assumptions. Economists would also find Lakatos's portrayal of how testing takes place in the protective belt to be an accurate description of their practice. Lakatos claimed that scientists often seek confirmations rather than falsifications, that crucial tests are rare and instant rationality unavailable, and that appraisal of a programme's progressivity is only possible over long periods of time. All of these notions resonate with economists, for they seem to characterize accurately the way empirical work is actually done, the frustrations associated with it, and the importance of being cautious about drawing conclusions from data whose interpretation is often ambiguous. Neoclassicals also work with a set of positive and negative heuristics which guide their research, suggesting which lines of questioning might hold the most promise. To be sure, the heuristics vary across the discipline, depending upon such things as whether one is principally a theorist or an applied economist, or whether one was trained at MIT or Minnesota or Chicago. But their presence is evident.

Thus the Lakatosian framework not only solved certain philosophical problems associated with Popperian thought, it apparently provided a vehicle for analysing the science of economics. This completes the situational analysis of Mark Blaug's movement away from Popper and towards Lakatos, and rational indeed his exit seems to be.

The purpose of this paper is to suggest that another alternative might be preferable. As such, it may be helpful to point out first those areas where I am in agreement with Mark Blaug (or better, with my reconstruction of Blaug's views). I agree with Blaug that it is difficult to apply falsificationism in economics, and further that the tension between Popper$_n$ and Popper$_s$ is a real one. As far as I know, I also agree with most of Blaug's substantive judgements about which research programmes within economics are doing the best work and which are least impressive. What separates us is how best to characterize the process by which such judgements might be reached.

Rather than accepting the Lakatosian framework, I am an advocate of critical pluralism, which is a modified version of Popper's critical rationalism. Like Blaug's solution, my alternative remains squarely within the Popperian tradition. It may also be the case that critical rationalism provides a solution to the dilemma of the two Poppers (Caldwell 1991). I shall argue presently that it is more accurate to view critical rationalism as occupying a middle ground between Lakatos and his relativist opponents than it is to see Lakatos as the golden mean between Kuhn and Popper. And most important, I do not think that the Lakatosian framework fits economics very well at all, at least along the dimensions that really matter. Let us turn to this key question first.

THE MSRP AND ECONOMICS

One should be suspicious when a framework which was developed with the natural sciences in mind appears to rationalize the practice of economists so comfortably. Why does the MSRP work so well in economics?

At least one reason is that many of the Lakatosian categories, when interpreted broadly enough, would fit *any* discipline. For example, the hard core of a research programme is simply the starting point of an analysis. Such starting points are generally taken as given by those working within the programme, which is another way of saying that they are taken to be irrefutable. (Contingent starting points have a way of not remaining starting points for very long.) And because every analysis must start *somewhere*, every programme ends up having a hard core. Positive and negative heuristics are simply the instructions one follows to do the analysis: some approaches are favoured and others are ruled out. All reasoning is pursued in this way. Finally, the protective belt is where some connection with the world is made. And Lakatos is right: often when one holds a theory, one simply looks to the world to confirm it. His observation that sometimes people hold on to theories even in the face of disconfirming evidence is also clearly true. Neither behaviour is particularly exemplary, but both are commonly encountered.

The point is simple: the Lakatosian categories which seem to make so much sense of economics would also make sense of virtually any form of human inquiry. They make sense within the sciences, but they also make sense of astrology, of textual criticism and of the kind of casual empiricism which characterizes everyday reasoning. What form of human reasoning lacks a starting point, or a strategy for identifying which questions to ask, or some contact (usually with the intent of rationalizing one's prior views) with the world?

This would not constitute a criticism of Lakatos had he set for himself the task of providing a general description of how human reasoning works. But he claimed to do much more, to have developed a programme which would allow one to distinguish scientific from other forms of human reasoning. As such, in assessing the MSRP, we must ignore the characteristics which describe human reasoning in general, and focus on those elements which are unique to scientific reasoning. Given this goal, I submit that the part of the MSRP upon which we should focus all our attention is Lakatos's criterion for appraising scientific progress. A research programme is judged progressive if it is capable through time of generating novel facts, some of which are ultimately corroborated. If we wish to see how well the MSRP works in economics, we must do so not by looking for hard cores and protective belts, or for positive and negative heuristics, but for instances of progressive problem-shifts. What does the evidence suggest?

Mark Blaug and Neil de Marchi co-directed a conference in Capri in 1989, and one of the goals of the conference was to answer just this question. I participated in the conference as a discussant, and my impression at the time was that too few authors had really tried to answer it. A conference volume is forthcoming (Blaug and de Marchi 1991), however, and perhaps if some of the papers are revised, more attention will be paid to whether and when economists have, through the process of theory revision, come across novel facts, some of which were confirmed.

Of course, the Capri conference was not the first time the question had been asked. In his introduction to the volume, de Marchi (1991) summarizes some of the findings contained in the already large Lakatosian literature in economics. One of his conclusions is that 'methodological analysis . . . has given us a better appreciation of the difficulties in applying the criterion of empirical progress in economics' (p. 10). In his assessment of the literature, Wade Hands (1985b) reaches much the same conclusion. At least so far there is reason to doubt that there exist many examples of progressive research programmes in economics.[2]

BLAUG'S CASE STUDY: THE KEYNESIAN REVOLUTION

I think that Mark Blaug would accept the argument that the best test of the MSRP is to see whether there are instances of progressive problem-shifts in economics. This would at least explain why he seems unconvinced by Roy Weintraub's (1985) ingenious reconstruction of the development of existence and stability proofs within general equilibrium theory as constituting a Lakatosian 'hardening of the hard core' (Blaug 1990a: note 2). But Blaug answers the charge that there are no instances of progressive problem-shifts in economics by providing an example of one in his detailed study, 'Second Thoughts on the Keynesian Revolution' (1992). An assessment of Blaug's paper is thus in order.

Blaug chronicles the meteoric rise of Keynesian ideas in the 1930s and 1940s, as well as the equally rapid collapse of that research programme in the 1970s. He does a masterful job of documenting the multitude of factors responsible for the ascendancy of the Keynesian monolith (1992). Blaug notes that Keynesian theory appealed to those who had been radicalized by the Great Depression. Its comparative static presentation conveyed both a sense of rigorous simplicity and of determinateness. The theory fits nicely with categories already being developed by national-income statisticians. When compared with its rivals, it gave clear and directly applicable policy advice. The Keynesian message was delivered at 'the optimum level of difficulty'. And its fecundity and appeal to puzzle-solvers guaranteed that followers would have much work to do. Blaug corrects the still-popular myth that Keynes stood alone in calling for public works to counteract the Depression. About the only point that he neglects to mention was Keynes's flair for self-promotion.

In addition to all this, Blaug mentions that Keynes predicted a novel fact, indeed, a number of them (some of which later turned out not to be true). The chief novel fact was that the multiplier exceeds unity; this implies the prediction that government can spend us out of a recession, which the Second World War soon corroborated. Having cited all the other causes, Blaug settles on this as the decisive one: it was responsible for the quick successes of the Keynesian Revolution. And because it was *an empirical fact* that was corroborated the Keynesian Revolution represents a Lakatosian problem-shift. I wish to raise three criticisms of this account.

(a)   It should first be noted that Mark Blaug is too good an intellectual historian to be anything more than a lousy Lakatosian. A good Lakatosian would have emphasized the novel fact in the text and relegated the rest of Blaug's fascinating discussion to the footnotes. This is not a mere quibble. Were historians to take Lakatos's advice seriously, the resultant history would look bizarre indeed: pages of footnotes would have to be appended to every paragraph of text. Alternatively, if the footnotes were left off, Lakatosian history would devolve into just another variant of monocausal explanation. Is the history of science written from the point of view of the discovery of novel facts any more substantial than the history of mankind written from the point of view of the class struggle? Is the causal nexus ever so neat and simple?

(b)   Blaug demonstrates convincingly that Keynes produced a corroborated novel fact, that a progressive problem-shift occurred within the Keynesian research programme. But the rest of his excellent account raises doubts as to whether the Keynesian programme as a whole was progressive. In the last part of his article Blaug (1992) documents how the programme generated not one but a number of novel facts. Unfortunately, most of the rest of these facts turned out not to be true. Is a programme to be considered progressive if one out of a number of its novel predictions turns out right while the rest turn out wrong? This is important because one suspects that in most empirical sciences one is bound to stumble across an occasional corroborated novel fact. Isolated progressive problem-shifts will be found. Much rarer in economics are sustained periods of progress in which a series of corroborated novel facts are unearthed within a single research programme.[3]

Blaug seems to anticipate this kind of objection when he points out (1992) that many of Keynes's predictions, though incorrect, were none the less fruitful: they inspired much theoretical and empirical work, both in the immediate aftermath of the revolution and in more recent years. Most economists would consider this later work to be evidence of the richness of the Keynesian programme. It is less clear how it would fit into a straight Lakatosian account, however, except to provide more material for the footnotes.

(c)   Blaug asserts somewhat provocatively that the novel fact predicted by Keynesian theory and corroborated by the war experience *was the most important factor* in persuading the profession of the truth of Keynesian ideas. His own rich, detailed account of the revolution provides the ammunition if one chose to pose the counter-argument: other factors were also present that might account for Keynes's quick success. But by emphasizing the significance accorded by economists to the discovery of novel facts, Blaug gets at a very important point. Unexpected empirical discoveries sometimes have a huge impact on the profession.[4] Where Blaug goes wrong is to attribute the size of the impact to the discovery of a novel fact.

Economists are sometimes swayed by the discovery of unexpected facts, but not in the way Lakatos imagines. The sorts of 'facts' that produce reactions among economists are broad historical confirmations or disconfirmations of a particular dominant world-view. The Great Depression (which challenged the efficiency-of-markets view) and the stagflation of the 1970s (which challenged the efficacy-of-demand-management view) are two excellent examples. Future historians will probably add the widely heralded 'collapse' of communist regimes in Eastern Europe to our list of paradigm-shattering episodes.

Such events give rise to large and sometimes extreme reactions among the various sciences which study social phenomena. These reactions are not well-described by models which emphasize the rationality of scientists responding to novel empirical evidence. Indeed, the ascendancy of the Keynesian programme and its desertion in the face of the stagflation of the 1970s illustrates convincingly just how coarse the evidence can be and still be capable of swaying virtually an entire profession. As Blaug demonstrates, a good Lakatosian would have to judge the Keynesian episode as a theoretically and empirically progressive problem-shift. It would count as *scientific progress*. But the actual history suggests that economists (and other social scientists) over-react to the sorts of disruptions which occasionally transform the social world. Bandwagons are jumped upon. A methodology which ends up characterizing such responses as scientifically progressive is fundamentally flawed.

On a more positive note, I think that progress *does* occur within economics. Progress takes many different forms, not all of them having to do with the empirical. But I would also agree with Mark Blaug's fundamental intuition that the most important sorts of progress within economics must be linked to the empirical. What the precise links are constitutes the sixty-four dollar question.

Blaug himself points out (1992) that the most common form of economic research involves trying to explain a known set of facts better. This usually occurs when a model is modified so that previously anomalous facts can be incorporated into it. If one employs the Popperian situational analysis framework, it is the description of the agent and of his situation which typically get modified. This is theoretical work, but it is guided by empirical anomalies. Judging by the reward structure of the profession, this sort of work is highly regarded by most economists.

I end this section with a conjecture. It seems to me that the ability to explain an ever-broader number of facts (by developing ever-more-general theories) typically also involves a diminution of one's ability to predict specific outcomes. In a way, and contrary to many expressly empirical methodological doctrines, progress in economics is often associated with the use of models of heightened explanatory power but of decreased predictive adequacy. As a result, it may be that the increases in knowledge that economists gain involve in a fundamental way a better understanding of the limitations of economics as a predictive science. Some may think it strange to characterize a better understanding of a discipline's limitations as a form of progress. But it is not an unprecedented view: Hayek certainly understood it very well. In any case, it is a view which cannot be easily discussed within the Lakatosian framework, nor within any framework in which progress is equated with increased predictive ability.

THE QUEST FOR UNIVERSAL CRITERIA OF APPRAISAL

Blaug's paper on the Keynesian revolution was a response to an earlier paper by Wade Hands. Hands has been a frequent critic of attempts to apply the MSRP in economics, and his exchanges with Blaug have been illuminating (Hands 1985b, 1990, 1991 a and b; Blaug 1976b, 1991, 1990a). But on at least one issue Hands (1985b: 2) agrees with Blaug, as may be seen from his assertion 'that economists should start not with Lakatos' methodology itself – i.e., not with his result – but with his questions, with the problem which originally motivated his methodology'. Hands suggests that though Lakatos's answers are less than satisfactory, the questions he pursued (namely, a search for specific criteria for appraising the progress of science) are the right ones. Both Blaug and Hands agree that coming up with a set of criteria for demarcating science from non-science and for appraising scientific theories as better or worse is a proper and important goal of methodology. They disagree only on how well Lakatos's MSRP fits the bill.

Why is the search for a specific set of criteria so important? There are some very good reasons. On the positive side, such a set of criteria, if ever attained, would make the job of methodologists much easier. And the goal seems a reasonable one. After all, most scientists believe that they know what science is, even if they are not able to come up with a list of necessary and sufficient conditions for identifying it. Astrology seems categorically different from astronomy, and creationist science seems categorically different from evolutionary theory. A universal set of criteria would not only allow one to distinguish pseudo-science from real science, it might even allow one to determine ahead of time which research programmes were most likely to lead to positive results and which were not.

Another good reason for coming up with such standards is to provide a buttress against the forces of relativism. This is a pressing problem in the current environment. As is well known, despite the efforts of many great minds the search for universal criteria of appraisal within the philosophy of science has so far yielded no success stories. This has led some to conclude that the quest is chimerical. It was mentioned earlier that the relativism in Thomas Kuhn's model of science was unacceptable to Mark Blaug. In the intervening years, other models for analysing science have been developed which make Kuhn's analysis seem absolutist in comparison. Some have responded to the failures of prescriptivist programmes by renouncing all prescription. Others have taken the failure to discover universal criteria of appraisal to imply that all criteria are equally valid, and the inability to measure progress to imply that sciences do not progress. Some have presumed that the absence of a demarcation criterion implies that science is no different from any other form of human activity. Others have concluded that the failure to come up with an unproblematical criterion of truth implies that truth is a meaningless concept. Most generally, these critics have taken the failures of prescriptivist philosophy of science to achieve its goals to imply that the philosophy of science should be replaced altogether by some other, non-epistemically based mode of inquiry. The doctrines of anti-foundationalism in philosophy and of deconstructionism in literary criticism have begun to make inroads into economics. Some economists have urged that we turn to fields like the sociology of science or rhetoric the better to understand theory choice, and often their arguments begin from the assumption that epistemology is a failed academic enterprise. The quest for standards embraced by methodologists like Mark Blaug and Wade Hands is meant as an antidote to these recent trends.[5]

CRITICAL PLURALISM AS THE MIDDLE GROUND

But it seems to me that there is another alternative, one which I view as a middle ground between relativism and the quest for universal criteria. The position that gradually emerged in a series of works (for example, Caldwell 1982, 1986, 1988, 1989) is one that I labelled critical pluralism. It is not a full-fledged epistemological position, but neither is it so vague that it cannot be articulated. The major tenets include:

1. A disavowal of quests for a single demarcation criterion or for universally applicable criteria of theory appraisal.
2. An emphasis on criticism: the role of the methodologist is to assess the strengths and weaknesses of various research programmes.
3. An objectivity constraint: in reconstructing a programme and its methodological content, one should try to give it its strongest possible portrayal.
4. An insistence on viewing all criticism as problem-dependent. The content of the criticism will depend on the sorts of problems the programme seeks to answer. A programme could be found to be adequate for the solution of certain problems and inadequate for the solution of others.
5. Finally, the critical pluralist values novelty. Though criticism is a key, new programmes should be encouraged to flourish and permitted a grace period in which they are not severely criticized. One a programme is established, though, the critical process begins.

I view critical pluralism as providing a rough set of guidelines for economic methodologists to follow. The sort of writers whose works I think are broadly supportive include a number of Popperians: Popper himself in his critical rationalist writings (this is why whenever I criticized Popper I always talked about the 'falsificationist Popper'); Kurt Klappholz and J. A. Agassi (1959) (reading this article first set me on the path towards critical pluralism); Larry Boland (1982); and Bill Bartley (1984). I would also include, somewhat paradoxically, the early Lakatos, the author of *Proofs and Refutations* (1976). Finally, certain people whose work lies outside of the Popperian tradition would also be included, especially Larry Laudan (1977), whose detailed discussion of science as a problem-solving enterprise is wholly compatible with critical pluralism.[6] That such different writers can provide inspiration indicate just how eclectic critical pluralism is.

Though I view critical pluralism as a middle ground, there is no time to offer an extended demonstration of how it is an improvement over both extremes. The focus of this paper has been on those who endorse a specific normative role for methodology. Continuing that theme, I shall offer two arguments, one practical and the other epistemological, for why accepting critical pluralism makes more sense than trying to resuscitate Lakatos (Blaug's route) or holding out the hope that some day a set of criteria of appraisal or of demarcation may be discovered (Hands's route).

TWO ARGUMENTS AGAINST THE QUEST FOR UNIVERSAL CRITERIA

(a) To make the practical argument, let us begin with an analogy. You are a professor and a student who is flunking your course comes into your office for a conference. What course of action do you recommend to the student? Drop the course and focus on doing better in other classes? Get a tutor? Improve attendance? Read more of the assigned materials? Improve note-taking? Join a study group? Another question is, what sort of attitude do you display towards the student? Concern? Sympathy? Encouragement? Or do you play 'tough cop', pointing out the student's reprehensible attendance record, poor attitude, laziness or absence of good study skills? Or are you coolly objective, stating simply but precisely what the student's situation is and laying out the options that are available? These are tough questions. And there is a further, distinctly methodological, question in all this, namely: how does one go about answering these questions?

Too often, of course, we as professors answer them according to our own moods, either our general dispositions or our moods as they happen to be on the day of the conference. For example, those whose time is short (or who do not want to get involved with students generally) remain coolly objective. Those who are having bad days (or who believe that most students are lazy) are indifferent or recriminating. And those who suddenly decide to make a difference in a student's life (or who are possessed with perpetual missionary zeal) are encouraging. If there is no feedback from students, such professors might continue their behaviour for years. It takes a severe anomaly (for example, a student suicide or a classroom revolt) to get them to question their procedures.

This sort of professor is analogous to economists who are not interested in methodology and who unselfconsciously practice the methods they learned in graduate school. They assume that those methods are the correct and scientific ones, and that identifying science is easy. They only turn to methodology when something happens to call all such beliefs into question: a major policy failure, for example, or the desertion of the paradigm by a number of prominent advocates.

Another way to answer these questions is to try to come up with some sort of optimal response, a set of instructions and a way of dealing with students which are universally applicable. The response might be based on case studies of past student successes and failures, or empirical data collected by departments of education on the prevalence of various student 'types' in the population, or on psychological studies of motivation, or (most likely) on some intuitive notion of what works. But the goal is to come up with an optimal response.

This, I suggest, is the analogue of the type of programme which Hands and Blaug are pursuing. They seek a universal set of criteria for demarcating and appraising scientific theories. This is not to suggest that they are inflexible about how such standards are to be applied. They may even be prepared to grant that the standards can change through time; for example, that the observation of practice can lead to 'corrections' of a particular set. But the *goal* is to find specific and universally applicable standards.

A third way to answer the question is to find out more about the student's problem situation, to begin asking the student questions, and to focus intently on what the student has to say. The goal of this process is to find the *source* (or sources) of the student's problem. Once the sources are identified, the number of appropriate responses are narrowed down considerably. Crucially, it will become apparent through this process that *some responses are better than others.* But as to which *particular* responses are best, that decision cannot be made until one specifies the student's problem: our responses are *problem-dependent.* Note finally that students with different problems may require responses which are *diametrically opposed:* for example, one encourages students with self-image problems and one confronts those with bad study habits. There is no room for such contradictory advice within a universalist framework.

This is the way of the critical pluralist. The critical pluralist is sensitive to the diversity of science, just as a good professor is sensitive to the diversity of students. The goals of the pluralist (make theories better, or get students to perform better) are the same as those of his universalist colleagues. But his problem-dependent methodological solution is very different. It is not a methodology of 'anything goes': standards are explicitly used. It is just that the pluralist refuses to announce the standards prior to the determination of the problem. Nor does the pluralist see much sense in trying to specify in advance the hundreds of types of problems that science might try to solve (or hundreds of types of students who might walk through his door). Case studies can be instructive and illuminating, but a methodology consisting of case law would be as dull as it was static.

(b)   The analogy presented above was meant to suggest not only how difficult it is, as a practical matter, to come up with some universal set of specific criteria for demarcating and appraising theories, but also that such a quest may be inappropriate, given the diversity of science. But let us assume that the search culminates in the discovery of a set of criteria which are widely supported by the scientific and methodological communities. Even then, a question remains. This epistemological question is the one that is dear to anti-foundationalist philosophers as well as to non-justificationists like Popper and Bartley: How does one justify, or defend, or ground these criteria? Do we look at the history of science? If so, history as written from which interpretative framework? Do we consult the scientific élite? If so, which élite? Do we consult our pre-analytic intuitions? If so, whose intuitions? More generally, how, without recourse to what John Losee (1987: chs 5,6) dubs 'a principle worthy of inviolable status', can such a set of criteria be defended? How, without knowledge of what knowledge in the future looks like, are we to come up with criteria to distinguish what should count as knowledge in the future?

Critical pluralism takes these questions seriously, and perhaps that is a mistake. But given that the forces of relativism have grown rather strong of late it is important to formulate a response to them. One of the virtues of Popper's critical rationalism is that it is an attempt to meet the anti-foundationalist, the non-justificationist, on his own ground, and to show him that there still is a place for critical discourse. Critical pluralism follows Popper on this question.

It may be that Popper is unsuccessful in this venture, or that his thought leads to a dead end, or that, if successful, his success is bought at too high a price. It seems to me that his programme, though radical, is at least consistent, and it has the further virtue of focusing our attention on the questions the relativists pose. And it seems to me that if one insists, as I think Blaug and Hands do, that we must seek out a universal set of criteria, then one is at least obligated to address this conundrum explicitly and to try to offer a solution to it.

And perhaps such a solution will some day be forthcoming. I am prepared to be open and to pursue critical pluralism until that day. And if they agree that no such candidate is currently on the scene, I invite Professors Blaug and Hands to join me in the meantime in the middle ground provided by critical pluralism. It is not so uncongenial a place as they might imagine.

NOTES

1.   Samuelson's borrowings from philosophy have been criticized by Caldwell (1982), and his use of analogies from physics has been attacked by Mirowski (1989). Ironically, though the value of his explicitly methodological writings have been called into question, Samuelson's *practice* of economics has obviously

had a profound effect on the actual methods followed by economists. Machlup's methodological articles are collected in Machlup (1978).

2. Of course, one might conclude from this that economics is not a science. This option is not open to a Lakatosian economist, however, who is forced to judge the MSRP as deficient if it cannot rationalize the history of his discipline.

   As an aside, if we use another demarcation criterion (namely, the presence of causal arguments) to determine whether a discipline is a science, the literature on folk psychology raises some serious doubts concerning the scientific status of many of the social sciences (Rosenberg 1988). I think that much might be gained if the term 'social science' was changed to 'social studies'. By denying such studies scientific status, the hubris of many practitioners would be reduced. For their part, philosophers and methodologists would be forced to address the new and more difficult question of what is worthwhile in social studies rather than to continue mouthing the (rather easily demonstrable) proposition that the social sciences are in various ways inadequate. Perhaps best of all, since acronyms would be unaffected, such a move could be accomplished economically.

3. A framework provided by Larry Laudan (1977) may be a better vehicle for discussing the Keynesian Revolution. Laudan's crucial move is to uncouple the notions of progress and truth, which has important implications for the assessment of the Keynesian programme. For example, at the time of its development the Keynesian Revolution was viewed as progressive by scientists. And as Blaug points out, even in retrospect the programme was progressive in terms of its fecundity. Laudan's model would allow one to judge the Keynesian programme as progressive even though it was later recognized that certain of the claims of the programme were not true.

4. Obviously, sometimes empirical anomalies are simply ignored. The ubiquitous presence of preference reversals has had little impact on textbook presentations of choice theory, for example.

5. In the opening chapters of his book on rhetoric, Donald McCloskey (1985) grounds his approach, at least in part, on the anti-foundationalist philosophy of Richard Rorty. This is why many methodologists, most of whom one assumes would otherwise be sympathetic to McCloskey's general message, reacted critically to the rhetoric programme. It is ironic that McCloskey (by grounding his work on the writings of anti-foundationalists) provoked the ire of those who insist on foundations and who therefore oppose the philosophy of anti-foundationalism!

6. One reason Laudan is able to discuss problem-solving in so detailed a way is because of his willingness to disengage the notion of progress from truth. Popper and Popperians are not prepared to do this. As a result, although they emphasize that science solves problems and that progress occurs when problems are solved, Popperians seldom extend the analysis of problem-solving much further. If problems are solved only by the discovery of the truth, there is not much more to say.

9. Popper, the Rationality Principle and Economic Explanation

D. Wade Hands

INTRODUCTION

In earlier work (1985a, 1990) I have argued that an inconsistency exists between Karl Popper's falsificationist philosophy of natural science and the type of methodological advice he gives to social scientists in his writings on situational analysis. To emphasize this point I introduced (1985a: 90) the appellation Popper$_n$ for the well-known views of Popper the falsificationist philosopher of *n*atural science, and Popper$_s$ for the lesser known views expressed in Popper's writings on *s*ocial science and situational analysis.[1] While I have not been alone in calling attention to this potential contradiction, there does not seem to be any consensus in the literature regarding either the significance of this tension or how it might be alleviated.[2] Mark Blaug for instance, in his response to my paper, recognized the 'clash' between the two positions, but resolved the conflict by simply dismissing Popper's writings on social science: 'The fact is that Popper knew little about social science and even less about economics' (1985: 287).

In this paper I should like to continue the examination of Popper$_n$, Popper$_s$ and the implications for social science and economics. I will argue that the tension in Popper is in fact an essential tension and that it stems from Popper's unfailing commitment to the covering-law model of scientific explanation; Popper's meta-commitment to this model forced him to characterize social science explanations in a way that clashed with his support of the 'unity of science' thesis and certain other aspects of his philosophical programme. This essential tension has important implications for the overall success of Popper's philosophical project as well as for the social science that Popper used as his general model: neoclassical microeconomics. In order to make my case for the essential tension it will be necessary to review Popper's perspective on scientific explanation, the unity of science and situational analysis. This review will be contained in the first two sections below. Possible philosophical 'solutions', some Popperian and some non-Popperian, as well as the implications for economic methodology will be examined in the last two sections.

POPPER ON SCIENTIFIC EXPLANATION AND THE UNITY OF SCIENCE

Although philosophical discussion on the nature of scientific explanation goes back to at least Aristotle, it is Hempel and Oppenheim (1948) who are usually given credit for the first definitive statement of what now constitutes the received view on scientific explanation: the deductive-nomological (D-N) or covering-law model.[3] According to the D-N model the key to scientific explanation is the deductive subsumption of the explanandum (the thing to be explained) under general laws; the explanandum should be deductively 'expected', given the initial conditions and the relevant general laws.

For example, suppose we wish to explain why a particular piece of wire expanded. A D-N explanation of this phenomenon might take the following form:

(a) The wire was made of metal.
(b) The wire was heated.
(c) *All metals expand when heated.*
(d) The wire expanded.

The *explanandum*, a statement describing the phenomenon to be explained, is given by sentence (d). It is *logically deduced* from the *explanans*, the explanation of the phenomenon, given by sentences (a) to (c). Notice that the explanans is composed of two different types of sentence – sentences (a) and (b) which state the *initial* (or *antecedent*) *conditions* and sentence (c) which states a *general scientific law*. Any D-N explanation must contain at least one general law and, according to the original Hempel and Oppenheim characterization, the general laws as well as the initial conditions must all be *true*. In general then, a legitimate D-N explanation must take the following deductive form:

$$\frac{C_1, C_2, ..., C_n \quad \text{explanans (or explicans)}}{C_1, C_2, ..., C_n} \quad \text{explanandum (or explicandum)}$$

$$\frac{L_1, L_2, ..., L_m}{E}$$

where each C_i represents a sentence describing one of the initial conditions and each L_i represents a general law.

Now, while it is standard to credit Hempel and Oppenheim with first delineating D-N schema, Karl Popper may in fact have a legitimate claim to priority. In the *Logic of Scientific Discovery* (1968), a work originally published in 1935, Popper clearly sets out the covering-law model of scientific explanation:[4]

> To give a *causal explanation* of an event means to deduce a statement which describes it, using as premises of the deduction one or more *universal laws*, together with certain singular statements, the *initial conditions*. (1966: 59)

> We have thus two different kinds of statement, both of which are necessary ingredients of a complete causal explanation. They are (1) *universal statements*, i.e. hypotheses of the character of natural laws, and (2) *singular statements*, which apply to the specific event in question and which I shall call 'initial conditions'. It is from universal statements in conjunction with initial conditions that we *deduce* the singular statement. . . . (Ibid.: 60)

The question of whether Popper was actually the first to characterize the D-N model is not really the point; the point is that Popper clearly *accepts* the D-N framework as the proper way of characterizing scientific explanations.[5] In fact, not only does Popper accept the covering-law view, he is actually a much stronger advocate of the model then Hempel (despite the fact that it is often called the 'Hempelian' theory). There are at least two reasons to believe that Popper is a stronger advocate. One is that for Popper this is the *only* legitimate form of scientific explanation;[6] for Hempel other types of scientific explanation are possible. In particular, Hempel accepts both deductive-statistical (D-S) explanations and inductive statistical (I-S) explanations.[7] Secondly, for Popper such explanations provide the *aim* of science: 'I suggest that it is the aim of science to find *satisfactory explanations* of whatever strikes us as being in need of explanation' (Popper 1972: 191).[8] Thus for Popper covering law explanations are uniquely important; they provide the only legitimate form of scientific explanation and explanation is the aim of science.

Now, as mentioned above, in the Hempelian characterization a true scientific explanation is only obtained when both the laws and the initial conditions in the explanans are true. But Popper could not possibly endorse such a requirement. According to Popper's fallibilist theory of knowledge we never know when a scientific law (or even an initial condition) is true – all we have is a way for (we hope) eliminating error. All we can do is to test the theory empirically, and provisionally accept those theories that have passed severe tests.

> The *explicans* in order to be satisfactory (satisfactoriness may be a matter of degree), must satisfy a number of conditions. First it must logically entail the *explicandum*. Secondly, the *explicans* ought to be true although it will not, in general, be known to be true; in any case, it must not be known to be false – not even after the most critical examination. If it is not known to be true (as will usually be the case) there must be *independent* evidence in its favour. In other words, it must be *independently* testable; and it will be the more satisfactory the greater the severity of the independent tests it has survived.   (Popper 1983: 132–3).

In this way Popper's acceptance of the D-N model of explanation connects up cleanly with his general falsificationist methodology. The aim of science is explanation, explanations require general laws, and the general laws must be scientific theories which have survived severe, independent, empirical tests. In terms of the language of Popperian falsificationism, the 'laws' in the explicans must be corroborated scientific theories. So what about social science? How are explanations and the theories involved in them different in social sciences than in natural science? Or are they?

The short answer is that for Popper there is no difference. Popper advocates the 'unity of science' or methodological monism: the position that the method employed in social science is fundamentally the same method as that employed in natural science. Social science might be a little more difficult, the data might not be as clean or as available, but the basic methodology is the same for both social and natural science.

> I am going to propose a doctrine of the unity of method; that is to say, the view that all theoretical or generalizing sciences make use of the same method, whether they are natural sciences or social sciences. . . . The methods always consist in offering deductive causal explanations, and in testing them (by way of predictions).   (Popper 1961: 130–1)

Actually the unity-of-science thesis is such a fundamental part of the Popperian philosophical position that to abandon it could potentially undermine the entire programme. As Popper makes very clear in his autobiography (1976b) and elsewhere, one of his early motivations for the development of his philosophy of science, and of his demarcation criterion in particular, was to define 'science' in such a way that certain social sciences – specifically Marxism and Freudian psychology – would fall outside the domain of science.[9] For Popper successfully to *criticize* Marx and Freud as being 'unscientific' necessarily presupposes methodological monism for it presupposes that social science *can* and *should* be judged by the same methodological standards as the natural sciences. If social theorizing is fundamentally different from theorizing in the natural sciences then Popper's criticism of these two research programmes is simply a category mistake.

In summary then, the Popperian position seems quite clear. The aim of theoretical science, either natural or social, is to provide causal explanations. These causal explanations must conform to the D-N model and the universal statements (the laws) involved must live up to falsificationist methodological standards. In particular, these theories need to be 'scientific' – they must be potentially falsifiable by empirical basic statements – and they must have survived severe independent testing. This all seems relatively straightforward; now let us consider Popper's writings on situational analysis.

SITUATIONAL ANALYSIS AND THE RATIONALITY PRINCIPLE

Only a small fraction of Popper's written work is concerned explicitly with social science.[10] His approach to social science is called 'situational analysis' and it was developed as 'an attempt to generalize the method of economic theory (marginal utility theory) so as to become applicable to the other theoretical social sciences' (Popper 1976b: 117–18). It is not entirely clear whether Popper considers situational analysis to be merely one approach to human science or whether he considers it to be the 'only' method available to social science.[11]

The basic method of situational analysis is to specify the 'situation' the agent is in – this includes the individual's beliefs and desires as well as objective constraints and information – and then deduce the behaviour of the agent on the basis of the *rationality principle* (RP) that all individuals act 'appropriately' (rationally), given their situation. Since the situational description, no matter how detailed, is simply a description, the rationality principle is necessary to 'animate' that description into action. In general, 'there is only one animating law involved – the principle of acting appropriately to the situation', it 'is known in the literature under the name "*rationality principle*" ' (1985: 359).

In schematic form, then, if we want to use situational analysis (SA) to explain why a particular agent A did action X our explanation would take the following form:[12]

Description of the situation:	Agent A was in situation S.
Analysis of the situation:	In situation S the appropriate (rational) thing to do is X.
The RP:	Agents always act appropriately (rationally) given their situations.
Explanandum:	Therefore: A did X.

Comparing this SA explanation with the D-N explanatory schema presented above we have the first two parts – the description and the analysis – serve as the initial conditions and the RP serve as the general law. Popper generally, though he is not entirely consistent on this, calls the first two parts the 'model' of the situation; thus 'the premises of the explanation usually consist of a situational model and of the so-called rationality principle' (Popper 1976a: 100 note). Given Popper's use of the term 'model' the two explanatory schemata can be compared in the following way:[13]

D-N explanation   *SA explanation*
Explanans: Initial conditions theory (or law)   Explanans: Model (or theory)
                                                                    RP

Explanandum: Event   Explanandum: Action

So far so good; nothing seems to be inconsistent with what was said about Popper in the previous section. Popper requires D-N explanations for all sciences – he advocates SA for social science – but SA just seems to be a special form of the D-N model. So why should there be a conflict between Popper$_n$ (the advocate of the left-hand D-N schema) and Popper$_s$ (the advocate of the right hand SA schema)?

The key to this question *lies in the nature of the rationality principle.* Since the RP serves as the general law in a D-N explanation then it needs to be a corroborated scientific theory and 'it must not be known to be false' (Popper 1983: 132), but this requirement presents severe difficulties for the RP. First of all, Popper is never clear whether the RP requires the agent to act appropriately in some *objective* sense, or whether it only requires the agent to act appropriately in the *subjective* sense of acting appropriately 'as they see it'.[14] For this reason Nadeau (1990: 10) considers to separate rationality principles: RP$_o$, the objective rationality principle that agents act appropriately to the situation in some objective (ideal observer) sense, and RP$_s$, the subjective rationality principle that all agents act appropriately as they see the situation (however distorted their viewpoint may be to any other observer). I shall argue that the RP runs into problems with Popper's demarcation criterion, and thus Popper$_n$ is in conflict with Popper$_s$, on *either one* of these characteristics.

First consider the RP$_s$. The problem with the subjective interpretation of RP is that it is empirically *unfalsifiable.* What possible observation could we make of an individual's behaviour that would falsify the claim that the individual was acting appropriately to the situation 'as they saw it'? The only way to falsify such a claim would be to have independent (and objective) information about the individual's beliefs: if we knew his beliefs and the (observable) action he took, we could then evaluate whether he did in fact act appropriately given his beliefs.[15] But we do not read minds. The only way we might possibly find out about a person's beliefs would be to ask him, but this entails a vicious regress. A speech act is no less an intentional action as any other human action. How someone will respond to a question about his beliefs will in fact depend on his beliefs; in particular how he responds will be what is appropriate for him to say given the conversational situation as he sees it.[16] Any way we might test RP$_s$ necessarily pre-supposes it and thus the rationality principle in its subjective interpretation is unfalsifiable.

Now consider RP$_o$. The problem with the objective interpretation of RP is that it is empirically *false*, people do not always act in a way that is objectively appropriate given their situation. Popper (1985: 361) clearly admits the falsity of the RP$_o$:

> I think one can see very easily that this is not so. One has only to observe a flustered driver, desperately trying to park his car when there is no parking space to be found, in order to see that we do not always act in accordance with the rationality principle. . . . But a principle that is not universally true is false. Thus the rationality principle is false. I think there is no way out of this.[17]

Thus we clearly have a tension between Popper$_n$ and Popper$_s$. The best social science explanations, those involving the rationality priniciple and situational analysis, employ a general law that is either *unfalsifiable* (on the RP$_s$ interpretation) or *false* (on the RP$_o$ interpretation). In either case situational analysis does not provide explanations that are bona fide scientific explanations. If scientific explanations are the aim of science and the best social science cannot provide such explanations, then it must be the case that all of social science falls on the non-science side of the demarcational fence. Thus economics, Popper's model for situational analysis, is indicted, and Popper's entire argument against Marx and Freud is defused. This ultimately must undermine the unity of science thesis and the internal integrity of the entire Popperian philosophical programme.

SOME WAYS OUT

I should like to discuss a number of ways in which one might philosophically get around the negative conclusion of the previous section. These 'solutions' will be divided into two separate groups. The first group constitutes solutions which could be called 'Popperian' in spirit; that is, they are solutions that are generally consistent with the fundamental tenets of the Popperian programme. The second group of possible solutions are non-Popperian in that they require the sacrifice of at least one important part of the Popperian ensemble.

The first of these Popperian solutions is what I would call the *verisimilitude solution* and there seems to be reasonably good evidence that this was in fact Popper's own solution to the problem.[18] During the 1960s Popper developed the concept of 'verisimilitude' or 'truthlikeness'.[19] The basic idea was, first, to formalize the notion of being 'closer' to the truth or approximately true and, secondly, to demonstrate that scientific theories consistent with Popper's falsificationist methodology exhibited this property. It is easy to see how the concept of verisimilitude might provide a solution to Popper's problem. Even though the RP is false, if it could be shown to be closer to the truth than other 'laws' which might be used in social science explanations, then situational analysis would be vindicated. In the verisimilitude scenario the unity of science continues to hold; the only difference between Popper$_s$ and Popper$_n$ is that the former is more approximate, has less verisimilitude, than the latter. As Popper himself (1976a: 103) says:

> The explanations of situational logic described here are rational, theoretical reconstructions. They are oversimplified and overschematized and consequently in general *false*. Nevertheless, they can possess a considerable truth content and they can, in the strictly logical sense, be good approximations to the truth, and better than certain other testable explanations. In this sense, the logical concept of approximation to the truth is indispensable for a social science using the method of situational analysis.

There are at least two reasons why the verisimilitude solution fails to be successful. One of these is simply that Popper's general programme in verisimilitude was a failure.[20] Not only did Popper's formal concept of a 'measure' of verisimilitude run into insurmountable difficulties, but even in a less formal guise the concept was never linked up with the rest of the Popperian programme; in particular it was never demonstrated that increasing the degree of corroboration increased the verisimilitude of a theory. Secondly, even if Popper's concept of verisimilitude had been a complete success there are still problems with defending SA in this way. Suppose Popper had clearly established a link between passing severe tests (being corroborated) and being approximately true (having verisimilitude). For this to help SA it would be necessary to actually corroborate the RP

– it would be fine for the RP to be false in a number of specific cases – but it would continually need to be challenged with severe tests and pass them. This is *not* what Popper recommends for the RP. In fact Popper argues that the RP should not itself be tested; the arrow of *modus tollens* should be aimed at the 'model' and not at the RP.

> Now if a theory is tested, and found faulty, then we have always to decide which of its various constituent parts we shall make accountable for its failure. My thesis is that it is sound methodological policy to decide not to make the rationality principle accountable but the rest of the theory; that is, the model.   (Popper 1985: 362)

Since Popper does not recommend testing the RP, it cannot be corroborated and thus it cannot be shown to have increasing verisimilitude even if the concept of verisimilitude were unproblematic.

The second Popperian solution could be called the *Lakatosian solution*. Suppose we treat the RP as a hard-core proposition in the situational analysis research programme in social science. Since according to Lakatos's 'Methodology of Scientific Research Programmes' (1970), the hard-core propositions are never tested, Popper's defensive strategy regarding the RP would be entirely appropriate.[21] Given Lakatosian standards for 'progressive problem shifts' we could examine the overall progress of the general SA research programme or the progress of a particular specialized version of it, such as microeconomics. For example, if large portions of the neoclassical research programme could be reconstructed as progressive by Lakatos's standards it would certainly diminish the impact of the conflict between Popper$_s$ and Popper$_n$. I say diminish rather than eliminate for a number of reasons, the most important of these being that no one has ever argued convincingly that the theories extracted from progressive Lakatosian research programmes can legitimately serve as the general laws in D-N explanations. But such issues are probably just 'in-house' debates between those of a more old-fashioned Popperian persuasion and those in the Lakatosian wing of the programme. Ultimately whether the Lakatosian solution will be viable or not will depend on the overall success of the Lakatosian programme and that is a topic which is surely beyond the scope of the current chapter.[22]

It should probably be noted that the Lakatosian solution is the solution endorsed by Mark Blaug.[23] Since Blaug has never actually admitted that the tension between Popper$_n$ and Popper$_s$ is an issue of major significance it might be better to say that because Blaug has endorsed Lakatos's methodology as the proper way to apply Popper to economics for over a decade,[24] it seems reasonable to argue that he would endorse Lakatos's work as the solution to any problems that one might uncover relating Popper's philosophy to the social sciences.

The third and final Popperian solution I shall examine is the *critical rationalist solution*. It is the solution recently endorsed by Bruce Caldwell (1991). Critical rationalism is an alternative interpretation of Popperian philosophy due primarily to W. W. Bartley (1984).[25] It is an interpretation which Popper himself seemed to support in later years, especially in (1983). The basic argument of critical rationalism is that the 'method of science' consists of criticism and being open to criticism. 'Scientific theories are distinguished from myths merely in being criticizable, and in being open to modifications in the light of criticism' (Popper 1983: 7). On this view, empirical falsifiability is simply one of many different forms of criticism; it is the form most important in scientific discourse, but it is simply one form of criticism. According to critical rationalism the issue is not demarcation, where something either is or is not science, but rather criticizability which is not yes or no but a continuum from very criticizable to not criticizable (or dogmatic). Since critical rationalism blurs the distinction between science and non-science it provides a way out of the tension between Popper$_n$ and Popper$_s$. As Caldwell (1991: 48–9) argues:

> Critical rationalism is a problem-solving approach which itself appears to resolve a problem within Popper's philosophy of science, the tension between situational analysis and falsification-ism. Critical rationalism states that sometimes it is appropriate to evaluate a theory using the strict empirical criteria of falsificationism. But at other times, especially within the social sciences, one is better able to criticize a theory by applying the canons of situational logic. And there are still other circumstances, particularly when metaphysical theories are considered, when other routes to criticism are preferable. Which methods of criticism are most appropriate cannot be specified in advance: that will depend on the subject matter and the problem to be solved.

Caldwell is entirely correct that *if* one accepts critical rationalism then the tension between the two Poppers seems to dissolve. The real question is not about whether it solves the problem, but about critical rationalism itself. In earlier work I have expressed some scepticism about this approach[26] and I still tend to think of it as an epistemically retreatist position (as some of Popper's generals advising him to fall back to a region of such philosophically unstable terrain that his critics will be unwilling to continue their pursuit), but none the less I must also admit that critical rationalism is a position on which the jury is still out. The argument is relatively new and both its general philosophical adequacy as well as its Popperian fidelity are still open questions.[27]

Turning now to philosophical solutions that cannot properly be called 'Popperian', I should like to examine two possibilities (there are of course many more that could legitimately be discussed). The first of these non-Popperian solutions could be called *social science instrumentalism*. Many of the criticisms raised against the RP and SA are general criticisms of any 'action' explanations that utilize beliefs, desires and other intentional notions in their explanans. Such explanations are called 'folk psychology' and a fairly extensive philosophical literature has developed which considers the explanations given by folk psychology to be something less than bona fide scientific explanations.[28] This literature has not as yet addressed itself explicitly to Popper's situational analysis but since many of the criticisms of folk psychology apply directly to Popper's SA, those things proposed to circumvent the problems of folk psychology could also serve as a solution to the tension between the two Poppers. Now, one of the most discussed responses to the problem of folk psychology is social science instrumentalism; it is a position usually associated with Daniel Dennett.[29] The argument is that while social sciences that utilize belief and desire in their explanans do not provide us with causal scientific explanations, they might none the less be instrumentally quite good when judged solely on the basis of their predictive adequacy. Maybe the involvement of intentional notions prevents scientific explanation, but such notions do not preclude the instrumental usefulness of the theories in which they are embedded. In addition, so the argument goes, maybe such instrumental usefulness is all that we can expect from any social science – at least for the immediate future. This instrumentalist view of social science is certainly non-Popperian, both because it violates the unity of science thesis and because it supports instrumental-ism, a view that Popper has long criticized (in any science). Obviously, whether one is Popperian or not, the degree to which one finds this solution acceptable will ultimately depend on one's views about instrumentalism and one's commitment to the unity of science.

The second non-Popperian solution is what I shall call the *alternative views of explanation* solution. The basic argument is that the tension between Popper$_s$ and Popper$_n$ is a tension created by Popper's too-strong adherence to the D-N model of explanation. The covering-law model has been under almost continuous siege for the last 40 years and while no new consensus has emerged to replace the received view of the D-N model, a few points of consensus have surfaced. One of the points of consensus, the one most relevant to the question at hand, is that our concept of a scientific explanation needs to be more pragmatic or context-dependent.[30] The D-N model was a purely formal, *a priori* framework for appraising scientific explanations; its replacement should be sensitive to the pragmatic context in which explanations are proposed. In the last few years a number of different approaches to scientific explanation have been suggested which try in various ways to accommodate this pragmatic component. These approaches include the explicitly pragmatic approach of van Fraassen (1980), the explanatory unification account of Kitcher (1989) and the causal explanation view of Miller (1987).[31] While I do not intend to endorse any particular one of the alternative views, I would argue that with a less rigid, more pragmatic notion of explanation the criticisms of SA explanations may disappear. As I discussed above, if SA is to be forced into the D-N framework then the RP must satisfy the requirements for being a general scientific law; on a more pragmatic characterization this very strict requirement would no longer need to be met. For example, on Richard Miller's (1987: 91) causal view, explanations are judged in part by the much weaker criterion of whether they satisfy certain field-specific 'standard causal patterns'.

Now, of course, it is possible that SA will fail to live up to the standards of even a more context-dependent view of explanation. It is also possible that these pragmatic notions of explanation simply surrender too much, that they will accommodate 'explanations' of a clearly non-scientific type. Both these questions will be a matter for further research. My point is simply that if the D-N model is now generally accepted as being too rigid even for natural science – if our best examples of successful scientific explanation fail to fit the D-N model – why should such standards continue to be used in the indictment of social science explanations, SA or otherwise?

IMPLICATIONS FOR ECONOMIC METHODOLOGY

While it is very unlikely that awareness of the tension between the two Poppers or its origin in Popper's strict adherence to the D-N model will have a profound impact on most practising economists, it should have an impact on the kinds of issues that concern economic methodologists. For those of the Popperian persuasion such as Blaug and Hutchison the issue is obvious; as Blaug himself (1985: 287) admits, 'Those like myself who claim that modern economists largely subscribe to Popperian falsificationism have a little difficulty here that they have not squarely faced up to.' But even for those who do not consider Popper to be a useful guide to the philosophical investigation of economics, the issue should also be of substantial concern. As the above discussion of folk psychology indicated, this is not simply a problem of an inconsistency or tension within the Popperian tradition; it is potentially a problem for any social science that appeals to intentional notions such as beliefs and desires in an attempt to provide covering-law explanations of human action. And given that most standard microeconomic explanations are considered to be just this kind of intentional yet nomic explanation, the real issue is the general question of the explanatory adequacy of microeconomics.[32] While Alexander Rosenberg (1980, 1983, 1988) seems to be the only author who has applied this critique of folk psychology directly to economics, the issue is substantive and independent of one's commitment to Popperian philosophy.

Now, one could argue that even though these issues are substantive, their impact on economic methodology will be small since most of the 'solutions' are already standard positions within the methodological literature. Lakatos's methodology of scientific research programmes provides a possible solution and has certainly received a lot of attention from economists – no doubt for reasons other than those discussed above. On the other hand, Caldwell's support of critical rationalism seems to be motivated by precisely these concerns. Instrumentalism offers a solution and it certainly has a wide following within the economics profession. While some of instrumentalism's support may come from blind adherence to Friedman's famous essay (1953), far more of it comes from instrumentalism's ability to provide a solution to the problems examined here. This is not to say that practising economists have adopted an instrumentalist position because they care about the essential tension within Popperian philosophy – they most certainly do not. The point is simply that practising economists adopt instrumentalism because they know that the basic assumptions of their models (including the RP) are false and yet they find these models to be very useful in predicting economic behaviour.[33] Finally, the new literature on pragmatic explanation has not explicitly been applied to economics, but none the less the economics profession has a long tradition of resisting attempts to force economic explanation into the procrustean bed of the covering-law model.

Despite the fact that many of these solutions are already in the literature, the essential tension within the Popperian tradition and the implied critique of microeconomic explanations constitutes more than a new way of interpreting the existing work in economic methodology. These issues also raise fundamentally new methodological questions that require our attention in future research. I should like to close this chapter by examining one of these questions.

The question is: Are microeconomic explanations really SA explanations? Certainly Popper thought so since he considered microeconomics to be the model for his character-ization of SA. And certainly those like Rosenberg who apply the critique of folk psychology to microeconomics must believe that economic explanations are of this general intentional form. In fact the entire discussion of 'solutions' was implicitly based on the argument that real social science explanations, particularly those in microeconomics, were of this type. But are they?

I frankly do not have a firm answer to this question, but I do think it is a topic that deserves serious investigation. Consider the issues. The explanandum of an SA explana-tion is the action of an individual; in terms of the schema in the third section above, 'A did X'. Now it is possible that microeconomics could be used to explain why an individual consumer purchased a particular good or why an individual worker offered to work at a particular wage, but this is certainly not the only, or even the most common, type of microeconomic explanation. More commonly, microeconomics is used to explain phenomena that emerge from the actions of a large number of individuals – things like market prices and quantities. Even in the realm of purely *micro*economics, it is aggregated (market) variables that are usually the topic of investigation, not the action of an individual economic agent. The event to be explained is often an *un*intended consequence of the actions of the individual agents and since, according to SA, the actions of the individual agents are intentional, the event to be explained must necessarily be subject to laws that emerge at a higher level than that of the individual agent. Now Popper clearly pays lip service to the unintended consequences of individual action. He says (1965: 342), in fact, that the main task of theoretical social science is 'to trace the unintended social repercussions of intentional human actions'[34] and he even uses supply and demand as an example (1965: 124), but this is not really what SA explains. SA, like any folk psychology explanation in terms of the beliefs and desires of agents, explains only the actions of individuals. If unintended consequences or other emergent properties are to be explained it seems that 'laws' other than the RP and 'causes' other than individual beliefs must be involved. It is possible that such an argument can be used to extricate social sciences like microeconomics from the general critique of SA and intentional psychology.[35] If this is the case, the tension is simply a problem for the internal integrity of the Popperian programme and not necessarily a general problem about the way economists explain. Such an argument would of course lend credence to Blaug's (1985b: 287) original response that 'Popper knew little about social science and even less about economics'.

NOTES

1. The Popper$_n$ position is best represented by *The Logic of Scientific Discovery* (1968) and the essays in *Conjectures and Refutations* (1965); Popper$_s$ is best represented by Popper (1976a) and (1985).
2. Some of the contributors to this literature include: Blaug (1985b), Caldwell (1991), Farr (1983), Koertge (1974, 1975, 1979, 1985), Lagueux (1990), Latsis (1976, 1983), Nadeau (1990), Pepin (1990), Schmid (1988) and Watkins (1970).
3. Hempel and Oppenheim (1948) is reprinted in Hempel (1965). Salmon (1989) provides a detailed history of the D-N model and the philosophical literature that has surrounded it. The D-N model is also summarized in Blaug (1980a) and Caldwell (1982).
4. Hempel does in fact recognize Popper's early contribution to the literature although he does not actually go so far as to give Popper priority (1965: 251 note 7, and 337 note 2). Popper himself, though, seems to be quite clear on the matter: 'To my knowledge, the theory of causality sketched here in the text was first presented in my book, *Logik der Forschung* (1935) – now translated as *The Logic of Scientific Discovery*' (1966: 362).
5. In case someone might attribute Popper's support for the D-N model to mere youthful exuberance, it should be noted that almost 50 years later in the 'Postscript to the Logic of Scientific Discovery' his view is unchanged (see Popper 1983: 132).
6. Because of this position Salmon (1988: 95) finds Popper guilty of 'explanatory deductive chauvinism'.
7. See Hempel (1965: 376–412); the topic is also given a detailed discussion in the Salmon (1989) survey on explanation.
8. Also see Popper (1968: 61 note, and 1983: 132).
9. See Popper (1976b: 36–7, 41–2; and 1965: 33–5).
10. In addition to Popper (1976a and 1985) listed in note 1, the other places where social science is given more than a passing comment are (1961, 1966, 1976b).
11. Certainly in (1985: 358) he says, 'My thesis is that only in this way can we explain and understand what happens in society. Similar comments are on 361.
12. This schematic form is based on Koertge (1975: 87; 1979: 440). The scheme goes back at least to Hempel (1962: 12), a paper where Popper is not cited but which some have called 'Hempel's attempt to codify the main features of Popper's "logic of the situation" ' (Leach 1968: 260).
13. This way of comparing the two explanatory schemata is given in Nadeau (1990: 4).
14. Popper is *really* unclear on this; Latsis (1983: 133) claims, I think rightly, that Popper is either 'confused or deliberately elusive' on this issue. For example, in 1985 Popper clearly takes the subjective interpretation saying that rationality is only 'as they see it' and thus SA can be applied to the behaviour of a 'madman' (1985: 363). On the other hand, he calls SA 'a purely objective method' which 'can be developed independently of all subjective or psychological ideas' (1976a: 102), and in 1966 he says the RP is the 'general law that *sane* persons as a rule act more or less rationally' (1966: 265).
15. 'The only way to falsify such a statement would be to prove that an agent did not act in accordance with his own beliefs. Such a proof would only be possible if the observer could have access to the beliefs of an agent *other than by observing his behavior*; but this is clearly impossible' (Nadeau 1990: 14).
16. This argument is presented in greater detail in Rosenberg (1988: 30–6).
17. Similar remark in Popper (1976a: 103).
18. Although here, as elsewhere in Popper's discussion of SA, the issue is hardly clear cut.
19. Popper's primary discussion of verisimilitude is contained in chapters 2 and 9 of (1972) and chapter 10 of (1965). Verisimilitude is discussed in much greater detail in Hands (1991 a and b).

20. Popper himself discusses this in (1983: xxxv–xxxvi); the problem is also surveyed in Watkins (1984: 279–88).
21. To the best of my knowledge this solution was first applied to microeconomics in Latsis (1972) and SA in general in Koertge (1975).
22. The literature surrounding Lakatos's programme is far too extensive to cite here but two important volumes of essays are: Cohen, Feyerabend and Wartofsky (1976) and Gavroglu, Goudaroulis and Nicolacopoulous (1989). The literature on Lakatos and economics is also extensive but the two most important volumes are probably Latsis (1976) and Blaug and de Marchi (1991).
23. This is how Blaug is interpreted in Caldwell (1991: 40).
24. Blaug (1976, 1980, 1985, 1987, 1990).
25. Caldwell provides a very careful discussion of critical rationalism in (1991: 40–52).
26. Hands (1990: 30–1); also see Nola (1987).
27. A fourth Popperian solution which I did not discuss is that offered by Watkins (1984). Watkins is not really concerned with the tension between Popper$_s$ and Popper$_n$ but he is concerned with formulating a neo-Popperian programme that avoids some of the pitfalls of the Popperian original. At least two of the changes in the Popperian programme that Watkins proposes may actually help dissolve the tension discussed above. For one thing, Watkins proposes weaker adequacy requirements rather than a demarcation criterion, and secondly, Watkins weakens the concept of explanation, away from the D-N model and more toward explanatory unification.
28. This argument, a version of the view that reasons cannot be causes, is often traced to Wittgenstein; important recent works include Churchland, P. M. (1984), Churchland, P. S. (1986) and Stich (1983). Chapter 2 of Rosenberg (1988) summarizes the argument nicely.
29. See Dennett (1978); criticisms of this view include Baker (1989) and Stich (1983: 242–6).
30. Salmon (1989: 181) lists three other such points of consensus.
31. This is just a small sample of the literature on alternative theories of explanation. Many of the influential papers are reprinted in Pitt (1988), and Salmon (1989) provides a detailed survey.
32. I shall simply avoid the quite interesting topic of macroeconomics and how it related to all of these issues.
33. This argument for the popularity of instrumentalism is presented in Caldwell (1990).
34. For similar remarks see Popper (1966: 95, 323; 1972: 160; 1976b: 185).
35. Such an argument is presented in Nelson, A. (1990), but the author warns us (correctly) that his position does not automatically endorse the social sciences. It only says that the fate of the social sciences is *independent* of the fate of intentional psychology; the social sciences may still have problems of their own.

10. What's So Special about General Equilibrium Theory?

Alexander Rosenberg*

Along with an unshakeable attachment to the formalization of common sense as an explanatory theory, neoclassical economics has formed an equally irresistible attraction to the goal of explaining phenomena by deriving their existence as instances of an equilibrium, and if possible a unique and stable one at that. The fact that few economic processes appear to cry out for such treatment does little to distract economists from this goal. In this paper, I examine the motivation behind this attachment, and whether there is anything that does or could justify it. Understanding its grip on economists, together with the grip intentional variables have, should explain much about the cognitive status of economic theory. Both the question of what general equilibrium theory is all about and a good deal of help in understanding its importance are to be found in the work of Mark Blaug, as will become apparent below.

Given the announced attachment of economic method to falsifiability as a methodological stricture, the unmovable position of general equilibrium as a theoretical desideratum, should come as something of a shock. For, more than any other style of theorizing, equilibrium claims are least open to being falsified, at least in theory.

The existence and stability of a general equilibrium are like the unicorn: things we could go on looking for ever without falsifying the hypotheses that there are such things. Of course, once we have established that a general equilibrium exists and that it is stable, falsifying the claim that it is unique is much less difficult: simply find another set of prices at which all markets clear and we have falsified the claim of uniqueness. This is small comfort in the circumstances.

But if the chief theoretical ornament of economic theory is in principle unfalsifiable when treated as a contingent hypothesis, to what can we attribute the attachment scientific economists feel for it? There are of course claims about ideological causes, as well as sociological, historical or biographical explanations, not to mention rhetorical explanations for the prominence of general equilibrium analysis. What we need, however, is an epistemological or a methodological explanation, which identifies a goal otherwise unattainable than by constructing general equilibrium models.

It will not suffice to answer this question by appealing to the place of general equilibrium in the hard core of a Lakatosian research programme, even if there is such a thing. Our question is prior to the explanation the Lakatosian claim answers: Why don't economists give up general equilibrium thinking very easily? Our question is why *should* they find it attractive in the first place. We can all agree that general equilibrium analysis constitutes the hard core of what seems to satisfy Lakatos's characterization of a scientific research programme. But the question to be examined is why it should be chosen for this honour. This is not the historical question of why it was chosen. Presumably that question is answered by appeal to the intellectual biography of Walras and the influence he has exercised on twentieth-century economics. In *Economic Theory in Retrospect* Blaug (1978: 603) suggests that before Walras

> Economists . . . were still capable of asking: Are prices first determined in the market by demand and supply and then passed on to consumers to permit them to reach an optimum quantity adjustment, or do consumers first decide how much to purchase and do these decisions result in market demand prices? Even if we start with given factor supplies and fixed input coefficients or production, factor prices are not determined until firms have decided to produce certain levels of output: but this decision implies knowledge of product prices, and these are not determined until households have received income from the sales of factor services at certain prices. Obviously [*sic*] product and factor prices are determined simultaneously [*sic*]. Many contemporaries of Walras found this proposition difficult to comprehend. They never quite overcame the suspicion that the argument constituted a vicious circle. They understood the validity of partial equilibrium analysis, based on the assumption that certain variables in the analysis are treated as parameters, but they could not grasp the idea that the existence of n partial equilibria each involving n variables did not in any way guarantee general equilibrium for the whole economy made up of n markets.

It is not obvious that all prices are in fact determined simultaneously, but what was needed was an account of how they possibly could be; for without such a possibility, economic theory would apparently be mired in an infinite regress. So Walras took the first steps towards showing how it was possible for all these processes to operate simultaneously, and interact with one another. What he did was solve a 'how possible' problem. The question remains by what right this solution to a 'how possible' problem became the touchstone of theory in the discipline of economics, why it should have become an adequacy criterion on 'why actual' explanations of what is really happening in a market, industry or whole economy.

Blaug's (1980a: 192) answer to this question is that there was no reason for it to become such a criterion at all:

> What may be doubted is the notion that [general equilibrium theory] provides a fruitful starting point from which to approach a substantive explanation of the workings of an economic system. Its leading characteristic has been the endless formalization of purely logical problems without the slightest regard for the production of falsifiable theorems about actual economic behavior, which, we insist, remains the fundamental task of economics. The widespread belief that every economic theory must be fitted into the G[eneral] E[quilibrium] mold if it is to qualify as rigorous science has perhaps been more responsible than any other intellectual force for the purely abstract and nonempirical character of so much of modern economic reasoning.

But if this diagnosis is right, then the mystery of why general equilibrium analysis has assumed this role is even greater.

Let's put aside the simplest and most tendentious answer: that not only does general equilibrium theory show how something is possible, it also explains the actuality of that possibility. It would be nice if we had much good evidence that a general equilibrium obtains. This answer is the most obvious, and if it were accepted would put to rest the question of why pursue general equilibrium analysis. If the hypothesis that there is a unique stable market-clearing general equilibrium were obviously well-confirmed, then it would be found attractive for the best of all reasons: it would be our best guess as to what the truth is about our economy. Alas, the jury is still out on this issue, to say the least.

In fact, the most vocal defenders of the role and significance of general equilibrium thinking in economics are among the first to admit that the importance of general equilibrium is not a matter of the factual adequacy of the theory. Their justification for pursuing general equilibrium strategies in economics involves a sort of persuasive definition of economics: economics just is what we can extract from the equilibrium approach. Thus in *Equilibrium and Macroeconomics*, Hahn (1984) repeatedly says that the equilibrium notion 'serves to make precise the limits of economic analysis', that when we have translated some action into 'equilibrium behavior' we have gone as far as economists can, in the present state of knowledge, go. If equilibrium thinking defines economic theorizing, general equilibrium is afforded *ipso facto* a central role as the limiting case of this approach, and perhaps even more, as the necessary condition for partial equilibrium analysis (cf. pp. 124–5).

This sort of definitional claim is not much more than a bald version of the Lakatosian claim that general equilibrium is the hard core of a research programme. The mere fact that equilibrium thinking defines economics is no reason to suppose it is a fruitful approach to any real problem. If there were anything to this argument a similar one could be erected to justify an obsession with demons on the ground that without it demonology is impossible. If without equilibrium 'economics' is impossible, it doesn't follow that the problems that what we call 'economics' must deal with will disappear. And so long as they remain there is a discipline that concerns itself with them, whether we recognize it as economics or under another name.

Another approach invokes the success of other equilibrium theories and urges economics to emulate the disciplines in which such theories have succeeded, on the grounds that what has worked so well in physics or biology should be given a good run for its money in economics. Well, there is something to this argument, especially when we tease it away from the versions associated with mere physics-envy.

The fact that a successful physical theory is cast in a certain form is no good reason in and of itself to cast an economic theory in that form. After all, there's no reason to suppose that economic phenomena are like physical phenomena, and it is the data of each domain which ultimately should arbitrate the nature of theory in each. To let styles of theorizing in physics dictate economic styles is to let the motion of pendula, cannon balls and comets dictate our best guesses about the choices of consumers, the motion of markets and the shape of economic theory.

On the other hand, there are reasons why physicists and biologists have found equilibrium strategies attractive, independently of the fact that they have worked predictively. And in the case of biology at least the attraction must have been largely independent of the predictive success of the theory, since by itself evolutionary theory has little predictive success. These independent reasons for the attractiveness of equilibrium explanations are so general they might almost seem metaphysical.

How can we explain change? One answer to this question which has attracted attention literally since Plato's time is that change is explained when it is revealed to be merely apparent, when we can show that underneath the changes there is some unchanging fact which accounts for it. An enlightenment version of this idea is that the persistence of arrangements over time without change is in and by itself intelligible, and not in need of explanation. Accordingly, such persistence can serve to explain change, if we can show that apparent change is really the result of the persistence. As J. L. Mackie (1974: 222) writes, in his qualified defence of this view:

A match is struck on a matchbox and a flame appears: on the face of it this effect has nothing in common with its cause. But if we were to replace the macroscopic picture with a detailed description of the molecular and atomic movements with which the perceived processes are identified by an adequate physico-chemical theory, we should find far more continuity and persistence. . . . What is called a causal mechanism is a process which underlies a regular sequence and each phase of which exhibits qualitative as well as spatio-temporal persistence.

I do not mean to endorse this view, only to note that it is a widespread though rarely expressed presumption that still operates in our search for explanations. General equilibrium approaches, whether in physical science, biological science or social science, have the virtue of satisfying this presumption most fully. For in a state of general equilibrium there is no change to be explained, there is just persistence. And if systems remain in equilibrium or tend towards it, then the amount of change that requires explanation is minimized.

All this makes equilibrium explanations particularly attractive independent of their success in other disciplines, and independent of the prospects of harnessing them to well-worn mathematical techniques drawn from differential calculus. They provide a natural stopping point for inquiry, and so an obvious target in theory construction. This, I think, is the strongest purely intellectual source of their attraction in the sciences, both natural and social.

But these considerations only explain why eccccooonomists might in fact emulate other scientists in initially seeking equilibrium explanations of the ceaseless change that appears to characterize economic phenomena. At most it justifies the attempt to find an equilibrium explanation for the apparent chaos of economic exchange. But it will not justify general-equilibrium theorizing as a long-term research programme. Only empirically substantiating the equilibrium explanations it suggests, and improvements in their predictive power, will do this; and that is just what is missing from general equilibrium theory. So, a purely methodological argument for general equilibrium theory from the nature of equilibrium explanations is insufficient.

There are two recent arguments for the cognitive importance of general equilibrium theory in economics which don't lean on any controversial prior claims about its evidential basis or methodological provenance. They seem to be about the best around, and they have the special advantage of being offered by economists whose credentials as general equilibrium theorists are unimpeachable. First, there is Frank Hahn's claim that Arrow–Debreu equilibrium has a negative role that by itself is, in Hahn's words 'almost' a 'sufficient justification' for it: Arrow and Debreu showed that for a general market clearing equilibrium, it is necessary to have futures markets in every commodity, where commodities are distinguished from one another by date and place of availability, as well as by the usual differences. But no such futures market obtains, except for a few stock options and bulk commodities. And even in these instances, the markets hardly have the fineness of grain Arrow and Debreu require. After all, you can only trade in pork-bellies deliverable at one place and just four times year, and you can't buy or sell less than 20,000 lb. Now, according to Hahn this is important, because pointing it out will forestall jejune claims that market prices will effectively ration non-renewable resources. He writes (1984: 52):

The argument here will turn on the absence of futures markets and contingent futures markets and on the inadequate treatment of time and uncertainty by the [Arrow–Debreu] construction. This negative role of the Arrow Debreu equilibrium I consider almost to be sufficient justification for it, since practical men and ill-trained economists everywhere in the world do not understand what they are claiming to be the case, when they claim a beneficent and coherent role for the invisible hand.[1]

   This is really not much of an argument for the role general equilibrium analysis plays in modern economic theory. After all, even without it we can explain what is wrong with the claim that price will allocate scarce goods with perfect efficiency. The absence of a complete set of continent futures markets is in fact well down on the list of reasons why market prices are not market-clearing.

   This purely negative role for general equilibrium theory no more justifies its relevance to an issue like the future availability of a resource like oil than the claim that the special theory of relativity is relevant to aerodynamics because it sets a limit on the maximum velocity of airplanes. If this were all that the special theory of relativity did it would not be enough to sustain its centrality to physics. *Mutatis mutandis* for general equilibrium theory.

   Hahn's justification is, if anything, an irony, since, as Alan Nelson (1986a: 149) has noted, the allocation claim refuted by careful general equilibrium analysis is almost always one advanced on the basis of the assumption that general equilibrium theory is at least approximately right as a claim about the workings of the economy. It's hardly a justification of the theory, when we use it to show the theory's boundary conditions are *not* realized by any real economy.

   Another unconvincing reason for the importance of general equilibrium is offered by Weintraub (1985).[2] Roughly, the argument is that partial equilibrium analysis is impossible except against the background of an assurance of general equilibrium. Comparative statics involves inferring from a change in one variable, like demand, to another variable, like price, or in the case of complements or substitutes, from the price of one to the price of another. But we can make no such inference without the assurance that the first change leaves other variables unaffected, or affects them in ways that cancel out in compensating ways, and without the assurance that the second change will not affect other prices in an avalanche of cascading ways that ultimately undermine the entire price system, so that comparative statics is impossible.

   This argument is a double-edged sword, however. If it is right, it will also support the claim that if we know that the conditions for a market-clearing general equilibrium do not obtain, then perhaps even so innocent an enterprise as comparative statics is compromised. But if this argument is a double-edged sword, it is one with blunt edges. For the fact is we have a great deal of empirical, anecdotal, factual, relatively non-theoretical evidence that the price system is stable enough so that changes in the price of one commodity will not send ever-increasing effects throughout the economy leading to some catastrophic explosion of prices. Even given money illusions and hyperinflations, relative prices remain relatively constant, despite the uncertainties produced. It would of course be nice to have a theoretical assurance that partial equilibrium analysis is possible. But in its absence there is still considerable reason for confidence in its employment.

   Indeed, the shoe may be on the other foot. That is, according to some accounts, it is partial equilibrium analysis that is the more basic or fundamental component of economic theorizing, and general equilibrium theory that which is the derivative application. Daniel Hausman (1981) has long argued that what he calls 'equilibrium theory' is the fundamental theory in microeconomics: it is composed of the recognizably basic assumptions about consumers and producers that every economics text recounts, plus assumptions about decreasing returns to scale, the convexity of production functions and the assumption that entrepreneurs maximize profits. According to Hausman the application of these assumptions to undertake comparative static analysis requires only that markets be relatively independent of one another – a fairly reasonable assumption. Such analysis constitutes a 'partial equilibrium model'.

Now, if we add some *further* assumptions, restrictions or complications to the basic ones of 'equilibrium theory', the result must be a derivative theory, not a more fundamental one, or so Hausman claims. And indeed, partial and general equilibrium theories are both derivative in this sense; the latter involves applying the basic components of microeconomics under two such further assumptions: that there are many commodities and that there is a general interdependence among all markets.

If Hausman is right, then not only is general equilibrium theory not required to underwrite partial equilibrium analysis, but they are both further specifications on another distinct and more fundamental theory, 'equilibrium theory', which we need to start with if we are to have a hope of proving general equilibrium.

I am inclined to think that this counter-argument is inconclusive, however. It is by no means clear that 'equilibrium theory' *sans phrase* makes no assumptions about the independence or interdependence of prices. The last of nine 'lawlike statements' which Hausman (1981: 109) takes to constitute 'equilibrium theory' is: '(9) Through exchange the economic choices of individuals become compatible.' This assumption of 'equilibrium theory' will only be true if prices are so related as to provide for stability, and this in turn will obtain only if they are independent of one another – as partial equilibrium assumes – or market-clearing, as general equilibrium assumes. If one argues that independence of prices is more basic a case than the partial or complete interdependence of them, then partial equilibrium turns out to be more basic than general equilibrium, *pace* Weintraub. But if independence of all markets from one another is a special case from a general range of possibilities, such that we can prove existence, stability and uniqueness of equilibria for the most extreme case of complete interdependence and for all less extreme cases of partial interdependence down to the null-case, then complete interdependence will be no less basic an assumption than complete independence. Indeed, proofs for the former case will be more general and in effect include the latter case as a degenerate case. So it is not clear either that there is some third, more basic, sense of equilibrium besides partial and general, nor is it clear which of them is really a further restriction on the other. General equilibrium may after all be a special case of partial equilibrium, or partial equilibrium a restriction on the general case. But this hardly vindicates Weintraub's argument. For, Hausman rightly argues, no matter whether derivative or fundamental, general equilibrium proofs have no explanatory role, because there is no equilibrium to explain. This is a point to which I return below.

In other disciplines partial equilibrium analyses are conducted not only in the absence of any assurance of general equilibrium, but in the open recognition that no such equilibrium obtains. For example, in evolutionary theory we can trace the effects on the gene-pool of the immigration of new genotypes by comparing gene-frequencies before and after immigration. But we can be sure that for every immigration into a gene-pool there is an equal emigration from another gene-pool, with a concomitant change in its gene-frequencies. It is always theoretically possible that this latter change can have further ramifications on the equilibrium level of the former population, preventing it from reaching any stable equilibrium. But this theoretical possibility provides no real basis for anxiety about local genetic equilibrium. Similarly, in Newtonian mechanics the effects of a disturbance on a system are calculated on the assumption that it is 'closed'. For example, position and momentum calculations for the solar system are made on the assumption that the distant stars are fixed in their positions and unaffected by these disturbances. Yet we know that since gravitational forces are transmitted instantaneously and infinitely, this assumption is false. Nevertheless, observation is sufficient to assure us that no untoward consequences follow from the assumption that the disturbance's effects are not propagated outward in such a way as to result in chaos.

Most discussions of general equilibrium theory begin with the assumption that, like any theory which proceeds as an existence proof, the objective of general equilibrium theory is to explain why there is a unique stable market-clearing equilibrium and do so by proving its existence. Since it is, to say the least, doubtful that such an equilibrium exists, perplexity about the cognitive status and systematic role of general equilibrium theory emerges. Thus, solutions to the problem of explaining why general equilibrium theory is central to economics presuppose two things: that, like any scientific theory, general equilibrium theory has an explanatory function, and that its explanandum phenomenon is the equilibrium whose existence it establishes.

Both of these assumptions can be questioned. In 'The Explanatory Role of Existence Proofs' (Rosenberg 1986), I challenged the second one and suggested that the cognitive status of general equilibrium theory might become clearer if we realized that its explanandum was not equilibrium, but something else: *stability* of the price system.[3] Part of the reason to seek an alternative explanandum for general equilibrium theory is, of course, the fact that the existence of a general equilibrium is completely unsuitable as the explanandum phenomenon of general equilibrium theory. First of all, it is pretty obvious to everyone except a few rational-expectation theorists that there is no general equilibrium to explain, still less a market-clearing one. Secondly, there is more to general equilibrium theory than just the existence of a market-clearing price vector, there is also the proof that the equilibrium this price vector generates is unique. And there is the proof that it is a stable price vector: changes in the price of one good will generate compensating changes in the rest of the market relations that bring the economy back to the equilibrium level of prices. Finally, there are also its welfare economic consequences, of which more later. All in all, general equilibrium theory is more than an explanation for something that doesn't occur.

Now, the existence and uniqueness of equilibrium are highly theoretical matters about which there is much debate – so much that the claim they constitute the explanandum phenomenon of general equilibrium theory must be suspect. We normally demand explanations for events or states we know actually to take place. Hypothesized facts, like the existence and uniqueness of general equilibrium, are usually to be found in the explanans, not the explanandum, of an explanation. For instance, in evolutionary biology the existence and stability of an equilibrium figures as part of the explanation for observed adaptations and their evolutionary stability. Here equilibrium is not a fact to be explained. It is a claim which does the explaining.

But the same cannot be said of the stability of prices. Here we have an explanandum phenomenon that all parties agree obtains and that needs explanation. The fact is that though prices are interconnected, the price system is not unstable: when one price changes the result is not a catastrophic collapse of the whole set of interrelationships; changes do not accelerate and feed back on themselves in such a way as to destroy the basis for exchange; changes in one market do not send shock waves through all other markets, though they do produce readjustments in them. As noted above, even in hyperinflations, the relative prices among commodities remain remarkably stable. Here is something that definitely needs explaining. This fact, which undermines Weintraub's argument for indispensability because it is not one we need further assurance of, nevertheless demands explanation. So, perhaps we can treat the existence of price stability as the explanandum phenomenon of general equilibrium theory, and view the proofs of existence and uniqueness as parts of an explanation of this fact of stability.

The overarching importance of price stability for general equilibrium theory is illustrated by passages like the following from Quirk and Saposnik (1968: 198–9):

> Stability of equilibrium positions occupies a special place in the study of comparative statics. This is because comparative static theorems, which are statements about changes in the equilibrium values of economic variables when equilibrium is disturbed, have no predictive content, if equilibrium is dynamically unstable.

But if existence and uniqueness of a general equilibrium are not what are to be explained, what are their roles in an explanation? How can a theory which turns on their existence explain what does obtain, when they do not obtain?

One possible answer turns on the notion that a theory is explanatory if it describes a process leading to the fact to be explained which *would* produce what actually obtains – price stability – were it not *pre-empted* by other processes that do produce stability.[4]

But can we make much of a case for viewing general equilibrium theory as part of a pre-empted process that begins with arbitrary endowments and ends with price stability via equilibration over time? This may seem doubtful. After all, it is a persistent criticism of general equilibrium theory that it provides no coherent theory of the process by which equilibrium originates (cf. Blaug 1978: 610–12). The Walrasian explanation of equilibrium in terms of *tâtonnement* cannot be viewed as a series of temporally sequential trades from initial positions through a succession of exchanges to a final equilibriating one. Non-equilibrium trading could just as well keep altering the equilibrium solution instead of converging toward it. In Walrasian *tâtonnement* there is no process of approximation to equilibrium; nothing happens until the price vector that clears all markets is found. Only then does exchange take place. There is nothing in this that could be a pre-empted but possible history through which price stability originated. The situation envisioned by *tâtonnement* is one of bargaining behind a veil of ignorance until the participants choose the price vector the economist hopes for.[5]

But even if we assume, along with the exponents of general equilibrium theory that there is at least in principle some way to realize the price vector that current theory can only identify in a *tâtonnement* process, some sort of Edgworthian groping process that finds its way towards equilibrium and keeps us in its vicinity, the most we are going to have is a pre-empted explanation. Why? Because this groping operates to attain stability through the vehicle of achieving a unique equilibrium. And there is no such thing. That's why we say the general equilibrium theory mechanism is pre-empted.

But how much use can a pre-empted explanation be? This is a debatable question. Still, the exponents of the centrality of general equilibrium theory are going to have to give a very strong and implausible answer to this question. They will have to say that though pre-empted and bereft of a real mechanism to secure stability, this theory is the most central part of neoclassical economics. And to make this claim they will have to show how in general a pre-empted explanation can be explanatory at all. A pre-empted explanation may be a useful predictive device and as such be an important scientific accomplishment, like Ptolemaic astronomy. But general equilibrium theory certainly can make no such claim. On the other hand, pre-empted theories are generally viewed as non-explanatory just because the processes they envision have been pre-empted by other ones. After all, it is easy to dream up alternative scenarios about how we get from one state of affairs to another. But no such scenarios have explanatory power unless they bear a more robust relation to the actual scenario than the relation of being pre-empted by it.

What this suggests is that even changing the explanandum phenomenon of general equilibrium theory so that it's aimed at explaining something that really obtains – stability – instead of something that doesn't – equilibrium – doesn't seem able to circumvent the problems facing the theory.

So if the pre-empted mechanisms of general equilibrium theory are going to be of any interest to us, we need to find another function for them to serve. That is, we need to challenge the assumption that they have an explanatory purpose to begin with.

Our discussion of general equilibrium theory and its content has so far been silent on the welfare economic dimensions of the subject. Yet we know that the two theorems of welfare economics that can be extracted from general equilibrium theory are a major intellectual achievement and a powerful reflection of its charms for economists. On the other hand, it behoves the economist to remain silent on the role of these theorems in the context of any inquiry into the explanatory role of general equilibrium theory. For at most, they show that if one endorses a certain distribution of commodities, one can secure it through a certain market mechanism, and if one establishes a market mechanism among rational consumers one can be sure that the result will be desirable according to at least one very weak normative principle of desirability. The former claim is a hypothetical imperative, and therefore without explanatory content. The latter a conditional claim about the attainment of a morally approved goal *ceteris paribus*, and its relevance to the real world is suspect for the same reason as the theory as a whole. Neither will make much of a contribution to justifying general equilibrium theory as an explanatory enterprise. Nor will other normative considerations.

But now we seek a non-explanatory rationale for the centrality of general equilibrium theory in economic theory. Let us consider whether the rationale might in the end be normative. At any rate, in what follows I shall sketch what such a rationale might look like. It is worth noting that the rationale trades on the intellectual attractions that general equilibrium theory has held for economists, even economists initially unsympathetic to the welfare-economic hypothetical imperative derivable from the theory. And the rationale helps itself to the most compelling of all strategies for the establishment of political philosophies: the social contract.

What is so seductive about general equilibrium theory is that it is a formal proof of an apparently surprising possibility. As Arrow and Hahn (1971) have noted, 'The immediate "common sense" answer to the question "What will an economy motivated by individual greed and controlled by a very large number of different agents look like?" is probably: there will be chaos.' This is right, and it is probably the chief source of the attractions of a centrally planned economy, one in which the planners can reconcile everyone's conflicting wants and decide on a schedule of production that meets these wants optimally, given the constraints of available resources. Let us hazard a guess that most intelligent persons thinking abstractly about the need for co-ordination, efficiency and equity in a society will be attracted to some form of collectivism.[6]

Arrow and Hahn (1971: vi), however, note in a tone of understatement and technicality that the contrary is the case:

> a decentralized economy motivated by self-interest and guided by price signals would be compatible with a coherent disposition of economic resources that could be regarded, in a

well-defined sense, as superior to a large class of possible alternative dispositions. . . . It is important to understand how surprising this claim must be to anyone not exposed to this tradition.

Now, imagine a large number of rational agents who have already come to an agreement about the advantages that each will accrue from the existence of a state with political authority to coerce each of them as necessary to enforce rules on which they have also agreed. I grant that we do not as yet have a good 'reconstruction' of exactly what argument will convince all our agents to concur in these rules, or exactly what rules they will concur in. That is to say, contractarian political philosophy has not yet entirely solved its own problems. So let's assume it has solved them.

Now, having agreed on political rules, these individuals fall to arguing about what commercial institutions they will establish. What arrangement will recommend itself? Given the assumption contractarian political philosophy makes, that they are rational and not altruistic in their preferences, and given some undeniable facts about information, incentives and scarcity, it is not difficult to establish the preferability for society as a whole of decentralized market mechanisms over centralized planning ones.

Except in the case of public goods, what seems most remarkable about a market economy is that by accepting the inevitability of surpluses and shortfalls, it does better at mitigating them than a planned economy which denies their inevitability. That is, it not only avoids shortages and surpluses more frequently, but when it does result in them, they are smaller. This will be especially true in the case of innovations. These it brings to market quickly. If we can prove that by arranging a scheme that will mitigate gluts and shortages to the maximum extent, we do better than we should if we simply aimed directly at eliminating them through the central collection of information and rational planning in the use of it, we shall have provided a powerful incentive for rational agents to adopt such a scheme. If we can show that there is too much information from consumers and producers for a planner to process, and too much information that consumers and producers have an incentive to hide, so that gluts and shortages will be inevitable and that a market mechanism takes advantage of both these facts about information, then we shall have little difficulty convincing the parties to a social contract that the market is the way to go. These are the kinds of considerations that seduce intelligent young minds from socialism to capitalism. Because they work, because they actually move people, we should accord them considerable respect in any account of why general equilibrium should have any claims on our attention.

For general equilibrium theory is the formalized approach to the systematic study of this claim about how the unintended consequences of unco-ordinated selfishness results in the most efficient exploitation of scarce resources in the satisfaction of wants. It is, of course, an inquiry with many limitations, ones which so far have prevented it from securing the agreement of all students of the matter. But at least now we can understand why economists continue to lavish attention on general equilibrium theory. It's not because they think it can be improved in the direction of a descriptively and predictively accurate explanation of economic activity, but because they believe it is already part of the best contractarian argument for the adoption of the market as a social institution, and more important, stands a chance of becoming an even better one, as its assumptions are weakened, changed and varied.

This suggests that general equilibrium theory is one important component in the research programme of contractarian political philosophy. It helps explain two other features of neoclassical theory: its remarkably *a priori* character and the temptation felt by philosophers, among others, to view it as a body of prescription about rational conduct.

Among others, I have long sought an explanation of the centrality of general equilibrium theory for economics in the notion that economic theory is a branch of applied mathematics, the study of the mathematical properties of transitivity among the elements of a set (Rosenberg 1983). The reasons I sought such an explanation reflect the conviction that the psychological theory which serves as the natural interpretation of neoclassical assumptions about agents is a scientific dead-end. In spite of this fact, economists are not about to give up microeconomics. The simplest explanation of this attitude is to suppose that, like other applied mathematicians, economists were relatively unconcerned by the factual application of their most central theoretical accomplishment.

But the facts that might lead one to view economic theory as a branch of applied mathematics are also accommodated by the conclusion that economic theory is an exercise in the formal development of a solution to the problem of what economic institutions will be agreed upon by agents who must enter into a contract to establish them. Any solution to the contractarian problem must be relatively *a priori* because it can assume little about the actual details which the parties to the contract will face after agreement is reached and lives must be carried on. Probably it can assume no more than what is assumed in neoclassical theory. And the theory will also have to disregard the dim prospects for a scientific psychology that trades on expectations and preferences, for no matter how doubtful the scientific status of these intentional concepts, individual agents calculating their own interests will certainly have to make use of them. So, the contractarian approach absorbs those very features which might suggest that neoclassical theory is best assimilated to applied mathematics.

Of course, the two interpretations of economic theory, as a component of applied mathematics and part of the research programme of contractarian political philosophy are perfectly complementary. They may jointly overdetermine the centrality of general equilibrium theory to the enterprise of economics.

But contractarianism has one advantage over applied mathematics as a justification for the fascination general equilibrium theory has exercised for economists. Whereas the appeal of a problem in applied mathematics is relatively limited, the problem of choosing the optimal institution for our economic lives is a problem that should be of interest to everyone except Robinson Crusoe. Accordingly, a theory which stands the chance of providing the firmest theoretical foundations for the claim that one particular choice is the best one *should* certainly be the focus of attention that general equilibrium theory in fact has become. For now, at any rate, I am convinced that this is the best answer we can give to the question: Why should general equilibrium theory be the hard core of the research programme that constitutes neoclassical economics.

In effect, this approach to general equilibrium theory assimilates neoclassical economics to what James Buchanan (1985) identifies as one of its subdivisions: 'constitutional economics'. Buchanan distinguishes 'orthodox economic analysis' and 'constitutional economic analysis':

> Orthodox economic analysis, whether this be interpreted in Marshallian or Walrasian terms, attempts to explain the choices of economic agents, their interactions with one another, and the results of these interactions.

So far, we must disagree with Buchanan, for interpreted as an explanatory project, orthodox economic analysis or its core at any rate just isn't explanatory. But Buchanan (1985: 64) goes on:

> By contrast . . . constitutional economic analysis attempts to explain the working properties of alternative sets of legal-institutional-political rules that constrain the choices and activities of economic agents, the rules that define the framework within which the ordinary choices of economic and political agents are made.
>   . . . the whole exercise is aimed at offering guidance to those who participate in discussions of constitutional change. . . . constitutional economics offers a potential for normative advice to members of the constitutional convention. . . . it examines the *choice of constraints* as opposed to the *choice within constraints*.

But to decide on choice of constraints, we need information about the effects of choice within those constraints. To the extent that orthodox economics provides information about those choices within constraints, it will be a compartment of what Buchanan calls orthodox economic analysis. But suppose that the *only* information it reliably provides is information relevant to the choice among constraints, that is, to what rules rational agents would contract, were they required to do so, then there would be no other role for what Buchanan calls orthodox economic analysis.

Now, the doubts about the explanatory relevance of general equilibrium theory suggest that it cannot explain choice within constraints. That's, so to speak, how the problem of justifying general equilibrium theory starts. But these doubts are irrelevant to its role in a search for optimal constraints. For in this search there is every reason to assume that agents ruthlessly maximize their utilities everywhere and always, that they dissimulate when it is to their advantage, free-ride where they can. For this is just the sort of behaviour against which a polity must protect itself. Therefore, as Hume (1985: 42) writes (and Buchanan is fond of quoting):

> Political writers have established it as a maxim that, in contriving any system of government, and fixing several checks and controls of the constitution, every man ought to be supposed a *knave*, and to have no other end, in all his actions, than private interest.

There is a prudential requirement that for purposes of institution design we treat all agents as utility maximizers, and assure ourselves that each of us is willing to live with the consequences of doing so. This requirement is honoured in an especially clear and powerful way by general equilibrium theory, as its game-theoretical development reveals.

As Weintraub's (1985: ch. 6) history makes clear, it was early recognized that the existence of a general equilibrium was also the solution to an n-person generalization of the von Neumann–Morgenstern solution for a two-person zero-sum competitive game. Arrow and Debreu's version of this realization is particularly instructive for the assimilation of general equilibrium to a contractarian agenda. We are given two kinds of agents, price-taking budget-constrained utility maximizers and an omniscient auctioneer, whose only aim is to minimize excess demand among the other agents. The second agent announces price-vectors, for which the other players each announce their best response. The auctioneer chooses one which clears the markets most fully. His position is little different from Hobbes's sovereign. The auctioneer and his institution are thus shown to be the most advantageous arrangement parties to a contract about the rules for economic activity can adopt in the abstract.

For the equilibrium whose existence it establishes can be shown to be a Nash equilibrium – one in which each such egotistical agent has an optimal strategy, regardless of the strategies of other agents. The market in which an equilibrium-producing price-vector exists thus has an especially desirable property from the point of view of contractarian political philosophy: no one can do better by adopting another strategy and the strategies result in an informationally efficient market-clearing Pareto-optimal unique stable equilibrium.

It remains possible on this view to cavil at the abstractness of general equilibrium theory, at the demanding assumptions required to prove that there is a market-clearing price-vector. But the evident desirability of such a price-vector makes it worth attempting to identify the institutional constraints under which the equilibrium such a vector produces is attainable, no matter how unbridled the egoism of Hume's knave.

Of course, the trouble with this account of the nature and centrality of general equilibrium theory is that it still leaves an important aim of an economic science undone. For by assigning general equilibrium theory to contractarian political philosophy, we find ourselves lacking a good general theory that explains actual economic phenomena. But then, this is something that general equilibrium theories never really offered us under any interpretation anyway. But if economic theory in general has little explanatory and predictive power, whence comes its right to claim the prudential role assigned to it by a contractarian political philosophy? The answer is roughly that for purposes of institutional choice generic prediction of existence is enough (Rosenberg 1987)[7]. Since our aim is to protect ourselves against worse-case scenarios, and these are ones that a pure theory that proves the existence of possibilities can identify, we may find an important use for this theory despite its infirmities.

NOTES

*   My thanks to Daniel Hausman and Phillipe Mongin for reading and commenting on an earlier draft of this paper. My intellectual debts to Mark Blaug are evident. His work has helped me not to miss the forest for the trees, but also to recognize the trees as well.

1. It is hard to know exactly how much force to attach to this argument. For on the one hand, it is not clear what it means for a justification to be almost sufficient. On the other hand, Hahn goes on to write: 'But for descriptive purposes this negative rule is hardly a recommendation.' Which side is Hahn on?

2. Perhaps Weintraub does not fully endorse the argument to follow, for he puts it into the mouth of one of the interlocutors in a dialogue. The fact that the interlocutor who offers this argument is the economist and the others are his students emboldens me to attribute it to him.

3. This is a notion that Weintraub explores in *Stabilizing Dynamics: Constructing Economic Knowledge* (forthcoming).

4. The idea derives from Robert Nozick (1975) and is explored in Nelson (1986b).

5. There are, of course, theorems in general equilibrium theory to the effect that under certain circumstances non-*tâtonnement* processes involving a sequence of non-equilibrium exchanges beginning with arbitrary endowments can converge on an equilibrium. See, for instance, Hahn and Negish (1962). But these theorems do not guarantee stability, only an equilibrium and only under restrictive conditions.

6. One reason to think this is right is the large number of autobiographical admissions of neoclassical economists that they were attracted to economics by the socialist vision. But as Stigler is infamous for noting, nothing makes an intelligent person an opponent of central planning faster than a good dose of microeconomics.

7. They are not enough for other purposes, but they may be sufficient for political philosophy.

11. On Interpretative and Feminist Economics

Arjo Klamer

During the last few decades feminism has been a fact of western life. There is no way around women's questions, not at home, not in business life and not in academia. The impact is also visible in the world of economists. The mainstream of economists has attempted to increase the status of women in the profession, and at the margin there are calls for a feminist economics. Even methodological discourse in economics cannot escape the feminist questioning.

Feminism in life has been a somewhat bewildering experience. At least, it has been for me. A white male, I have been exposed as a member of a privileged group or, to rub it in properly, of the dominant and exploiting class. Feminist criticisms have forced me to confront my roles in academic and personal life. I am not sure where that has left me – politically, intellectually and personally. Regarding the politics of gender I have to agree with Sandra Harding (1986: 658) when she writes:

> [O]bjectively, no individual men can succeed in renouncing sexist privilege any more than individual whites can succeed in renouncing racist privilege – the benefits of gender and race accrue regardless of the wishes of the individuals who bear them. Gender, like race and class, is not a voluntarily disposable individual characteristic.

Intellectually, I cannot pretend to know what a feminist economics should be or what precisely the consequences of feminist criticisms will be. Yet I discern in feminist criticisms certain themes and arguments that closely resemble themes and arguments that have emerged in recent conversations about the nature and purposes of economic discourse. I furthermore anticipate that feminist inquiry may produce another impulse for the interpretative approach to economics that I, along with others, am advocating.[1]

This essay explores commonalities between feminist and interpretative economics. I do not have the illusion that I can sway my feminist colleagues and friends – they are in no need for another male voice to tell them what to think. The intended audience are colleagues who are, as I am, engaged in the conversation about the nature and purposes of economic discourse. With them I should like to concur on the merits of feminist criticisms and the desirability of an interpretative approach to economics.

TWO OR THREE SEPARATE ISSUES

Janet Seiz, in 'Gender and Economic Language and Research' (forthcoming), has put some order into what seems a widely spread confusion on feminisms and their conceivable consequences for the ways in which economists operate, think and argue. The separation of the political issue – the position of women in science – from the ontological issue – the representation of women in economic discourses clarifies the situation.

The *political issue* concerns the under-representation of women in the ranks of academic economists. Carolyn Shaw Bell, Barbara Bergman, Heidi Hartmann, Nancy Folbre, Robin Bartlett and Teresa Amott come to mind as the women who, along with many others, have fought the fight for equal treatment of women in the profession. This fight is not just about the recruitment of more women as graduate students and assistant professors, as Seiz emphatically states in her article. I can see that. The rituals of academic life appear to affirm and exploit gender differences. Women end up, willingly or unwilling, doing a disproportionately greater amount of committee work and attending to the needs of their students than their male counterparts. Probably as a consequence the tenure and publication game seems to advantage men. Listening to women who feel excluded in 'aggressive and confrontative' seminars and who face uphill tenure battles, one would say that the academic world is androcentric, revolving around masculine games.

The focus on academic politics suggests that feminist concerns are met with changes in academic practices. But we are not let off the hook so easily. The feminist critique of the status quo extends further, into ontological issues. This critique compromises the truth about economic phenomena as it is represented by neoclassical theorizing. Feminist economists point at a 'male' bias in the questions that (male) economists ask and the modelling they do to answer their questions.

The theorizing of the household has been a prime target of feminist scholarship. An extensive literature exposes the repression of intra-household activities in dominant neoclassical theorizing, a repression that is attributed to the conceptualization of the household as an unproblematic entity.[2] Since the household has been in recent times the major life-world for many women, more so than for men, its problematization is an obvious move in feminist inquiry. The purpose has been to pierce the myth of the household as a seamless whole with its individual members living in peaceful coexistence, with interdependent utility functions or well-defined production functions, and to present in its stead a vision of families or households – the definition of these entities is already problematic, given the rich variety of arrangements – as sites of relations of oppression and domination, of gender hierarchies and of gender conflicts. The result is certainly a different world from the one that neoclassical discourse produces.

The test of this feminist research programme should be, according to the conventional methodological norm, its empirical and theoretical progressiveness. One strategy in feminist research has been to respond to this norm and to develop neoclassical types of models that incorporate the feminist vision. (In Sandra Harding's (1986a) terminology this is a successor science project.) Seiz discusses as an example game-theoretic models of intra-family behaviour. She wonders, however, whether the neoclassical heuristic as well as its language are biased towards a male perspective. Thus the discussion veers towards epistemological issues.

Donna Harroway, Sandra Harding, Evelyn Fox-Keller, Janet Seiz and Julie Nelson are among the feminist scholars who question the object–subject split that allegedly underlies the dominant scientific strategy, its reductionistic thinking that directs the gaze away from contingent and concrete phenomena to universal entities, its language that excludes outsiders, its one-sidedly mechanistic metaphors, and a general vision that rationalizes and thus shackles the world and everything that lives in it. They view in these characteristics a privileging of the 'male' gaze. On that much these scholars concur.

Disagreement emerges on the question whether reductionistic and universalizing thinking necessarily precludes a 'female' way of seeing the world.

A radical feminist line of argument strategy has been to expose the 'male' gaze for its shortsightedness and to depict positivistic and reductionistic methodology as an exploitative and repressive (male) strategy. A female way of knowing, an emphatic knowing that recognizes and allows for significant connections between the subject and her object(s), is presented as the superior alternative. The *feminist standpoint epistemology*, as Harding has called this line of argument, seems, however, to produce a position that it is intended to subvert, namely, a position of privilege and exclusion. The feminist standpoint epistemology essentializes the female way of knowing. At least this is the argument of Haraway, Seiz, Harding and others. They point out that such a radical stance runs in the face of the growing postmodernist awareness that any privileging and any claim to universal knowledge is a power move without epistemological foundation.

At this place in the argumentation the commonalities emerge with the postmodernist turn in the conversation about science and economics. Sandra Harding (1986a: 655) concludes, after establishing that 'many feminists share a rejection of the value of the forms of rationality, of dispassionate objectivity, of the Archimedian perspective' that they 'are ambivalently related to such other sceptics of modernism as Nietzsche, Wittgenstein, Derrida, Foucault, Lacan, Feyerabend, Rorty, Gadamer, and the discourses of semiotics, psychoanalysis, structuralism, and deconstructionism'. Donna Haraway (1988: 581), after having negotiated feminist epistemology away from the relativist position, decides that she would like 'a doctrine of embodied objectivity that accommodates paradoxical and critical feminist science projects: Feminist objectivity means quite simply *situated knowledges*'. Janet Seiz writes of the rhetoric of economics. All this sounds quite familiar: these scholars appear to reach conclusions that are remarkably similar to the ones that predominantly male reflexive discourses on disciplines such as economics have produced.

THE PROBLEM OF KNOWLEDGE

Reflections on neoclassical economics are invariably provoked by its aura of an objective and unreflexive science. We experience a discourse that is couched in mathematical language, and a stylized theorizing devoid from the drama that stirs emotions. The classroom presentation of this discourse suggests that agreement among economists prevails. The confusion sets in when the world of economists turns out to be divided.[3] Such a confusion is bound to make economists self-conscious of their discipline and engender ruminations about the nature and purpose of economic theory.

The reflexive ruminations have led to awareness of methodological weaknesses. Scientific standards, which can adjudicate competing claims to the truth, seem hard to come by. Disagreements persist on what constitutes good economics. Some theorists, the new classicals among them, demand rigour based on consistency with the constrained maximization set-up for economic behaviour. Others, such as the last of the Keynesians, are willing to loosen up the theory and let in less-well-specified hypotheses that vaguely allude to sociological and psychological factors. But virtually no self-respecting economist challenges the heavy emphasis on analysis as is expressed in the modelling strategy. The construction of a model is a *sine qua non* for participation in the academic conversation on economics. Interpretative methods are beyond the collective imagination of economists. Yet the weaknesses in the science of economics suggest the need for just those types of methods.

Analysis focuses on 'what if' statements. Neoclassical analysis comprises the construction of models that specify the conditions for rational decisions as fully as conceivable. The result is an algorithm that tells *what* the agent will do *if* the conditions are such and such. Ricardo used the 'what if' set-up when he thought about *what* an economy would be like *if* its only product were to be corn.

In contrast, Adam Smith wondered *how* a nation should conduct its affairs in order to increase its wealth. To answer this moral question he investigated the world as it appeared to him, produced anecdotes, critically examined ideas of others and circumscribed the 'character' of commercial society and of those inhabiting it. Smith engaged only sporadically in a 'what if' form of reasoning, and where he did, as in his attempts to explain value, he was less than rigorous and consistent. I would call Smith's approach interpretative.

The 'what if' reasoning in neoclassical economics relies heavily on a particular and somewhat peculiar metaphor of abstract agents who solve constrained maximization problems. The metaphor has proven to be very productive, allowing the incorporation of stochastic elements, the treatment of (imperfect) information and assumptions on decision strategies of other agents. But – and this is the key to the major weakness in the neoclassical analysis – the metaphor and the analytical discourse that it generates are speechless in the face of the problem of knowledge.

That the constrained-optimization metaphor necessitates abstraction from the problem of knowledge has been observed by many (male) critics of the neoclassical heuristics. Interesting are, in particular, the comments of critics who support the political dimension of the neoclassical vision. 'Fully rational action', Shackle (1966: 20) asserts, 'can only occur in a momentary or timeless system.' He argues that in historical time, economic agents do not necessarily know their constraints, the actions of others and the possible outcomes of their actions. Hayek concurs. In his well-known article 'The Use of Knowledge in Society' he writes (1945: 530): 'The problem is thus in no way solved if we can show that all the facts, if they were known to a single mind (as we hypothetically assume them to be given to the observing economist), would uniquely determine the solution; instead we must show how a solution is produced by the interactions of people each of whom possesses only partial knowledge.' The thinking about the process is crucial to him. The optimization approach, he argues, 'disregards an essential part of the phenomena with which we have to deal: the unavoidable imperfection of man's knowledge and the consequent need for a process by which knowledge is constantly communicated and acquired' (*idem*).

The problem of knowledge to which Shackle and Hayek point appears to permeate all aspects of economic life. Its presence is obvious in deliberations on the relocation of a family, a change in career plans, the decision on a career or a new investment project. But we are confronted with the problem even in mundane circumstances, such as the moment at which we have to order a meal at a Chinese restaurant – at least I am. Although I know the prices, I do not quite know my budget constraint. (How far do the $22 in my wallet have to go?) More serious is the problem of finding out what I want. The preference ordering commonly does not come neatly arranged on a platter or in a table. I am forced to weigh the alternatives – going for the usual, being adventurous this time, feeling out what others want, not asking for the sweet-and-sour to avoid the scorn of your companion and so on. I will deliberate with myself and, if the company allows it, will discuss their preferences in the hope of finding mine. These internal and external deliberations involve and represent *interpretations* of the situation at hand. There are no algorithms for such interpretations; a few rules maybe – 'when you don't know, choose that which is familiar', or 'always choose that what is different and unknown', but the choice ultimately rests on a negotiated judgement.

So far, economic discourse has produced little insight into these deliberations. One might expect that game theory takes the analysis to these types of deliberation; but that has not yet not happened. Game theory presumes the maximizing individual in the conventional neoclassical sense. Its main feature is the possibility of interaction between individual decision strategies. Individuals become players because they not only need to 'know' the market price and allocations, but also the strategies of the other participants. Game-theoretic models commonly assume given preferences and goals of the individual players. Accordingly, players in these game models will not change their preferences in the course of the game. Furthermore, players are assumed to work with well-specified information on the behaviour of other agents and on the pay-off structure. They are pictured as individuals who process the information analytically and calculate their optimal strategy. If there is ambiguity in the model, it is caused by the imperfection of information and by stochastic elements. The analytical set-up, however, does not allow for interpretation, judgement, opinion, or other non-analytical thought-processes in which 'normal' people engage.

THE SQUARE AND THE CIRCLE

Among the few economists who have done some serious thinking about the problem of knowledge are economic methodologists such as T. W. Hutchison, Mark Blaug, J. J. Klant and Bruce Caldwell. Thinking about the problem in the context of economic science, these economic methodologists basically follow the neoclassical heuristic. Accordingly, they concentrate on the conditions of rational choice among competing claims to truth. The goal of economists is supposed to be the approximation of truth (cf. maximization of utility); the constraints are the logical structure of theories (cf. the budget constraint) and their correspondence with facts (cf. prices). Analysis along these lines leads to criteria for rational-theory choice, such as the Lakatosian criteria of empirical and theoretical progressiveness.

The heuristic of analysing the *logic of choice* in both neoclassical and methodological analysis befits the Cartesian world view. Picture this view thus:[4]

the objective
logic
fact

the
subjective
will

The circle is the domain of the personal, the subjective. Following the example of neoclassicals, economic methodologists relegate feelings, morals, (religious) beliefs and preferences (taste) to this domain. These are the factors left out of their analysis. The (scientific) interest is directed at the square, the domain of the logical, of all that can be analysed in systematic (or scientific) manner. It is where analysis takes place – the deduction of propositions from well-specified assumptions and axioms – as well as the (econometric) testing of the propositions with data.

Ironically, Klant, Blaug and other economic methodologists who have tried to study what economists do in square terms, discovered that their square analysis has not produced a positive understanding of economic knowledge. Their findings have been mainly negative. The main conclusion is that the square does not cover all of economics. We now understand that logic and facts do not exhaust the constraints under which economists operate, that square standards are inadequate and not beyond dispute, and that the scholarly pursuit is about more than truth alone.

It is here that the rhetorical perspective comes in. The perception that economists are engaged in argumentation takes the analysis beyond the square and circle and shows the discursive domain that envelops both.[5] The rhetorical perspective calls not only for the detection of the metaphors, analogies, stories and other rhetorical devices that sustain conversations among economists, but also for an interpretation of the meanings that economists produce through these devices. This takes us away from the (idealized) realm where fixed and foundational standards determine the validity of arguments to the more pragmatic realm where arguments derive their persuasiveness from the context in which they get expressed. It is a move away from analysis in terms of the logic of choice towards an interpretation of the texts economists produce. Instead of being philosophers who design algorithms for rational choice, students of economics have become interpreters of the norms and values that economists generate and consolidate through their discourse.[6]

FROM ANALYSIS TO INTERPRETATION

Accordingly, thinking about the problem of knowledge in economics produces the image of economists as rhetors and draws attention to the discursive process. What if we follow the same track in thinking about the problem of knowledge in the economy?

The first implication is the shift of focus away from the logic of choice to thinking in terms of human action and activities. What do people do?: that is the opening question.

Much of what people do is a matter of routine. Going to the refrigerator, the store or the office we do what we usually do, without giving it much, if any, thought. Ignorance prevails, but we have learned to cope with it. Habitually we respond to the signals that invade our organs, habitually ignoring most of them.

When do activities cease to be habitual? Schumpeter, in his 'interpretation' of entrepreneurial behaviour, sidesteps the question, even though he stresses that entrepreneurs break routines. We do not have a good response either. One could say that action that can be described in 'square' terms is routine. That makes any action based on calculation according to well-specified strategies (such as cost-benefit calculations) routine. But very few activities are likely to meet that standard. Much of what people do is a matter of mimesis: we follow examples – do what others do – or act by analogy – do what we did in an analogous situation. All this is part of a routine, but cannot be captured in square terms only. Routines often express rules or conventions which can be conscious and tacit, individual and social.

The distinction between social and individual routine appears to be important when it comes to entrepreneurial behaviour. Steve Jobs, one of the two founders of Apple computers and the founder of NextInc corporation may habitually violate commonly held standards: the important point is that he does not do what others would do in a similar situation. He starts up a new firm when other 'knowledgeable' persons advise him against it. (In other words he acts upon a divergence in interpretation of the situation in the computer industry.)

Why people break routines is an intriguing question. The promise of abnormal profit is elusive, a reward *ex post*. Schumpeter alludes to non-rational motives, among which are the desire to acquire power, the excitement of conquering and the joy of creating. Personal motivations, however, become a less pressing issue once we recognize the discursive content as the dominant factor.

The study of actions of economists has suggested other possibilities. We discovered, namely, the promise of discourse analysis, that is, the careful reading of the texts economists produce, and of close observations. We have come to appreciate the significance of beliefs that economists hold, the meanings of concepts that they recognize or dismiss, and their perceptions of other economists and their arguments. To those who are used to square reasoning these studies may seem ambiguous and undisciplined but they provide us with a different and, I think, better understanding of what economists do. They get us to the native's point of view.

The native's point of view is the subject in ethnography. It is the view that Clifford Geertz tries to uncover in 'thick descriptions' of the life in specific communities. He elects to enter the 'life-worlds' of Indonesian and Moroccan villages and thus goes beyond the square models of economic growth and development to show a world in which rituals, myths, beliefs and economic constraints interact to produce a rich and dynamic reality. We could follow his example and enter the 'life-world' of the Chicago tradefloor, IBM's boardroom, General Motor's shopfloor, Iowa City's households or Boston's fishmarket. (To the sceptic: nobody says that such research is easy; learning Arabic is certainly not easy and living in and finding out about a foreign culture is not easy either. Some may find mathematics easy in comparison.) Doing so we move away from the analytical models and become interpretative social scientists. The goal is not just to 'explain' the natives but to 'understand' them. Pursuing this track we are bound to discover worlds that are as yet unknown in the world of economists.

Take savings behaviour as an example. The neoclassical model has told us much about the constraining role of current and future income in decisions to save. But it tells us all but nothing about attitudes towards saving and variations in such attitudes across cultures and through time. Mary Douglas and Baron Isherwood (1979) argue that in their decision to save, people communicate not only their time-preference but also certain beliefs and values. In Puritan families thriftiness was equated with prudent behaviour; in some communities it has the stigma of anti-social behaviour.[7] The neoclassical economist could retort that it is all in the preferences, but to understand savings behaviour in a *serious* way we need to go beyond the model of logical choice and the statistics and dare to look close.

In another close-up look Michael Buroway (1979) offers surprising insights into the life-world of the shopfloor. Researches generally emphasize either harmony or conflict on the shopfloor, depending on their political affiliation. Buroway places himself in the Marxist camp, but rejects Harry Braverman's deterministic theory of conflict and exploitation. Having been a machine-worker himself he presents the native's point of view. His interpretation tells about the game workers play on the shopfloor: the game of *making out*. In order to make their quotas machine-workers enter into intricate arrangements with the truck drivers who supply the materials, and develop strategies for getting the most-profitable assignments. These games get the workers deeply involved, compel them to work hard and account for their consent with the process and resistance against union efforts for change. His ethnographic description exposes the squareness of the deterministic analysis of the labour process and ventures into the area beyond the square.

These interpretative studies are not the final answer; they are also not the only vehicle for traversing the shifting grounds beyond the square. But they appear to get onto a track that promises new vistas on the economic life-world. In such studies we, social scientists, attempt to trace the webs of significance that people weave to sustain their lives. Influence on those lives is not the paramount concern. It is not as in the analytical approach that we want to explain the natives in order to find out how we can regulate and manipulate their lives. First of all we want to understand human action in their social and cultural environment.

BACK TO THE CONNECTION WITH FEMINISM

Nearly all the authors I have cited in the preceding motivation of the interpretative approach to economics are male. It goes to show that the discourse of males can reach a position that is at least sympathetic to the position that female economists have been arguing. After all, the interpretative approach as I understand it also poses the distance that the analytical approach imposes between the 'scientists' and their subjects as a problem. The decision to investigate the texts that the 'natives' produce defies the neoclassical metaphor of an autonomous individual 'which' makes calculated choices.

The interpretative turn, as proposed here, involves a focus on language, text, discourse. Some versions of feminist inquiry are taking the same turn. According to Evelyn Fox Keller (1983: 112):

> Over and over, feminists have found it necessary, in seeking to reinstate women as agents and subjects, to question the very canons of their fields. They have turned their attention, accordingly, to the operation of patriarchial bias on ever deeper levels of social structure, even of language and thought.

Phyllis Rooney (1989), a feminist philosopher, investigates the male biases in the metaphors that constrain the talk about reason; and in the context of economics both Janet Seiz and Julie Nelson target the language, or, as Seiz puts it, the rhetoric of economics.

All these feminist criticisms of the dominant discourse in science undermine the Cartesian dualisms – as the males do who question positivism in science. In the words of Sandra Harding (1986a: 25):

> Mind vs. nature and the body, reason vs. emotion and social commitment, subject vs. object and objectivity vs. subjectivity, the abstract and the general vs. the concrete and the particular – in each case we are told that the former must dominate the latter lest human life be overwhelmed by irrational and alien forces, forces symbolized in science as the feminine. All these dichotomies play important roles in the intellectual structures of science, and all appear to be associated both historically and in contemporary psyches with distinctively masculine sexual and gender identity projects.

These dualisms can be mapped into the square/circle picture of the universe. Accordingly, hard science pertains to the square, and so do rationality, rigour, reason, masculinity; and soft science, the humanities, irrationality, fuzziness, emotion and femininity are relegated to the circle. At least in the Cartesian world view they do. Harding, Haraway and others view a radical break with this world-view as a precondition for a feminist science.

Men such as McCloskey and myself agree with the feminist dismissal of the Cartesian picture as being unnecessarily constraining and discriminatory.[8] Both of us perceive in the rhetorical approach a way of changing the picture. It would recognize the non-logical and non-irrational elements in economic discourse, such as metaphors, authority and judgement. McCloskey finds in the rhetorical picture the message that we need to improve our conversation. Feminine economics contributes, according to him, to such an improvement of the economic conversation. My interpretation of the consequences takes me to the interpretative approach which would affect both the discourse about economics and the discourse about the economy. Such an approach would meet the feminist subversion of the object–subject split.

These commonalities on epistemological issues notwithstanding, we shall not necessarily produce a similar economic discourse. Men such as myself may fall short of contributing to the feminist project. After recognizing the need for interpretations of economic phenomena and the importance of the meanings that we ourselves and our subjects produce, we are still likely to produce different meanings. At any rate, this is not a time to expect a great deal of clarity. Some degree of bewilderment is inevitable in this postmodern stage, with its self-consciousness, its recognition of epistemological uncertainties, its acknowledgement and celebration of differences and pluralities, and its rediscovery of texts and discourses that call for interpretation. Some of us, both men and women, agree on at least this much. I would expect that we will sustain a productive dialogue when we are taking the interpretative turn away from the rigid, hard-nosed and discriminatory analytical approach that currently overpowers economic discourse.[9] And sustaining the conversation about economics is what our efforts are all about.

NOTES

1. See, for example, Lavoie (forthcoming), and Rabinow and Sullivan (1979). Interestingly enough, the editors of the latter volume count historians, sociologists, anthropologists, psychologists, historians of religion, scientists and philosophers among their audience, but not economists.
2. See for example Klamer (1983) and Klamer and Colander (1990).
3. For instance Hartmann (1981), Guyer and Peters (1987), Folbre (1982), and Dwyer and Bruce (1988).
4. This is worked out in Klamer (1991).
5. For example, McCloskey (1985), and Klamer, McCloskey and Solow (1988).
6. Klamer, McCloskey and Solow (1988) contains many examples of this work.
7. They refer to a study of a mineworkers' community in England where the men expect that each will spend extra money on beer for his mates.
8. This point is made forcefully in McCloskey (1988).
9. Together with Donald Lavoie, I am currently editing a series on Interpretative Economics for Basil Blackwell. It is intended to be an outlet for such a dialogue.

12. The Economics of Education and the Education of Policy-makers: Reflections on Full-cost Fees for Overseas Students

Maureen Woodhall[1]

THE INFLUENCE OF THE ECONOMICS OF EDUCATION

The economics of education emerged as a distinctive discipline in the early 1960s, although its theoretical antecedents lie in the eighteenth and nineteenth centuries, with both Adam Smith and Alfred Marshall drawing attention to the importance of education as investment in human capital. It was not until 1961, however, when Theodore Schultz (1961) gave his presidential address to the American Economic Association on 'Investment in Human Capital', Edward Denison (1962) was engaged in analysing *The Sources of Economic Growth in the US* and Gary Becker (1964) was measuring the rate of return to investment in education, training and other forms of human capital, that the policy implications of the economics of education began to be explored seriously.

Mark Blaug (1985: 17) has described the development of the subject in terms of 'phoenix-like' birth in the early 1960s, the 'golden years' of 1960–70, 'when no self-respecting Minister of Education would have dreamed of making educational decisions without an economist sitting at his right hand' to the 'deepening pessimism' of the 1980s until he delivered (1989: 331–2) the damning verdict:

> One might almost go so far as to say that the economics of education now lies dead in the minds of both professional economists and professional educators. . . . The simple fact is that the field has failed to deliver the goods.

This picture of a rapid decline in only 30 years from birth to a brief 'heyday', followed by a period of disillusion characterized by 'the antipathy of educators toward economists and the public disdain of economists in current controversies about education' (ibid.) reflects Mark Blaug's own perceived progression which he describes in *The Economics of Education and Education of an Economist* (1987a). He clearly believes that the development of the subject and his own attitude toward it marched in parallel. In the early 1960s his own interest in the economics of education was born; this was followed by a decade when he was a 'True Believer in human capital theory and rate of return analysis' (Blaug 1987: vii), with the publication of his *Introduction to the Economics of Education* (1970) representing the 'apogee of my "faith" in human capital theory' (ibid.). His 'slightly jaundiced' view of human capital theory (1976a) was followed by what he describes as a 'revisionist' position which emphasizes the importance of the 'screening' hypothesis and an analysis of labour-market trends for an understanding of the 'new' economics of education (1985a). Finally comes the 'general sense of boredom of economists with a subject that has remained relatively stagnant for more than a decade' (1989: 332).

Despite this gloom, Blaug declares: 'I come not to praise the economics of education but also not to bury it' (1989: 333), and in an attack on 'the outrageous manner in which virtually all European governments finance higher education to the benefit of a privileged minority' he concludes that 'So long as such scandals prevail, the economics of education will continue to have policy relevance' (1987a: ix).

Finally, on the economics of education in developing countries, he argues (Blaug 1979: 83) that:

> There is still something left for economists to say on educational planning in poor countries, and some of the lessons that economists can teach are absolutely fundamental in their implications for government policy.

The main argument of this paper is that the economics of education does indeed continue to be relevant for policy and that Mark Blaug's own writings on the subject have played a considerable role in the education of policy-makers. In fact, it is ironic that at the very time when he published his own pessimistic conclusions about a subject that had 'failed to deliver the goods', there were a number of indications that in more than one country educational policy makers were once again turning to the economics of education for guidance or for justification for new policy directions.

Elsewhere in this volume Nicholas Barr describes the sudden explosion of interest in the idea of income-contingent loans that occurred in 1989 in Australia, Sweden and the United States as well as in Britain. The government's proposals to introduce student loans in Britain were justified in terms of the profitability of public and private investment:

> Economic analysis suggests that, in financial terms alone, higher education would be worthwhile to the student even if no maintenance grant were available. . . . the return on the individual graduate's personal investment in higher education (earnings forgone, offset by the maintenance grant) in recent years has been in the region of 25 per cent, taking all subjects together. The same analysis shows that the return to society on its investment in the graduate's higher education has been much lower; between 5 per cent and 8 per cent. The individual graduate benefits more than the community as a whole from the latter's investment in the former's higher education. The division of costs, on the other hand, goes the other way. That is why there is scope for the individual student to bear more of the cost of the investment. (Department of Education and Science 1988: 10)

Although, as Nicholas Barr argues, the precise form of student loans introduced in Britain is open to criticism, and, indeed, Mark Blaug (1990: 19) recently wrote that 'the British government, after years of resisting any student loan scheme whatsoever, is now about to introduce the wrong kind of scheme', the fact that government ministers and policy documents now quote rates of return in advocating a shift of financial burdens from taxpayers to individual students can be seen as belated recognition of the validity of Blaug's (1970: 296) criticism of mandatory grants as a system which 'without splitting hairs . . . simply gives to those who already have . . . to defend grants in higher education on grounds of social equality is a monstrous perversion of the truth'. The same justification was given by the Wran Committee (Australia 1988) in Australia which argued that:

> The advantaged who use and benefit directly from higher education ought to contribute more

directly to the cost of the system and Australian taxpayers should not be expected to carry the burden of financing the growth envisaged in higher education, particularly since few directly enjoy its financial benefits.

There are many other examples to show that the economics of education has had considerable influence on policy-making in both developed and developing countries. The World Bank has argued in recent reports (1986, 1988) that in developing countries there should be a shift in government budget-priorities away from higher education towards primary and secondary education. Policy statements following the World Conference on Education for All, held in Bangkok in March 1990, suggest that a number of countries in Africa and Asia are now attempting to put into practice a realignment of priorities, as indicated by increased investment in primary schooling and basic education and a trend towards greater cost recovery in higher education. Blaug recommended such a policy shift in 1979 and again in 1987:

> The first priority in educational planning in the Third World is somehow to reduce the rates of growth of secondary and higher education, shifting resources from the upper to the lower levels of the educational system.   (1979: 346)

> The over-expansion of higher education in the Third World is associated with under-investment in primary education and the vital importance of primary education in the development process is perhaps the principal point of agreement among virtually all economists who have ever studied the problems of education in the Third World.   (1987a: ix)

Manpower forecasting, once so popular as a guide to educational planning, although Blaug (1970: 168) dismissed it as a modern form of 'crystal-ball gazing', is now recognized as providing only very rough estimates of future demand for educated manpower. Dougherty (1985: 89) in a review of manpower forecasting and manpower development planning in the UK since 1950 refers to the 'celebrated collection of manpower forecasting evaluations' by Ahamad and Blaug (1973):

> This had an enormous impact because it confirmed comprehensively that attempts to forecast demands in quantitative terms were liable to large margins of error. This had been widely suspected on theoretical grounds, and it had been demonstrated to be the case in a number of isolated retrospective studies, but here it was shown that regardless of the country or its level of development, the story was the same: quantitative projections tended to be depressingly inaccurate. . . . Rate of return analysis took over as the dominant planning approach among academics. and the few subsequent attempts at making quantitative forecasts have received very limited attention. In Britain the impact of Ahamad and Blaug has been felt as strongly as anywhere else.

While many would question Dougherty's assertion that 'rate of return analysis took over as the dominant planning approach', it is certainly true that in Britain, as in most market economies, there are few planners today who put their faith in detailed manpower forecasting. Here is one more example of economists playing a key role in the education of policy makers.

One of the most interesting examples of the influence of the economics of education on educational policy, not only in Britain but in Australia, Canada and the USA, is the growing interest in market mechanisms as a means of financing education and particularly in the effects of different tuition-fee policies on the demand for education and the internal efficiency of educational institutions. In Australia the reintroduction of tuition fees or a higher education contribution covering about 20 per cent of the costs of higher education was justified by the Wran Committee (Australia 1988: 5) on the grounds that:

> fee abolition had a marginal effect at best, on the accessibility of higher education for socially and economically disadvantaged groups; at worst, it provided a further benefit to the economically advantaged.

In Canada a number of government commissions have recommended an increase in tuition fees, accompanied by an increase in student aid, particularly student loan programmes and a recent review of alternative policies on university tuition fees (Stager 1989) showed that there was an emerging consensus in Canada that tuition fees should contribute about one-quarter to one-third of total revenue for undergraduate education and that universities should have more flexibility in setting their fees.

In the USA there has been considerable research on the effects of alternative fee policies on demand for higher education (summarized by Leslie and Brinkman 1988) and advocates of differential tuition pricing argue that greater reliance on tuition fees and greater flexibility in setting fees will improve efficiency and make institutions more responsive to students' and employers' needs. The idea of education vouchers has recently been reactivated in the USA, and economic analysis has been used to support or refute various claims about the effects of alternative financing mechanisms.

A comparison of trends in funding higher education in eleven OECD countries suggests that policy-makers in many countries have been influenced by the argument of economists that mechanisms of funding can have a powerful influence on how institutions operate:

> It is only recently that policy makers have begun to understand the critical links between expenditure patterns, costs and efficiency in higher education and the mechanisms by which institutions receive funds. . . . Many governments now see financial incentives as a more effective way of influencing the pattern of activities in higher education institutions than administrative intervention. (OECD 1990)

One trend noted in several of the countries included in the OECD study was a greater reliance on income from tuition fees and the use of other market mechanisms, such as competitive bidding for research contracts. This trend is already apparent in Britain (Williams 1991) and the government has promised further developments in this direction with increases in the level of tuition fees and competitive bidding for funds for both teaching and research. The government's proposals to increase tuition fees for home students to £1,600 in 1990–1, and thereafter to introduce differential fees in four 'subject bands' ranging from £1,600 to £3,200, argued that this would improve efficiency and make institutions more responsive and accountable:

> By making institutions' income dependent in larger measure on their ability to attract and satisfy student demand, this funding approach will both promote effectiveness in marketing and teaching, and enhance the scope of institutional independence. To the extent that the higher fee income covers marginal costs, it will assist in encouraging institutions to exploit spare capacity by taking in additional students, so contributing to the objective of widening access . . . while in the process reducing unit costs. (Department of Education and Science 1989: 2)

Increased reliance on market mechanisms, financial incentives and tuition fees as a means of financing education suggests that the economics of education still has considerable influence on policy-makers both in Britain and elsewhere, despite Blaug's (1989: 331) view that the 1980s saw a 'deepening pessimism about the importance of education and

. . . a pervasive disillusionment with the economics of education as an area of teaching and research'.

Furthermore, economic analysis will be even more necessary in the future, in order to evaluate the effects of the changes in patterns and mechanisms of finance for education that are now being proposed or introduced in so many countries. Will increased reliance on tuition fees increase the responsiveness of institutions as advocates, such as Barnes and Barr (1988) suggest? Or will it reduce access to higher education or lead to dilution of quality as the critics fear?

Some insights about the effect of an increase in tuition fees can be drawn from the British experience of the introduction of full-cost fees for overseas students in 1980. This is a policy area in which Mark Blaug himself made one of the first attempts at economic analysis, and his use of economic reasoning to analyse the costs and benefits of overseas students, the arguments for and against subsidies for overseas students and the effects of an increase in fees on demand for higher education in Britain had an influence on policy making not only in this country, but on a wider scale. His analysis has stimulated similar studies in Australia (Throsby 1985, 1986) and the USA (Winkler 1983). He made predictions about the effects of full-cost fees on overseas-student enrolment that proved remarkably accurate. Furthermore his conclusion that there is a strong case 'for not subsidising overseas students indiscriminately and directly subsidising only overseas students from the Third World under the foreign aid budget' finds echoes in ministerial pronouncements (Renton 1985) on the basis for government policy on overseas student fees and subsidies:

> Selective subsidies are more cost-effective than a policy of haphazard and indiscriminate subsidies which were not being directed to serve the aims of British policy at all closely.

In many ways, therefore, this represents an interesting case-study of how economic analysis can be used to illuminate policy issues, and how the economics of education can contribute to the education of policy-makers. On the other hand, the confusions that are still expressed about the relationship between average and marginal costs, about how 'full-cost fees' should be determined, and about how to measure the costs and benefits of overseas students, suggest that the educational process is still far from complete.

This chapter examines the introduction of full-cost fees from an economic perspective, considers the predictions made by Blaug and others when the policy was first announced by the new conservative government in 1979, and assesses the impact of this policy after a decade. It concludes that economic analysis has played an important role in influencing policy-making in this area not only in Britain but also in Australia. In the future, with increased reliance on tuition fees for home as well as overseas students, with increased student mobility as a result of programmes such as ERASMUS (the European Community Action Scheme for the Mobility of University Students), TEMPUS (designed to extend this programme to Eastern Europe) and increased competition for overseas students on the part of other host-countries, particularly Australia, Canada, Japan and the USA, there will remain a need for research and economic analysis. This is one of many areas where the economics of education will continue to provide lessons for policy-makers.

THE INTRODUCTION OF FULL-COST FEES FOR OVERSEAS STUDENTS

Until 1980 overseas-student fees were heavily subsidized, and both universities and public sector institutions received public funding for overseas as well as home students. The Robbins Committee (1963: 67) considered the question of the appropriate level of subsidy for overseas students and concluded that:

> It is not sufficiently recognised that, with fees at their present level, provision for overseas students costs the taxpayers of this country a very substantial amount . . . the annual subsidy involved amounts at the present time to something like £9 million. In our judgement this expenditure is well justified. It is a form of foreign aid that has a definite objective and yields a tangible return in benefit to the recipients and in general goodwill. It is, however, an open question whether the aid is best given by subsidising fees; and it is a further question to what extent Parliament of the future will permit it to grow without limit.

The calculation by the Robbins Committee of the cost of subsidising overseas students represented, according to Williams (1981: 4) 'the end of the age of innocence':

> All at once 'the subsidy to foreign students' became known about and treated as an option: something which was regarded for the time being as acceptable and outweighed by the benefits, but an item which in different circumstances might be manipulated. The sudden awareness in the first half of the 1960s of the existence and size of 'the subsidy' represented in a sense the end of the 'age of innocence' in respect of overseas students in Britain. Once the cost of educating overseas students stopped being seen as an uncalculated part of the natural order of things, and became instead a matter of cost and choice, the need for 'a national policy' was with us.

The question of how long the subsidy would be allowed to grow unchecked was quickly answered. In December 1966 Anthony Crosland, then Minister of Education, announced the introduction of differential fees for overseas students. From 1967–8 students from abroad paid £250 a year, compared with £70 for home students. This still represented a significant subsidy but the 'age of innocence' was over once and for all.

The introduction of differential fees caused some controversy at the time but had little effect on overseas student numbers, which continued to increase during the 1970s until by 1979 there were a total of 88,000 foreign students in British universities, polytechnics and colleges, and 11 per cent of all students in higher education were from overseas. There had been some attempt during the 1970s to limit the number of foreign students through voluntary quotas, but these were ignored in many institutions and were largely ineffective. By 1979 when the Conservative government was elected with a commitment to reduce public expenditure, there was mounting concern about the costs to the British taxpayer of subsidising increasing numbers of students from abroad.

The government estimated that the cost to public funds in 1978–9 was over £125 million. It was pointed out that many of these students came from countries with a higher national income than Britain's, yet they paid fees representing only a fraction of the true cost of their education. In the first round of spending cuts after the general election every government department had to make economies and the Department of Education announced that 'given the overriding need to reduce public expenditure while giving priority to home students', it would withdraw public subsidy for overseas students, and that from October 1980 all new students from overseas, except those from the European Community, would be expected to pay fees which covered the full costs of their higher education. This meant that annual fees increased from £940 for overseas undergraduates and £1,230 for postgraduates in 1979 to £2,000 for those studying Arts, Social Studies and Humanities, £3,000 for those studying science and engineering and £5,000 for students of medicine, dentistry and veterinary science. Home students, on the other hand, and those from the European Community (who were protected under the Treaty of Rome, which requires member states to charge students from other EC countries the same level of fees as their own nationals) were required to pay only £740 for undergraduate and £1,105 for postgraduate courses.

This decision provoked widespread opposition from critics in Britain and abroad, who argued that it would damage Britain's long-term political and commercial interests, that Britain still had obligations to former colonies and dependent territories, that higher education for students from developing countries was an important part of the British aid effort and that the presence of overseas students generated substantial economic benefits for Britain, not only in terms of foreign exchange and possible effects on future exports, but also through contributions to research. There were particularly strong protests from Commonwealth countries which had strong historical ties with British universities, and the Malaysian government retaliated by announcing a 'Buy British Last' policy designed to damage Britain's export trade.

Organizations such as the Overseas Students Trust (OST), the Commonwealth Secretariat and the United Kingdom Council for Overseas Student Affairs (UKCOSA) campaigned vigorously, and vice-chancellors predicted that universities would suffer a substantial reduction in income as a result of the new policy. The OST commissioned a series of studies on the likely impact of full-cost fees, and invited Mark Blaug and the Research Unit on the Economics of Education at the University of London Institute of Education to examine the economic costs and benefits of overseas students and the economic consequences of the proposed withdrawal of subsidy. This included a survey of 1,484 overseas students in universities and polytechnics in early 1980 and visits to 14 institutions to interview academic and administrative staff about the possible effects of the new fees (see Blaug 1981).

When full-cost fees were first announced in 1979, some vice-chancellors predicted a fall of as much as 70 per cent in first-year enrolments. At the time of the Institute of Education's survey in spring 1980, most institutions were predicting a fall of 30 per cent, but on the basis of an analysis of overseas student demand after 1967, when differential fees were first introduced, Blaug (1981: 60) predicted a more modest decline in first year enrolments: 'The true figure in the first year (1980/81) is more likely [to be] a fall of 5 per cent, building up to a fall of 16–17 per cent in the third year (1982/83).'

THE EFFECTS OF FULL-COST FEES ON DEMAND FROM OVERSEAS STUDENTS

In the event, Blaug's prediction of a 5 per cent fall in overseas enrolment in 1980 and a reduction of 16–17 per cent by 1982 proved to be very close to the mark in universities, although the numbers fell more sharply in polytechnics and colleges, and the numbers in non-advanced further education fell by 70 per cent between 1979 and 1982. Table 12.1 shows the numbers of overseas students in all publicly funded institutions in the UK between 1979 and 1988. In universities the introduction of full-cost fees led to a fall of almost exactly 5 per cent between 1979 and 1980 and by 1982 numbers had fallen by 17.8 per cent. Blaug's prediction, based on his estimates of the elasticity of demand between 1967, when differential fees were first introduced, and 1979, when full-cost fees were announced, was remarkably accurate, and much closer to reality than the gloomy forecasts of a 30–50 per cent decline which greeted the announcement of full-cost fees.

Table 12.1:   *Overseas students in publicly financed institutions in the United Kingdom, by sector and level of study, 1979 to 1988*

Sector/level of study	1979	1980	1981	1982	1983	1984	1988
Universities							
1. Postgraduate	18,433	17,445	16,431	16,233	17,044	17,998	n.a.
	(21)	(22)	(26)	(29)	(31)	(32)	
2. Undergraduate	21,578	20,538	17,505	16,661	16,464	16,931	n.a.
	(25)	(26)	(27)	(29)	(30)	(30)	
3. Total universities	40,011	37,983	33,936	32,894	33,508	34,929	49,100
(1) + (2)	(46)	(48)	(53)	(58)	(61)	(62)	(68)
4. Other advanced further education	21,313	19,998	18,924	15,555	14,154	13,580	16,000
	(24)	(26)	(30)	(27)	(25)	(24)	(22)
5. Total higher education	61,324	57,981	52,860	48,449	47,662	48,509	65,100
(3) + (4)	(70)	(74)	(83)	(85)	(86)	(86)	(90)
6. Non-advanced further education	26,713	19,649	11,211	8,216	7,946	7,612	7,100
	(30)	(26)	(17)	(15)	(14)	(14)	(10)
7. Grand total	88,037	77,630	64,071	56,665	55,608	56,121	72,200
(5) + (6)	(100)	(100)	(100)	(100)	(100)	(100)	(100)

Sources:
1979–84: Overseas Students Trust (1987); 1988 Department of Education and Science.

Note:
Figures in brackets denote percentage of grand total.

Commenting on these predictions, Blaug (1981: 58–61) pointed out: 'Considering that fees were going to rise on average by 111 per cent for undergraduates and by 177 per cent for postgraduates, a reduction of demand of 30 per cent would actually be rather modest', which implied that foreign demand for British higher education had a relatively low price elasticity, but he also observed: 'By and large polytechnics tended to be more pessimistic about the elasticity of overseas demand than universities, sensing perhaps that they faced a somewhat different clientele than the universities.' This also proved to be prophetic. Since 1983, when the government announced an increase in scholarships and awards for overseas students (known as the 'Pym Package', after the Foreign Secretary who introduced the programme), the number of foreign students in universities in the UK has risen steadily until in 1988 there were 49,100, which was 23 per cent higher than in 1979, whereas the number taking higher education courses in polytechnics and colleges at 16,000 was still 25 per cent below the 1979 figure of 21,313. The number in further education was only 7,100, which was 73 per cent below the 1979 enrolment of 26,713.

There have also been significant changes in the origins of overseas students. The number of European Community students, who continue to pay the same fees as home students, rose from 6,400 in 1980 to 11,600 in 1987, whereas the number from Commonwealth countries fell from 40,800 to 29,700. Numbers from the USA have increased, due in part to the growing popularity of 'Junior Year Abroad' programmes. Thus there has been a shift in the balance between rich and poor countries, despite the existence of scholarship programmes targeted specifically upon developing countries.

There are a number of possible explanations for the different trends in universities and polytechnics and colleges of higher education. First, it could demonstrate, as Blaug suggested, that demand for higher education is not highly sensitive to changes in price, whereas the elasticity of demand for non-advanced further education is much greater. One reason for this is that the capacity of domestic institutions overseas, particularly in developing countries, has grown substantially in the last decade which means that there are now many more substitutes available for British non-advanced courses, and the numbers following GCE and other similar courses have fallen by nearly 75 per cent since 1979 whereas the numbers following postgraduate courses, for which there are fewer substitutes, have increased until they are now well above their 1979 level.

Another reason for the difference between universities and polytechnics is that the number of home students in polytechnics rose sharply during the 1980s, leaving no room, in some cases, for students from overseas. But this is only part of the story. Another explanation for the marked difference between universities and polytechnics and colleges is the increased recruitment activity on the part of universities that followed the introduction of full-cost fees. A survey of 33 universities, polytechnics and colleges conducted by the Institute of Education in 1985 (Williams, Woodhall and O'Brien 1986) concluded that the introduction of full-cost fees had led to a remarkable increase in 'entrepreneurial activity' on the part of universities, which by 1985 relied on overseas students for between 5 and 16 per cent of their income. The survey found that since 1980 more than half the universities visited had introduced internal incentive schemes to encourage and reward departments for the recruitment of overseas fee-paying students and it found numerous instances of new courses being created and new recruitment initiatives in universities. However, they found that 'the public sector has been much less entrepreneurial', partly because many institutions had no financial incentive to increase overseas recruitment since they were required to transfer all income from overseas student fees to their local education authorities and partly because of the pressure of demand from home students between 1980 and 1985. The situation was changing, however, and by 1985 a number of polytechnics in particular were beginning to take active steps to recruit students from overseas.

By 1989, when we conducted another survey, both universities and polytechnics were extremely active in attempting to attract overseas students, whose fees accounted for over 10 per cent of total recurrent income in several institutions. Most universities are predicting further increases in income from overseas students by 1991–2.

Some of these forecasts may prove to be over-optimistic. There are several reasons why universities may find it hard to maintain the substantial increases that have occurred since 1983. Since most universities, and now an increasing number of polytechnics, are trying to increase overseas recruitment, there is growing competition between British higher education institutions. At the same time universities in other major host-countries, notably Australia, Canada, Japan and USA, are also trying to increase their market share, particularly in Asia. There were reports in our case-study universities of 'cut-throat competition' for students in Hong Kong and Malaysia.

Yet another factor is the change in the relative price of British higher education, compared with that in other host-countries, notably USA, as a result of fluctuations in the exchange rate between sterling and the dollar. *The Times Higher Education Supplement* recently reported a study which compared overseas student enrolments and the exchange rate two years previously (that is, when decisions are made about whether to study in Britain or elsewhere). If these trends shown in Figure 12.1 are extrapolated,

Figure 12.1

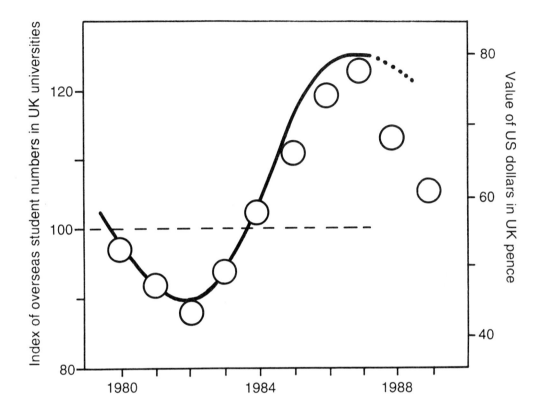

Source:
The Times Higher Education Supplement, 16 June 1989.

it suggests that overseas student enrolments may start to decline in the next few years, despite the increase in overseas student numbers in higher education between 1983 and 1988. Does this matter? It will certainly mean a significant loss of income for some individual universities. To answer the question for the country as a whole, we need to analyse the costs and benefits of overseas students, as Mark Blaug attempted in 1980.

THE ECONOMIC COSTS AND BENEFITS OF OVERSEAS STUDENTS

At the time when full-cost fees were first announced, many commentators argued that the benefits of having foreign students in Britain far outweighed the costs of subsidizing their tuition fees. Think of the future exports that would be generated after the students returned home! To some, the fact that Malaysia promptly announced a 'Buy British Last' campaign intended to damage British exports was proof of the fact that Britain would suffer, in economic terms, from the decision to charge full-cost fees. However, Blaug's analysis suggested that it was not so simple.

The economic benefits of overseas students to Britain can be classified in terms of contributions to (a) reseach; (b) exports, (c) balance of payments; (d) aggregate demand. Blaug concluded that in all cases the presence of overseas students does generate economic benefits, but that they are often overestimated. In particular he was not able to demonstrate that overseas students stimulate exports to any great degree and asked (Blaug 1981: 80): 'who is to say that factory visits and short in-plant training courses, geared to particular engineers, technicians, scientists, bankers, ministry officials, etc. might not achieve the same stimulus to British exports at a lower cost than full-time study in Britain?'.

On the other hand, he showed that the costs of overseas students often tend to be underestimated. Critics of the decision to introduce full-cost fees had argued that the marginal costs of educating one foreign student were considerably below the average costs that were used by DES to determine the level of 'full-cost' fees. However, Blaug argued that the fact that overseas students were heavily concentrated in high-cost courses, such as engineering, meant that long-run marginal costs of overseas students were fairly close to the average costs of all undergraduates.

The final conclusion of this fairly detailed comparison of costs and benefits was that the net costs of overseas students in Britain in 1979, before full-cost fees were charged, exceeded their economic benefits. It was recognized that this conclusion rested solely on his estimates of *economic* benefits. Overseas students also generate political costs and benefits as well as cultural and educational benefits through a widening of intellectual horizons of British students. On the other hand, a purely economic cost-benefit analysis did not justify the continuation of a general subsidy to all overseas students.

Instead, Blaug recommended subsidizing particular categories of student, for example, by charging full-cost fees but providing generous scholarship programmes for students from selected countries, or by directly subsidizing overseas students from developing countries under the foreign aid budget. 'In this way we would make transparent what is now opaque' (Blaug 1981: 86).

This is, in fact, what British government policy is now designed to do. A review of current policy on overseas students for a 1989 Round Table on Overseas Students (1989) summarized government policy as follows:

> In 1988/9 the Government provided more than £110 million to support more than 22,000 students from overseas. These resources have been deployed through a range of targeted schemes each designed to serve specific objectives within the Government's overall aim of bringing more overseas students to Britain. These objectives are:
>
> Win influential friends overseas by enabling future leaders, decision makers and opinion formers from all walks of life to study in the UK;
>
> Help the development of manpower skills and resources in developing countries;
>
> Promote the security and prosperity of the UK by cultivating good political and commercial relations with other countries;
>
> Ensure a continued supply of world class research students in UK universities.

The decision to replace indiscriminate subsidies for all overseas students by targeted schemes designed to achieve particular objectives is consistent not only with Blaug's advice to make transparent what was opaque, but with the conclusions of many economists of education, that explicit subsidies are more efficient than hidden subsidies.

The same conclusion has been drawn in other countries. In Australia, the Jackson Committee on the Australian Overseas Aid Programme in 1984 recommended a policy of full-cost fees combined with a selective scholarship programme and vigorous attempts to promote higher education in Australia as an 'export industry'. Economic analysis of costs and benefits of overseas students in Australia by Throsby (1985) supported this proposal and concluded that full-cost fees and an expanded scholarship programme would improve the efficiency and equity of allocation of Australian foreign aid, improve the trade potential of higher education and provide incentives to Australian universities to develop more effective programmes.

At about the same time, however, a second Committee on Overseas Student Policy, the Goldring Committee, recommended the continuation of subsidies for foreign students, on the grounds that they brought economic, political and cultural benefits to Australia (but without any detailed cost-benefit analysis). In the event, the Australian government chose a compromise and increased overseas-student fees but rejected the idea of full-cost fees, differentiated by subject. Quotas were also maintained, to attempt control of numbers by non-economic means.

In a subsequent analysis of the economic aspects of foreign student policy Throsby (1986: 412) concluded:

> In Australia, no less than elsewhere, shortcomings of policy towards foreign students are evident. The major aid impact of present policy, arising through subsidization of fees, is difficult to quantify and arbitrary in its incidence. . . . Proposals to introduce an expanded aid programme in tertiary education and a full economic fee for private overseas students are economically sound both in terms of national efficiency and international equity.

In 1988 a further review of Australia's overseas-student policies led to the decision to introduce full-cost fees and a new targeted scholarship programme in 1990. It was estimated that the total cost of public subsidies for overseas students in 1989 represented 45 per cent of the cost of a university place and the government announced that in future this will be redirected to a new targeted scholarship programme called the Equity and Merit Scholarship Scheme (EMSS) in which half the scholarships are awarded on grounds of merit and half on grounds of financial need, with students from developing countries receiving priority.

CONCLUSION

The introduction of full-cost fees for overseas students in Britain in 1980 and in Australia in 1990 provides two interesting examples of the influence of the economics of education on policy making. In Britain it was the increasing costs of subsidizing overseas students that eventually led to the decision to impose full-cost fees. Blaug's economic analysis of costs and benefits supported the idea of full-cost fees backed up by selective subsidies through targeted scholarships, but it was three years before the government announced an increase in targeted scholarships through the 'Pym Package' of 1983. This three-year gap was damaging to British interests abroad and led to strong criticism. In Australia the government first rejected the advice of economists to introduce full-cost fees linked with an expanded scholarship programme, but in 1990 this advice has been followed and the new level of fees and a new scholarship programme were announced simultaneously.

This chapter has attempted to show that the economics of education can contribute to the education of policy-makers, even though no one would suggest that economic considerations alone should guide public policy. The economics of education may indeed have 'failed to deliver the goods' in terms of precise measurement of the contribution of education to economic growth. It can, however, provide useful lessons for policy-makers about the effects of different forms and levels of subsidy. Cost-benefit analysis has not succeeded in quantifying the externalities of education, but it does provide a framework for the systematic evaluation of the economic impact of alternative policies. The introduction of full-cost fees for overseas students is just one example of a policy issue that requires economic analysis if the implications and consequences of educational decisions are to become transparent rather than opaque.

NOTE

1. The chapter draws on material collected as part of a study of the effects of new funding mechanisms in higher education, financed by the Department of Education and Science and carried out in the Centre for Higher Education Studies at the Institute of Education, University of London. The research, directed by Professor Gareth Williams, examined institutional responses to changing sources and mechanisms of finance in 25 universities, polytechnics and colleges of higher education. A full report of the research is to be published in Williams (1991).

13. Income-contingent Student Loans: An Idea Whose Time has Come*

Nicholas Barr

---

1 THE HISTORICAL BACKDROP

1.1 Introductory Matters

This paper tells a story with three elements. First is the development of a set of coherent theoretical propositions, emanating in part from the Robbins Report (1963), which underpin the intellectual case for income-contingent student loans. Second is the story of how long it took and how much campaigning until their gradual implementation in the late 1980s. Thirdly, and by way of a grace note (perhaps a disgrace note), is how the British government, in introducing an ill-conceived loan scheme in 1990, missed a golden opportunity to take the Robbins proposals a large step forward.

Section 1 summarizes the history of the student loans debate in Britain. The relevant economic theory is discussed in section 2, and its implications for policy design in section 3. Section 4 looks at loan schemes, actual or proposed, in Sweden, Australia, New Zealand and the USA, and describes recent British developments.

Funding for higher education derives from five broad sources: from government in the form of grants or scholarships:[1] from the student him/herself, largely out of future income; from the student's family; from the private sector, for example, contributions from industry; and from private charitable foundations. Though all these sources are discussed, the main emphasis is on the second, and in particular on income-contingent loans, that is, a loan whose repayment takes the form of x per cent of the individual borrower's subsequent annual income. This type of loan is in sharpest contrast with loans organized like a mortgage or bank overdraft, with repayment in fixed instalments over a fixed period.

Loans can cover the cost of tuition fees, living costs or both. Where tuition is tax-funded (as in much of Western Europe) loans are mainly for maintenance; in the USA they are for either or both. For economic purposes what matters is the total cost of higher education, and the assistance available to students in meeting that cost; little distinction is therefore made between tuition and maintenance costs.

1.2 Debates in the 1960s and 1970s

The British higher-education debate
It can be argued that higher education owes a great deal to Sputnik I, which motivated additional educational spending on both sides of the Atlantic. In Britain there were also

155

worries about poor economic performance. Both factors lay behind the appointment of the Robbins Committee in February 1961. In welcoming the publication of its Report, Sir Eric Ashby (1963) wrote:

> [it] is long overdue. It is at least a generation since we came to realise that Britain's stability in peace and safety in war depend on experts. We have created a world which cannot be run without graduates.

The Robbins Report should be read alongside the Anderson Report (UK 1960), which consolidated earlier arrangements by introducing a system of a mandatory, tax-funded maintenance grants, means-tested on parental income. The Robbins Committee's (1963: para. 31) conclusions rested on a number of principles of which, for present purposes, the most important was that:

> [t]hroughout our Report we have assumed as an axiom that courses of higher education should be available for all those who are qualified by ability and attainment to pursue them and who wish to do so.

Access to higher education, in other words, was a prime objective. In pursuit of that objective, among others, the Committee recommended *expansion* of higher education, from about one in twelve of 18-year olds to about one in six by 1980.

Among the written evidence to the Committee were the first two UK proposals for income-contingent student loans. Peacock and Wiseman (1962: para. 33) argued for:

> government or government-assisted . . . loans to students . . . at subsidised rates of interest and with fairly generous repayment terms. The loans could be paid off in the form of deductions through [income tax].

Prest (1962: 147) advocated publicly-funded loans to students:

> on condition that they enter into a contract to repay a specified proportion of their lifetime earnings to the government.

> [T]he obvious [repayment] mechanism is to gear this in with an individual's income tax payments, a fixed proportion of income being paid each year to amortise the original advance.   (148)

The idea was picked up in the Report, which acknowledged several advantages of loans, not least that tax-funded grants tend to be regressive, since higher education is disproportionately used by students from higher-income backgrounds (for the complexities underlying that argument, see Blaug 1982). The major worry about loans was their incentive effects, in particular the deleterious effects on access.

> On balance we do not recommend immediate recourse to a system of financing students by loans. At a time when many parents are only just beginning to acquire the habit of contemplating higher education for . . . their children . . . *we think it probable that it would have undesirable incentive effects*.   (Robbins Report 1963: para. 647, my emphasis).

The market-versus-the-state debate

The loans issue arose also in the broader debate about the proper role of government. In a general defence of the market mechanism, Friedman (1962) considered the government's role in vocational and professional training. He accepted the capital market imperfections discussed in section 2.2, in particular the riskiness of student loans (for example, the absence of any security). He (1962: 103) pointed out that:

[t]he device adopted to meet the corresponding problem for other risky investments is equity investment plus limited liability on the part of shareholders. The counter-part for education would be to 'buy' a share in an individual's earning prospects; to advance him the funds needed to finance his training on condition that he agree to pay the lender a specified fraction of his future earnings.

On that basis he (1962: 105) advocated loans from government, in return for which,

[t]he individual . . . would agree to pay to the government in each future year a specified percentage of his earnings in excess of a specified sum for each $1000 that he received. . . . The payment could easily be combined with payment of income tax and so involve a minimum of additional administrative expense.

These early student-loan proposals derived from the benefit principle (he who benefits should pay). A different approach starts from a predisposition towards free, tax-financed education, abandoning that model only because of its regressiveness when applied to higher education. Glennerster, Merrett and Wilson (1968: 26) point out that:

in the United Kingdom, higher education is now financed as a social service. Nearly all the costs are borne out of general taxation. . . . But it differs radically from other social services. It is reserved for a small and highly selected group. . . . It is exceptionally expensive. . . . [And] education confers benefits which reveal themselves in the form of higher earnings. A graduate tax would enable the community to recover the value of the resources devoted to higher education from those who have themselves derived such substantial benefit from it.

The conclusion is that the benefit principle and the ability-to-pay approach, despite their very different starting points, lead to identical policy prescriptions.

Subsequent history of the student loans debate in Britain
The idea of income-contingent loans slowly entered the academic literature. Blaug (1966) stressed again the distinction between mortgage-type and income-contingent loans, and made the link with the broader issue of the finance of all post-school education.

The early 1970s saw various proposals. It is rumoured that Margaret Thatcher, whilst Secretary of State for Education, brought a proposal to Cabinet which was summarily rejected by the then Prime Minister, Edward Heath. Outside government, Mark Blaug devised an income-contingent scheme for postgraduate students. It can be argued that this was the obvious way to begin: the numbers involved are smaller; mass access is less of an issue; and there is arguably less disincentive effect and less political opposition. The scheme, nevertheless, sank almost without trace (perhaps again the Prime Ministerial veto). A third proposal, by Maynard (1975) looked at loans in the broader context of the funding of higher education.

The election of a Labour government in 1974 effectively ended any likelihood of loans in the short run. The emphasis of higher education policy was to pursue expansion and improved access through the existing system of tax-funded maintenance grants though public spending cuts after the 1976 economic crisis ruled out any success.

The major event of the later 1970s on the loans front was Lord Robbins's conversion. In an article in the *Financial Times* (reprinted in Robbins, 1980: 35) he expressed regret that at the time of the Committee he had not sufficiently appreciated the advantages of income-contingent loans.

With the election of a Conservative government in 1979, loans came back on to the political agenda. The academic background was set by writers like Woodhall (1982). Keith

Joseph, then Secretary of State for Education, was committed to the policy, supported by politicians such as Rhodes Boyson. Any explanation of why no scheme was implemented can only be speculative. Three possible reasons suggest themselves: the high up-front-taxpayer cost of a loan scheme in its early years (coupled with a government committed to public spending cuts); the administrative difficulties cited by the Inland Revenue whenever the scheme was mooted; and the political dangers of reducing a middle-class perk.

The upshot is that by the early 1980s, though there was no political consensus, agreement outside the ranks of politicians was widespread. According to Blaug (1980: 45):

> virtually every advocate of student loans in Britain (Alan Peacock, Jack Wiseman, Alan Prest, Sir Charles Carter, Gareth Williams, Ernest Rudd, Anthony Flew, Donald Mackay, Michael Crew, Alistair Young, Arthur Seldon, Lord Robbins and Mark Blaug) . . . favours an income-related loans scheme . . . .

As discussed in section 4, similar debates were also a recurrent theme in other countries.

2 ANALYTICS

2.1 The Theoretical Case for Subsidizing Higher Education

The funding paradox
Higher education faces a painful and unavoidable tension. Large taxpayer-subsidies for tuition fees or maintenance can lead to supply-side constraints because of the desire to contain public spending. Where qualified students have no automatic entitlement to a place in higher education (for example, Britain), the constraint takes the form of a view (typically by the Treasury) about student numbers. The result can be a high quality system, but one which turns away at least some qualified applicants. In countries where students have a right to a place, the impact of cost containment is mainly on quality. With less public funding per student (for example, USA), there are no externally imposed supply-side constraints. However, unless limited taxpayer funding is sufficiently redistributive, students from lower-income backgrounds will be deterred from applying.

Thus high subsidies can harm access on the supply side but their absence can harm it on the demand side. This is the dilemma which a well-designed loan system should alleviate. To address the problem, two issues require discussion: does higher education have any benefits in production terms (the so-called screening issue); and if so, does it create benefits over and above those to the individual recipient (the externality issue)?

The screening problem
The investment case for higher education rests on the (usually unstated) assumption that it causes increased productivity. The screening hypothesis argues that education is *associated* with increased productivity, but does not *cause* it (the large literature on this and other aspects of the education literature is surveyed by Blaug (1976a, 1985a)).

The distribution of earnings depends on factors like sex, race, family circumstances, natural ability and the quantity and quality of education (Blaug 1970: 32–46). The screening hypothesis is a special case which argues, first, that education beyond a basic level does not increase individual productivity and, secondly, that firms seek high-ability workers but are unable, prior to employing them, to distinguish them from those with low ability. The problem is analytically identical to adverse selection in insurance markets, or more generally to 'lemons' (Akerlof 1970), in the sense that one side of the market has more information than the other. Individuals therefore have an incentive to make themselves distinctive by some sort of signal (Spence 1973; Varian 1984: ch. 8). According to the screening hypothesis, higher education fills exactly this function: it gives a signal to prospective employers, which it is in the *individual's* (though not necessarily in society's) interests to acquire. Just as an individual's good health may be due more to a naturally strong constitution than to medical care, so, according to this view, is productivity the result of natural ability rather than post-primary education.

There are various counter-arguments. Wherever higher education overlaps with professional training (for example, in medicine), there is a direct contribution to productivity. The strong form of the hypothesis also assumes that there is only one type of job. In practice, skills and job characteristics are heterogeneous, so that it is necessary to match workers and jobs, giving education an additional social return as a matching device.

Whether there is *some* validity in the hypothesis is an empirical matter. The verdict is undecided and likely to remain so, since individual productivity is determined in part by unmeasurable influences like natural ability and family background. Attempts to quantify the determinants of productivity which omit the unmeasurable factors are statistically flawed.[2]

A different argument for investment is higher education as a hedge against technological dynamism. Specific skills may become redundant in the face of technological progress, but higher education gives people *general* skills and can therefore be viewed as an investment which saves the resources which would otherwise have to be devoted to retraining labour whose skills had been made redundant by changing technology.

There is a genuine investment argument for higher education — but it must be made with circumspection.

Externality arguments
Higher education has at least one strong external benefit. By raising a student's earnings, it increases his/her future tax payments; in the absence of any subsidy, an individual's investment in a degree would confer a 'dividend' on taxpayers in the future. This is inefficient, in that investment in higher education would be inefficiently small, and is therefore the minimum case for a subsidy. This line of argument can be used as a justification for subsidizing *any* type of investment which raises future income; that is precisely what usually happens through the tax system, at least so far as business investment is concerned.

Does higher education create external benefits over and above this tax dividend? It is part of the conventional wisdom (Le Grand and Robinson 1984: 64–6) that it does. *Cultural benefits* arise out of shared experiences and common values. *Production benefits* arise if education not only makes someone more productive but also contributes to the productivity of others (if colleagues learn the same word-processing package they contribute to each other's productivity as well as to their own).

These effects, however, can go both ways. Higher education encourages questioning attitudes and so, it might be argued, can create negative cultural benefits (Grosvenor Square, Paris and Berkeley in 1968). If higher education unduly raises expectations, the result could be individuals who are discontented with their job, with possible ill-effects on their productivity.

These arguments are intended merely as a caution against blindly *assuming* that higher education creates external benefits. If there are potential costs as well as benefits, the issue must be resolved empirically. Again, however, measurement problems make a definitive answer impossible. The heart of the difficulty is that education might raise not only individual earnings (which can be measured), but also job satisfaction and enjoyment of life generally (which cannot). Estimates of the private rate of return to education are suspect because, of necessity, they omit all non-money returns. Estimates of the social rate of return are doubly suspect: they omit non-money returns and (since no other procedure is possible) they also ignore the screening problem.

The externality justification for subsidizing higher education is strong in presumptive terms, but wholly satisfactory empirical verification is still lacking. Because of the 'tax dividend' point there is an unarguable efficiency case for *some* subsidy, but it is not possible to show how much.

Whatever the size of the external benefit, higher education also confers private benefits on individuals: thus it is efficient that they (or their families) should make a contribution. Two questions arise: what is the efficient and equitable size of that contribution; and what form should it take? We have seen that no quantitative answer is possible to the first question. On the second, as discussed in section 3.1, it is possible to be rather more definite.

2.2   Capital Market Imperfections

When the Robbins Report (1963: para. 647) argued that student loans would discourage applicants, it implicitly assumed loans organized like a mortgage or bank overdraft, with repayment in equal annual instalments, possibly with some mitigation at low incomes. Such loans create problems on both sides of the market.

Demand-side-problems
Mortgage-type loans are risky from the individual student's viewpoint and so are likely to deter applicants, particularly from disadvantaged backgrounds. This is inefficient because it wastes talent, and inequitable because it reduces intergenerational mobility.

It is sometimes argued (Department of Education and Science 1988: Chart J) that people from lower socioeconomic groups will borrow to buy a house, so why not to buy a degree? Apart from the tax advantages, when someone buys a house (a) he knows what he is buying (since he has lived in a house all his life); (b) the house is unlikely to fall down; and (c) the value of the house is likely to go up. When people borrow for a degree, (a) they are not fully certain what they are buying (particularly if they come from a family with no graduates); (b) there is a high risk (or at least a high perceived risk) of failing the degree outright; and (c) not all degrees carry a high rate of return. More generally, though the *average* private return to a degree is positive (Department of Education and Science 1988: Annex D), there is a considerable variance around it. For all three reasons, borrowing to buy a degree is considerably more risky than borrowing to buy a house, and the risks are likely to be greater for people from poorer backgrounds and for women.

Supply-side problems

Long-term loans are risky also to the lender. There is no collateral (contrast the case of lending for house purchase). If the legalization of slavery is ruled out, the private sector will make long-term unsecured loans only with a government guarantee; and that guarantee will be costly (see the discussion of US default rates in section 4.4). A second form of risk to the lender is asymmetric information, in that students are better-informed than lenders whether they aspire to careers in arbitrage or the arts.

Because the guarantee is expensive, total lending will be strictly policed, creating the sorts of supply-side constraints discussed earlier. There are also high administrative costs, particularly for more risky students. Lending institutions have to keep detailed records of each borrower. The cost of chasing repayments is also substantial, the more so because the loan is unsecured.

3 IMPLICATIONS FOR POLICY DESIGN

3.1 Forms of Student Loan

Types of repayment

The fact of the matter is that private financial markets for long-run student loans do not work very well; if they did, such loans would already be on offer, as with loans for house purchase. For precisely the reasons just discussed, Friedman stressed the riskiness to both lender and borrower, and pointed to equity finance as a private-sector device for dealing with such problems.

The analogy with equity finance leads naturally to income-contingent loans. The graduate does not make fixed annual repayments; instead, the lender is entitled to a share of the graduate's subsequent earnings, analogous to dividend payments. The argument thus leads to a system in which the graduate pays the lending institution a fraction of his/ her income – that is, income-contingent repayments.

As discussed in section 1.2, the graduate tax approach, though drawing its main inspiration from egalitarian objectives, leads to precisely the same result. The first conclusion, and a very firm one, whether one starts from the benefit principle or from ability to pay, is that loan repayments should be a fraction of the individual graduate's subsequent income.

Subsidies for loans

Almost all loan systems are subsidized, creating a mixture of loan and implicit grant. Though the intuitive appeal is understandable, intuition in this case should be resisted. The resulting system is inequitable because the subsidy is generally regressive and usually large (for estimates in a US context, see Johnstone 1986: ch. 6). In equity terms it makes more sense to charge a market or near-market interest rate, and channel the saved resources into redistributive grants or scholarships.

Interest subsidies are also inefficient, first, if the interest rate bears on a student's choice between supporting him/herself by current earnings or out of future earnings. Secondly, the interest subsidy gives an incentive to borrow an inefficiently large amount, if only to benefit from the difference between the subsidized and the market interest rate. There is one counter-argument. If some students (particularly from poorer backgrounds) over-estimate the degree of risk, there might be an efficiency case for subsidy (see Williams and Gordon 1981). Again, however, such students might more effectively be encouraged into higher education by giving them a larger grant.

Even without the incentive to excessive borrowing, subsidized loans are expensive, creating supply-side constraints: either the amount each student can borrow is rationed; or the number of student places is restricted.

The role of private funds

Under appropriate conditions (market or near-market interest rates, secure repayment and/or government guarantee), the private sector would be prepared to lend the money students borrow, and to expand the system to meet demand, as with house purchase. What, if any, are the arguments in favour of loans from private-sector funds?

In theoretical terms it should not matter from which sector students borrow. Suppose it is efficient to expand higher education and that students borrow from public funds. If additional public borrowing crowds out private investment, it will only be less efficient private investment which is crowded out – a result which is itself efficient.

That theoretical conclusion, however, is valid only under stringent assumptions: in particular, government and taxpayers must be rational and well-informed about the future. Neither is true. Public funding requires that taxation is higher than would otherwise be the case, with possible disincentive effects; and higher public spending may affect financial and foreign-exchange markets. If students borrow from private funds no issue of taxation or incentives arises – we do not, after all, argue that the large and growing mortgage debt discourages work effort.

There are also political issues. There is virtually unanimous support for the principle of academic freedom, and considerable support for the view that excessive reliance on public funding threatens that freedom (Robbins himself warned against the dangers if universities received more than half of their income from government sources). It follows that diversifying the sources of funding contributes to the independence of higher education.

3.2   Other Aspects of Student Support

Student loans are only one aspect of funding. This section briefly discusses other sources.

The role of tax-funded grants and scholarships

Though most countries have maintenance grants of some sort, it is questionable whether heavy reliance on grants is the most efficient or equitable form of support. The much-vaunted UK system shows the potential pitfalls. Public spending constraints led to erosion of the basic grant, a problem exacerbated by the failure (discussed below) of many parents to contribute to student support. In consequence, some 8 per cent of students in 1982–3 were below the official poverty line (Barr and Low 1988: Table 6). But though many students are poor, their parents are usually well-off. UK students disproportionately come from better-off families (ibid: 51–9). Grants are also expensive in public-expenditure terms and so exert downward pressure on the size of the system.

The role of compulsory family support

Student support in most countries relies heavily on parents. When education was a concern mainly of the social élite, this approach was both natural and appropriate. The reliance on *compulsory* parental support is open to question today, when higher education is both a mass phenomenon and an economic necessity.

The arguments in favour of parental contributions are, first, that they save public spending thus allowing a larger higher education sector. Secondly, since parental support is generally means tested (see Johnstone 1986: 145–53) it can be argued that they are equitable. Thirdly, students cannot easily borrow from the private sector; but parents can borrow, and so parental contributions can be thought of as an indirect form of private-sector loan. Parental contributions, on this view, are an inter-generational attempt to correct a technical failure in capital markets. A counter-argument is that a well-constructed loan scheme is a more efficient and equitable way of correcting the market failure.

There are other counter-arguments. Parental contributions may constrain the system because attempts to enlarge it by increasing parental contributions can lead to a revolt amongst middle-class parents (as happened in Britain in 1985). Parental support can also be patchy: this is the case in the UK (Barr and Low 1988), though anecdotal evidence suggests that it works better in other countries.

This is not an attack on the idea of parents helping their children, merely on the idea of building a system of student support on the *assumption* that parents will contribute. With a well-constructed (for example, not heavily subsidized) loan system, students and their parents can make their own choices; parents who wish to help their children can do so; and children whose parents refuse have other options.

The role of employers
Since employers benefit from the education of their employees, it is efficient for at least two reasons that they contribute to its costs. It forces them to face the costs of trained manpower (given the declining number of younger workers, an increasingly scarce resource). It might be argued that the employer contribution, whatever form it takes, will be passed on to consumers. That, too, is efficient: it makes them face the costs of the scarce resources involved. It is efficient if a poor coffee harvest drives up the price of coffee; and it is efficient if employers, and through them consumers, pay higher prices after a poor brain harvest.

An employer contribution also helps to minimize an important market failure. Employers resist making donations on any substantial scale to education and training because the resulting graduates might subsequently work for another firm. Each firm thus faces an incentive to leave educational donations to other firms, that is, a free-rider problem. One solution is a user charge, possibly in the form of an additional payroll tax for each graduate employed. An employer thus pays only for graduates who are currently contributing to his profits and whom he finds it worthwhile to continue to employ. Given the free-rider problem it is no surprise that industry nowhere contributes on more than a trivial scale.

3.3 Principles
This section draws together the implications of the theory for policy design in the form of a set of propositions.

(a)   Higher education creates a 'dividend' for future taxpayers, and possibly also other external benefits (though the latter cannot be quantified), thus giving an efficiency case for taxpayer support. But there are also major private benefits, so the individual student should meet part of the costs of higher education.

(b)   There is a case for shifting the emphasis of support from the family to the individual student. It is both inefficient and inequitable that students should be compelled to depend on their families; students should have the option of borrowing against their future earnings.

(c)   Since taking a degree is risky, student support mechanisms, for both efficiency and equity reasons, should offer protection against risk both to the individual borrower and to the lender.

Proposition (a) implies a shift, in at least some countries, away from grants; proposition (b) suggests at least a partial shift away from compulsory reliance on parental contributions. The two together point towards loans, but proposition (c) implies that loans should not leave the individual student carrying all the risk. Hence:

(d)   Loan repayments should be related to the subsequent income of the individual student and, where necessary, should be government guaranteed.

(e)   There are strong arguments for the retention of some grants. Their main function, however, should not be *general* student support, but to bring about a level playing-field between different groups of students. There should be a larger grant for students from disadvantaged backgrounds (possibly starting at the minimum school-leaving age). Such a policy can be justified on equity grounds; there is also an efficiency argument for doing so if students from poorer backgrounds overestimate the degree of risk of doing a degree.

(f)   In the absence of strong *efficiency* reasons, loans should not be heavily subsidized; the same is true for equity reasons. Loans are a device for giving students access to their future earnings. Distributional goals should generally be pursued explicitly through grants.

(g)   Since employers are one of the main beneficiaries, it is efficient that industry contributes to the cost of higher education. Such a contribution should take the form of a payroll tax, rather than reliance on voluntary donations, which face free-rider problems.

What is needed, in conclusion, is a balance between grants, loans and parental support, a balance which will change over time and across countries. This is not a very dramatic conclusion: but non-economists seem to have a strong (and usually inappropriate) attraction to corner solutions.

4   POLICIES IN DIFFERENT COUNTRIES

4.1   Sweden

Sweden was early in the loans game (1965), was prepared to learn from experience and ended up with a system which conforms more than most with the seven propositions just outlined (for a survey, see Morris 1989). The 1965 measures were intended to expand higher education in the face of public-expenditure constraints, and to equalize participation rates across socioeconomic groups. The package provided support at 140 per cent of the official subsistence level, comprising a grant (25 per cent of the total) and a tax-funded loan. The grant was fixed in nominal terms, so that the loan became more important over time. Means testing against parental income was abolished.

After a two-year grace period, an individual's first repayment was his total debt divided by the repayment period (normally the number of years to his 51st birthday). Thereafter the nominal annual repayment was increased each year by the rate of inflation. The system was thus a publicly funded mortgage loan with a zero real interest rate. In 1975 the interest rate was changed from the rate of inflation to a (generally higher) nominal rate of 4.2 per cent.

By the early 1980s (a) inflation had eroded the fixed grant so that the loan element had increased to 94 per cent of student support; indebtedness for a three-year degree could reach £12,000. In addition, (b) there was increasing complaint that student support was inadequate. There was also (c) a reversal of the earlier improvement in the social composition of students. Because of worries that (c) was causally related to (a) and (b), a review of student support was established, leading to reform in 1989.

The main characteristics of the 1989 reforms were:

(a)   Total student support was increased by about one-fifth, from 140 per cent of subsistence to 170 per cent.
(b)   The grant element was increased from under 6 per cent to about 30 per cent of the total and was indexed, thus restoring a stable relativity between grant and loan.
(c)   Repayment terms were tightened somewhat: the grace period was reduced, and the interest rate set at half the market rate (generally higher than the previous rate of 4.2 per cent).
(d)   Loans are no longer funded from taxation, but out of borrowing by the National Debt Office; only the interest subsidy and written off loans are a budgetary charge.
(e)   Repayments are 4 per cent of gross income two years earlier.

The reforms explicitly or implicitly acknowledge a number of lessons:

(a)   *Interest subsidies*   The extent to which loans are subsidized has been steadily decreased by reducing the grace period and by gradual increases in the interest rate.
(b)   *The balance between grant and loan*   There was general agreement that the balance had tipped too far towards loans, acknowledging the need for multiple sources of support.
(c)   *Parental contributions*   Means-testing against parental income was abolished in 1965, and against a spouse's income in 1982.
(d)   *Private funding*   Loans continue to be publicly funded, but the 1989 transfer of loans to the government loan account is at least a step in the right direction.
(e)   *Income-contingent repayments*:   Large loans with mortgage-type repayments were associated with lower participation by the lower socioeconomic groups. The 1989 reforms therefore introduced explicit income-related repayments.

In 1965 Sweden had a publicly funded mortgage-type loan with heavy interest subsidies. Twenty five years later it had a much less heavily subsidized income-contingent loan scheme which allowed the possibility of partial private funding.

4.2   Australia

The Australian government appointed a Committee on Higher Education Funding in 1987, with terms of reference which made explicit mention of expansion and improved access. The Committee's Report (Australia 1988) (the Wran Report) was published in May 1988 and, as amended, took effect in January 1989 (for an analysis, see Chapman 1988; Chapman and Chia 1989).

The core of the reform package was a Higher Education Contribution Scheme, whereby students became liable to a contribution which is intended to be about one-fifth of the average tuition fee (that is, the contribution does not vary across subjects). Students have the option of paying the contribution on enrolment (at a 15 per cent discount). Otherwise the contribution is paid out of a loan at a zero real interest rate. Repayment is suspended for individuals with annual earnings below the national average. Thereafter, repayment is 1 per cent of taxable income, rising to 2 per cent and, at the highest incomes, to 3 per cent, collected through the tax system.[3]

Though often represented as a tax, the scheme is properly thought of as a loan for two reasons: it is voluntary in the sense that the fee charge can be paid upon enrolment; and the additional contribution is 'switched off' once the charge has been paid. Several points are noteworthy. The revenue from the scheme will finance expansion of higher education. Repayments are based on individual ability to pay, explicitly to avoid compromising access. Though the contribution is argued to be more equitable than the previous tax-funded system, the change should not be overstated: the effect of the interest subsidy is to reduce the contribution from 20 per cent of average tuition costs to closer to 10 per cent (see Hope and Miller 1988).

The Australian scheme, in short, is a tax-funded income-contingent loan scheme with subsidized interest rates, designed with the explicit aims of expansion and improved access.

4.3   New Zealand

The Report of the Working Group on Postcompulsory Education and Training (1988) (the Hawke Report) echoed earlier concern of the Report of the Universities Review Committee (1987) over New Zealand's low enrolment in higher education, and its underfunding. The Hawke Report considered, *inter alia*, how to pursue expansion and improved access without increased public spending. One of its main conclusions (para 3.10) was that

> [t]he most attractive way of obtaining private funding . . . is that recommended by the recent Wran Committee in Australia.
>   The Working Group, with the exception of Treasury, favours [the scheme] being seen as a means of acquiring additional resources for [higher education].
>   The particular merits of the Wran proposals are that it provides for funding for students independently from their family . . . while ensuring that repayments are required only when they have income levels which enable them to be sustained.

The Hawke Report went beyond the Wran Report in one important respect: it rejected interest subsidies. It proposed a real interest rate of about 3 per cent except for individuals caring for children, who would pay a zero real interest rate (that is, in the latter case real debt would not increase during time out of the labour force). The Report estimated that a user charge of 20 per cent of average tuition costs at a 3 per cent real interest rate could be repaid by a contribution of about 3 per cent of taxable income.

The Hawke proposal was thus a tax-funded income-contingent scheme without substantial interest subsidy, intended to encourage expansion without harming access. Though endorsed, with modifications, by government (New Zealand 1989: section 3.5), the scheme was not implemented. The New Zealand government failed to follow Australia's example by imposing the collection of repayments on the tax authorities. When the tax authorities demurred, the government turned to the banking sector. The banks, however, were reluctant to become involved, not least because the government was not prepared to give an unconditional guarantee to bank loans, whilst still requiring the banks to lend to all qualified applicants. In September 1989 they pulled out and the scheme was shelved. Three months later, as discussed shortly, exactly the same thing happened in Britain.

4.4 USA

The problems of student loans in the USA are well-known. Five stand out (see Reischauer 1989: 34–42).

(a) *Complexity* It is unduly kind to talk about a loan 'system': '[t]he complex range of grants and loans from federal, state and campus sources is a major administrative problem for most institutions. Students seldom understand all that is available' (Department of Education and Science 1989: para 123).
(b) *Mortgage-type repayments* apply almost without exception.
(c) *Interest subsidies* are pervasive.
(d) *High default rates* The largest scheme (Stafford Student Loans (formerly Guaranteed Student Loans)) gives a federal guarantee to loans to students by banks. The banks therefore have little incentive to chase defaulters. The result, in combination with the absence of any mechanism for suspending repayments when income is low, is high default rates (USA 1988: I-118).
(e) *Cost* The combined effect of interest subsidies and defaults is that the system is very costly and of only questionable benefit in encouraging participation from the lower-income groups (Bosworth, Carron and Rhyne 1987: ch. 6).

During his presidential campaign, Michael Dukakis proposed a new scheme (*New York Times*, 8 September 1988, A1 and B11, and Editorial, 11 September). Students would borrow from banks; the federal government would guarantee the loan. Repayment would be a percentage of the individual student's subsequent income, collected alongside the social security contribution. It was claimed that this 'Pay As You Went' scheme would save public money, be equitable, administratively simple, and have few defaults. The scheme went down with the Dukakis campaign.

Reischauer (1989), in what he describes as 'a first cut at a new approach', offers a much more fully articulated social insurance approach to student-loan policy. Students would borrow from a federal trust fund, it being left open whether the funds would be federal or private. Repayment, in the form of an addition to withholdings under the Federal Insurance Contributions Act (FICA), would be a percentage of the individual's income, varying with the amount borrowed. The loan would bear a positive real interest rate. Reischauer argues that real repayments are largely unaffected by fluctuations in nominal interest rates, since such fluctuations generally reflect the rate of inflation which in turn is captured by the buoyancy of wages; thus higher inflation causes higher interest rates, but also, through higher wages, leads to higher repayments. In the basic model it is assumed that repayment will be over an entire working life. Reischauer calculates that under those circumstances a 1 per cent additional contribution would repay a loan of $4 000.

The scheme is an income-contingent loan scheme with no substantial interest subsidy, and with the possibility of private-sector funding. Its main difference from the schemes discussed earlier is that the additional contribution is not 'switched off' once the loan has been repaid, thus introducing redistribution within cohorts of students. The use of the social security mechanism is a major administrative simplification, not least because of its well-defined and already-measured tax base (an option not available in Australia and New Zealand, which have no explicit social security contributions).

4.5 Britain

This section picks up the British story from section 1. It is more personal than the others since, with help and encouragement from Mark Blaug, Alan Peacock and others, I spent much of 1989 opposing an ill-designed government loan proposal and advocating an alternative.

The government loan scheme

This (Department of Education and Science 1988) was published (on the day after the US presidential election, ensuring muted coverage) with the stated objective of reducing the taxpayer cost per student. Under the proposals, students take out a loan to supplement the maintenance grant; the grant is frozen until student support comprises 50 per cent grant and parental contribution, and 50 per cent loan. The loan bears a zero real interest rate, and is repaid in (usually) ten instalments (that is, mortgage-type repayments), suspended for those earning below 85 per cent of the national average. Students borrow Treasury money, but in the original proposal both the issuing of the loan and the collection of repayments were to be administered by the banks.

The scheme has strategic flaws. First, mortgage-type loans are likely to harm access. Given the discussion in section 2.2 there is no need to labour the point. Secondly, the original proposal was that students borrow Treasury money, with repayment collected by the banks. Both legs were misspecified. If students borrow Treasury money, there is no public expenditure saving in the short- or medium-term: and the administrative costs of a completely new repayment system run by the banks are very high, eroding most of the long-term savings. The Government admitted (*Hansard*, WA, 24 July 1989, col. 441) that the scheme produces no cumulative net saving for at least 25 years; even that figure is a gross underestimate, in that it omits any interest charge on the cumulative deficit over those years. Thus the scheme yields no savings for a long time, and hence frees no resources for expansion; at the same time it risks harming access. Even in its own terms the White Paper fails to achieve any desirable objective.

Nor was it liked by the banks, both because they were not prepared to assume the administrative costs associated with a completely new repayment mechanism and because they were concerned about relations with their prospective best customers. For both reasons the banks contemplated participation only if repayments were collected by an arms-length institution, the Student Loans Company, owned jointly by the banks, whose costs would be met by government. The result was one of those peculiar animals designed by a committee – a private-sector publicly funded QUANGO (see Barr 1989b).

In December 1989, however, after a year of discussion with government, the banks pulled out. The Government decided to press ahead by running the Student Loans

Company itself, thus duplicating what the tax/social security authorities do already. As a companion-in-arms put it, the Government behaved just like its predecessors: faced with an ill-conceived loss-making enterprise, it nationalized it. The scheme took effect in October 1990.

The national insurance loan scheme
An alternative proposal (Barnes and Barr 1988; Barr 1989a) was designed with the explicit objectives of expansion and improved access. Its key characteristics are:

(a)   The loan would bear a real interest rate of 3 per cent.
(b)   Repayment would take the form of an addition to the individual's National Insurance Contribution (NIC); an indexed loan equal to half the maintenance grant could be repaid by a graduate with average earnings over 25 years by a 1 per cent addition to the NIC.
(c)   The additional repayment would be 'switched off' once the individual had repaid the loan plus interest. Thus no one would repay more than he/she had borrowed.
(d)   Because repayments (i) bear a realistic real interest rate, and (ii) are secure, it is possible for the money that students borrow (subject to a partial Treasury guarantee) to come from the private sector.

The scheme has various advantages:

(a)   *Expansion and access* are enhanced. Income-contingent repayments do not discourage applicants; and low earners, women working in the home, and unemployed individuals are automatically protected.
(b)   *Administration* is simple and cheap because it 'piggy-backs' on to an existing system and uses a well-established tax base.
(c)   *Security of repayment*:   Defaults are minimal: NICs are hard to evade; and, because they give title to future benefits, there is little incentive to evade. Security also facilitates repayment over an extended period, thus allowing a low repayment rate. Since the asset is long-lived, this arrangement is efficient. Secure repayment also facilitates private-sector funding.
(d)   *Private-sector funds*:   The possibility of funding loans largely from the private sector opens up the possibility of *immediate* public-expenditure savings, thus freeing resources for expansion and proactive measures to improve access.

The scheme, in short, conforms with the criteria set out in section 3.3 (in many ways a tautologous observation, since it was designed to do so).

An obvious question is why the scheme was not adopted (an early version was in ministers' hands several months before the White Paper was published). A possible answer (though one which it has not proved possible to verify) is that the idea of using National Insurance has a public-sector ring to it which is ideologically unacceptable. As in New Zealand, the scheme lives to fight another day.

5   CONCLUSION

Developments in the theoretical literature on the economics of information over the past

20 years have greatly enhanced our understanding of market failure. For instance, it is now possible to show why actuarial insurance is not readily applicable to risks like unemployment (Barr 1987: chs 5 and 8). With hindsight, it is easy to explain the catastrophic failure of unemployment compensation in Britain in the 1920s and early 1930s, and to understand the forces which led to the US Social Security Act of 1935 taking the form it did. The moral of the story is that policy will not work unless the underpinnings are right. The history of student loans illustrates the same point.

The Swedish reforms took effect in January 1989. The Australian reform took effect on the same date; from the same stable, New Zealand considered a very similar set of proposals in 1988 and 1989. The Dukakis – Reischauer proposals were a 1988–9 phenomenon. The British alternative proposals grew at the same time. All four sets of proposals – Swedish, Antipodean, American and British – have the same objectives: expansion and improved access; all derive, implicitly or explicitly, from the arguments in sections 2 and 3; and all, following the same logic, reach broadly the same conclusion. The four sets of proposals arose independently of each other, and the authors spent late-1989 writing letters of agreement to each other.

It is now nearly 30 years since income-contingent loans entered the literature. The theory is well-developed and supported both by the benefit principle and by ability to pay; its logic is producing well-articulated policy proposals; and there are now schemes in operation in at least two countries. Those, like Mark Blaug, who have fought for this outcome should take pleasure from the fact that the time for their idea has finally come.

NOTES

*   Financial support from the Esmée Fairbairn Charitable Trust and the Suntory-Toyota International Centre for Economics and Related Disciplines, London School of Economics and Political Science is gratefully acknowledged. Various colleagues have been very helpful. Gervas Huxley gave me immensely useful comments on earlier work and did much of the institutional research on which this essay draws. John Barnes and Iain Crawford were my companions-in-arms in pressing the case for an alternative to the British government proposals in 1989. Mark Blaug gave me much-needed tutorials on the economics of education literature, and both he and Sir Alan Peacock gave tremendous support as we took up their campaigns of earlier decades. I am grateful to Mark Blaug and Maureen Woodhall for filling in the events of the 1970s, and to Bruce Chapman, Howard Glennerster and Gary Hawke for helpful comments on an earlier draft. None of them should be blamed for remaining errors.

1. Though the use of the terms is often blurred, grants are awarded *inter alia* on the basis of an income test, scholarships on the basis of academic performance. Slightly to oversimplify, grants are income-related, scholarships performance-related.

2. It is a standard proposition in econometrics that omitted independent variables, unless they are orthogonal to the included variables, will cause biased ordinary least squares estimators. Similar problems generally arise with maximum likelihood estimation. The assumption of orthogonality is untenable in the present example, since educational attainments and family background are strongly related.

3. As the result of another 1989 reform, child support from an absent or divorced father in Australia is now also collected through the tax system.

14. The Concentration Process Revisited

Alan Peacock and Ilde Rizzo

INTRODUCTION

It was a happy inspiration on the part of the editors of the Cambridge Surveys of Economic Literature to invite Mark Blaug to write the volume on *The Methodology of Economics* (1980a). The attitude of many professional economists may be summed up in a paraphrase of Goethe's Faust: '*grau is alle Methodologie*', but a lack of attention to the issues which he raised about formulation of economic theories and empirical verification in his justly famous work is to risk falling into the trap of producing dangerously ambiguous conclusions.

This contribution in his honour offers a modest essay in an area of public sector economics in which there would appear to be a strong temptation to develop rather high-flown hypotheses concerning the determinants of the growth of the public sector, which lead to tests which have to rely on unsatisfactory measures of the variables entering the equations in the model. This is not an unusual situation encountered by economists, and Mark Blaug's book contains some graphic examples of members of the profession falling into temptation. It can at least be said by those who have sought explanations of the growth of the public sector that they have generally fought shy of matching grandiose explanations with striking predictions of the future growth of the public sector.

We devote attention to only one area of the debate on government expenditure growth – the relation between that growth and the change in the responsibilities of different layers of government. We begin by re-examining what Peacock and Wiseman (1961) labelled the concentration process (see the next section) which represents a particular way of defining and measuring the degree of centralization of government. The third section discusses and develops the hypotheses which might be derived from the observation of this process and the fourth section illustrates how these hypotheses might be tested. This means that we commit ourselves to the view that 'falsificationism' has a useful part to play in examining the robustness of a particular hypothesis, but that does not commit us to the view that 'goodness of fit' in regression equations would be the reliable, unique guide to the formulation of predictions. Peacock and Wiseman (1961), who might fairly be said to have set the agenda for the modern study of the determinants of government expenditure growth, only claim that the practical outcome may represent no more than 'informed speculation'. As it happens, our tentative conclusions drawn from the empirical evidence (in the fourth section) could not form a suitable basis for some dramatic statement about the interaction between government and citizen behaviour.

THE MEASUREMENT OF CONCENTRATION

The measurement of 'concentration' implies a distinction between those activities controlled by the central government and those controlled by lower layers of government.

To explain the problems encountered in measuring concentration, we take as a point of departure the solution offered by Pommerehne in a pathbreaking study (1977) on the quantitative aspects of federalism. He tests the proposition, amongst others, that the demand for decentralization of government is a function of the degree of inequality of income. Having rightly argued that there is no comprehensive measure of centralization which would satisfy political scientists and economists, he opts for 'an operating measure' of the proportion of central-government consumption in overall government consumption expenditure. Likewise, almost contemporaneously, Wallace Oates (1978), in examining the hypothesis that there is likely to be a historical trend towards centralization, used central government expenditure as a percentage of total government expenditure in order to derive a 'centralization ratio'. In remarking that the available evidence for the hypothesis was scant, he was quick to observe that 'there is no unambiguous, non-arbitrary measure of the extent of centralization'.

Whatever the arguments for these operating measures, they are not those adopted by Peacock and Wiseman. Influenced by British experience, they distinguished between the spending authority and the authority 'effectively responsible' for the expenditure. The distinction would not exist if central government were only responsible for financing its own expenditure, and, correspondingly, lower layers of government financed theirs only from their own revenue sources. The problem arises from the fact that, in many countries, lower layers of government receive grants from central government which, to a greater or lesser extent, are designed to encourage them to pursue policies laid down at the centre. They become 'agents' of the 'principal', that is, the central government. The measure of concentration, and indeed the measure of the degree of centralization, should take this problem into account, and one way of doing so would be to seek to determine the proportion of *centrally financed* consumption (or total) expenditure to total consumption expenditure or all forms of expenditure.

Whilst Peacock and Wiseman may seem a refinement of other measures which do not take into account the power structure within government, its degree of refinement will vary from case to case. As applied to a country such as the UK, it would reflect the change in the relative influence of the central government but in other countries this might not be the case. This could be true of the Federal Republic of Germany in which the division of total revenue is a reflection of the famous *Finanzausgleich*, the bargain struck between the Federal and Länder governments in which the latter play a major role. (For further elaboration, see Neumann 1978.)

Further problems are encountered in defining a satisfactory measure of concentration (or decentralization). In fact, inter-governmental relationships cannot be reduced to a dichotomy, having only financial content. Usually, many layers of government exist, each enjoying various degrees of autonomy, and it is difficult to measure concentration (or decentralization) unambiguously. The institutional features of such a relationship, as those derived from the existence of macroeconomic, legal and planning constraints on lower layers of governments, may play a relevant role as far as the allocation of power among different layers of government is concerned.

The attempts made in the literature to devise a concentration index do not incorporate all these features.

An interesting earlier example is one presented by Scotto (1950) in which the degree of concentration can vary theoretically from 1 (complete centralization) to 0 (complete decentralization) but, as pointed out by Fraschini and Rizzo (1987), it is based solely on the division of government expenditure between the central and lower layers of government. Scotto's approach anticipates the better-known measure of Breton and Scott (1978) who provide a concentration index which is based on the structure of the public sector as illustrated by the number and size of jurisdictions, but this index, too, does not incorporate the institutional features described above.

In addition, the choice of any comprehensive measure is severely constrained by the available data and information. When comparisons among countries are carried out, only the financial 'dimension' of the concentration (decentralization) process can be taken into account while other relevant 'dimensions' such as, for instance, the institutional 'dimension' (planning, legal and macroeconomic constraints imposed by higher layers of government) are left out. These factors can be relevant to countries such as Italy, in which local governments work within very close constraints of this kind.

Again, the Peacock and Wiseman measure, in common with others which concentrate on the public finances, cannot comprehend other ways in which the government may affect the division of resources between the public and private sector. An important problem is presented by the position of public corporations which sell goods and services directly to the private sector. Their operations are only picked up in the form of current transactions between the corporations and the various layers of government; for example, in public subsidies to public corporations' investment. Even in this case, it is normal practice to exclude borrowing and lending transactions. Peacock and Wiseman dealt with this problem by separate consideration of public corporations, but not within the context of the concentration process. A further problem is presented by the extent to which government control over the private sector is exercised by regulation, a point emphasized particularly by Frey (1985). It may be that growth in regulation as an instrument of the various layers of government may be picked up in the general growth in the size of government as conventionally measured, although regulation is normally treated in discussions of the economics of public policy as an alternative to public provision. This position has been strengthened by the growth of privatization measures which envisage the substitution of regulated private agencies and companies for publicly provided services through government departments or public corporations.

Our own view is that there must be sufficient intellectual as well as policy interest in reviewing the relation between the growth of public expenditure and concentration of its control to make it sensible to avoid extending the analysis to cover public corporations and regulation, though we recognize their importance. Moreover, we do not wish to be dogmatic about which measure of concentration is appropriate.

Consequently, within the limits imposed by the available data and information, we use a number of alternative measures in the ensuing analysis, looking at the expenditure as well as at the revenue side of the budget. The institutional dimension is left aside in our analysis except for an attempt to express the difference between countries with and those without a federal constitution. Details of these measures are provided in the fourth section.

HYPOTHESES

In the original analysis of the concentration process Peacock and Wiseman were concerned to show why the growth in public spending in the UK was not inhibited by the traditional institutional structure of government which assigned its different tasks of government to its different layers. Thus, major changes in the taste for government spending, as claimed to operate through a displacement effect, would not be held back by constitutional barriers. In the long run, the structure of government could cease to be a constraint and become a dependent variable. Nor need the removal of constitutional constraints be solely a function of some cataclysmic event such as a war. Long-term changes affecting voter preferences, including extension of the franchise, economic growth and changes in the distribution of income, could alter the relative importance of each layer of government as a system for delivering the service demanded by the electorate.

Peacock and Wiseman's concern to highlight the concentration process was limited to the analysis of an interesting phenomenon, namely, how the change in the relative economic importance of central and local government accompanied the change in the relative economic importance of the public and the private sector. They did indicate that the revelation of this process was of importance to contemporary British discussion on the 'need' to revive local government as a potent force in political life, because it cast doubt on whether this could be done without re-establishing local government control over sources of revenue. Latterly, interest has shifted to the influence of centralization of power on the growth of government spending itself. What we seek to do is to ascertain whether the thrust of this discussion might be affected by using a measure which locates that power in the *control of revenue sources*.

This brings us to our central proposition. We are interested in testing the hypothesis that growth in government expenditure relative to GDP is associated with a concentration process. This process is both the result of the influence of demand factors which confer a comparative advantage on the central government in the delivery of services and also of the effect of concentration of power on the ability of central government to influence the control of supply of services. Thus, as the concentration process gets under way, this offers the opportunity for tax authorities to promote 'fiscal illusion' more effectively, and makes it more difficult for government to police the efficiency of departments supplying the services. The converse of this hypothesis is that countries in which lower layers of government retain their taxing powers will experience a lower level of government expenditure growth relative to GDP. These countries are likely to have 'strong' federal constitutions.

We must make it clear that we are not offering some all-embracing theory of the growth of government expenditure. As both Peacock (forthcoming) and Wiseman (1989) have separately maintained, the search for some such theory is a fruitless task and the econometric techniques which might be used reveal a sterling example of the identification problem. This view, applied to the concentration process, must lead one to be wary about attaching cardinal importance to only one influence on the changing division of tasks between central and lower layers of government. Also, so far as the identification problem is concerned, it would clearly be very difficult, if not impossible, to specify for any country when precisely the concentration process enables the supply influences to assert themselves. For example, Kirchgassner and Pommerehne (1988) in a detailed comparison between two federal countries, the Federal Republic of Germany and Switzerland, find significant differences in their comparative government-expenditure growth, in the composition of government spending and in the division of spending between government authorities. It is conceivable that these differences, by any measure, could be greater than those found between these federations and unitary states – our observation not theirs.

Very sensibly, they inform the reader in detail about the differences in the structure of government, in voters' preferences and opportunities for expressing them, and in the size of country, which could account for differences in each country's experience of fiscal change.

TESTING

At the outset, the difficulty of developing a fully satisfactory measure of the extent of centralization (decentralization) has to be acknowledged. Notwithstanding the theoretical and conceptual relevance of the comprehensive measures of concentration described in the second section, available data limit us to fiscal measures and do not allow us to take into account more meaningful 'dimensions' of the concentration (decentralization) process.

The hypothesis that fiscal decentralization imposes constraints on the growth of public sector will be tested making use of a sample of 19 countries. The International Monetary Fund provides a rich set of data on public expenditure and revenue disaggregated by level of government. These data, however, are available only for a limited number of years, no more than nine or ten, and therefore they do not allow for carrying out a test on a long-run basis.

The international sample encompasses a variety of governmental structures; the relative roles of central and local governments vary both over time and across countries and, therefore, provide a considerable variation in the variables of interest.

In line with the empirical studies in this subject, the phenomenon of fiscal centralization (or decentralization) will be represented using centralization (or decentralization) ratios, given by the central (or local) layer of government share of total revenues or expenditures and by the shares of such an expenditure centrally (or locally) financed.

Some comments are in order. Unlike other studies in the field, this paper will pay attention to both centralization and decentralization ratios; as the empirical tests presented below show, when testing it makes a difference which of these two concepts is used. The plausible theoretical reason for such a conclusion is that in countries where fiscal inter-governmental relations are quantitatively and qualitatively important, neither central expenditure nor revenue necessarily represent the degree of centralization because part of these resources can be transferred (with or without constraints) to lower layers of government. The only indicator which is not affected by such an argument is centrally financed consumption expenditure, but its meaning, however, is likely to be undermined by the fact that a relevant component of the budget, that is, transfer expenditure, is left out. Nor does the reference to central-government consumption expenditure guarantee that concentration is measured correctly across countries. In fact, in some cases, central control on expenditure can be retained using conditional grants. For example, a concentration measure which yielded the same result for two countries could be misleading if the central control through conditional grants operated strictly in one country and not in the other.

In the literature the empirical evidence on the relation between fiscal centralization and the size of public sector is far from being conclusive. Among the ratios studied in the field, particular attention will be paid to Oates (1985), because his analysis is the closest to ours as far as the sample is concerned.

Oates (1985: 754) finds that 'government size seems to have little relation to the degree of centralization in the public sector'. Such a conclusion is reached using as explanatory variables only centralization ratios (that is, central government shares of total government revenue and of total public expenditure) which encounter the above-mentioned difficulties, for in each country such a ratio eventually implies a different degree of central–local fiscal relations. The fact that intergovernmental grants are excluded from the grantor's expenditure partially mitigates such a problem in so far as the centralization ratio based on the expenditure side of the budget is used. However, the fact that such exclusion obviously cannot take into account the nature of these grants must be borne in mind when using a cross-section sample; the relative weight of conditional and unconditional grants vary across countries and, therefore, the centralization ratio should take into account such a factor. It might therefore be argued that the results reached by Oates could be partially influenced by the indicators used.

For the same reasons put forward by Oates (1985: 751), the 'concentration' hypothesis is tested by using a series of *ad hoc* reduced form equations.

As in most studies in the field, the dependent variable is given by a measure of the size of the public sector and two different measures are used:

> REVGDP, the ratio of general government total revenue to GDP;
> EXPGDP, the ratio of general government total expenditure to GDP.

The appropriate measure of the extent of concentration (or decentralization) is less straightforward and, therefore, different plausible indicators of concentration (decentralization) will be used.

In line with Oates' study and also that of Peltzman, the fiscal measures of the extent of centralization used are:

> CRETRE, the fraction of total general revenues going to the central government;
> NCETEX, the fraction of total public expenditure attributable to the central government, net of the grants to lower layers of government.

Moreover, in order to represent centralization in a more complete way, a joint analysis of central expenditure and its means of financing is attempted and the following indicator is constructed:

> CTACEX, central expenditure centrally financed.

Furthermore, in line with the arguments expounded above, three different measures of the extent of decentralization are used:

> LRETRE, the fraction of total general revenue going to the local governments;
> LEXTEX, the fraction of total public expenditure attributable to local governments;
> LTALEX, local expenditure locally financed.

Revenue and expenditure data are presented, respectively, in Tables 14.1 and 14.2. Dependent as well as independent variables have been computed for the most recent year for which data were available for most of the countries, that is, 1986; in a few cases, however, these variables go back as far as 1981.

Table 14.1: Revenue by layers of government (1986) (millions or billions of national currencies)

	1	2 General govt total	3	4 Central govt total	5	6 Local govt total	7
	GDP	revenue	2/1 REVGDP	revenue	4/2 CRETRE	revenue	6/2 LRETRE
Australia*	246470	86242	0.350	65984	0.765	22612	0.262
Austria*	1432	684	0.478	494	0.722	197	0.288
Belgium	5148	2407	0.468	2233	0.928	142	0.059
Canada* (1985)	479450	192664	0.402	91100	0.473	101564	0.527
Denmark	667140	397191	0.595	279024	0.702	112714	0.284
Finland	357236	159142	0.445	111091	0.698	50095	0.315
France	5035	2349	0.467	2088	0.889	268	0.114
West Germany*	1937	897	0.463	573	0.639	317	0.353
Greece (1982)	2575	943	0.366	854	0.906	29	0.031
Ireland	18239	8409	0.461	7830	0.931	772	0.092
Luxembourg (1985)	251020	103633	0.413	103887	1.002	8333	0.080
Netherlands*	430	233	0.542	223	0.957	13	0.056
New Zealand (1981)	27831	10945	0.393	9753	0.891	1192	0.109
Norway	514580	297560	0.578	245670	0.826	58817	0.198
Spain	32085	10724	0.334	9353	0.872	1007	0.094
Sweden	934	519	0.556	378	0.728	184	0.355
Switzerland* (1984)	214100	82088	0.383	44215	0.539	38769	0.472
United Kingdom	377460	163418	0.433	142949	0.875	25141	0.154
United States*	4194	1397	0.333	823	0.589	458	0.328

Source: IMF, *Government Statistics, 1988* and *International Financial Statistics, 1988*

Note:
* in local government data state/provincial government figures are included.

Table 14.3 shows the summary statistics for the sample. The variable representing the size of the public sector in terms of expenditure varies from a maximum of 0.59 to a minimum of 0.37 with a mean value of 0.47. Similar variations occur when the size of the public sector is measured in terms of revenue: in this case, the indicator varies from 0.60 to 0.33, with a mean value of 0.44.

The extent of fiscal centralization exhibits more marked variations within the sample, going from a maximum of complete centralization of 1 to a minimum around 0.5. Marked variations also characterize the extent of decentralization, defined as local government share of total revenue and total expenditure: the former goes from 0.53 to 0.03, while the latter ranges from 0.72 to 0.04. Analogous variations characterize the extent of decentralization when it is measured in its 'purest' form, that is, in terms of the share of local expenditure locally financed; in this case, the indicator varies from 0.72 to 0.03, with a mean value of 0.41.

Table 14.3 also presents an analysis of the relationships existing among the above

Table 14.2: Public expenditure by layers of government (1986) (millions or billions of national currencies)

	1	2	3	4	5	6	7	8	9	10	11	12	13
	GDP	General govt total expend.	2/1	Central govt total expend.	Transfer to other level of govt	4-5	6/2	Local govt total expend.	8/2	Central govt tax revenue	10/4	Local govt tax revenue	12/8
			EXPGDP				NCETEX		LEXTEX		CTACEX		LTALEX
Australia*	246470	92859	0.377	70998	20997	50001	0.538	44567	0.480	58576	0.825	13625	0.306
Austria*	1432	742	0.518	569	46	523	0.705	198	0.267	455	0.800	143	0.722
Belgium	5148	2878	0.559	2713	181	2532	0.880	349	0.121	2152	0.793	119	0.341
Canada* (1985)	479450	180320	0.376	117202	23144	94058	0.522	129042	0.716	79277	0.676	81513	0.632
Denmark	667140	370636	0.556	251787	86955	164832	0.445	200333	0.541	242761	0.964	92193	0.460
Finland	357236	154497	0.432	110383	23724	86659	0.561	72874	0.472	100893	0.914	33092	0.454
France	5035	2494	0.495	2239	152	2087	0.837	433	0.174	1914	0.855	191	0.441
West Germany*	1937	919	0.474	583	31	552	0.601	365	0.397	531	0.911	223	0.611
Greece (1982)	2575	1475	0.573	1350	0	1350	0.915	54	0.037	834	0.618	5	0.093
Ireland	18239	10470	0.574	9791	2029	7762	0.741	3102	0.296	7035	0.719	167	0.054
Luxembourg (1985)	251020	93429	0.372	93193	7517	85676	0.917	15649	0.167	92711	0.995	6593	0.421
Netherlands*	430	256	0.595	243	63	180	0.703	80	0.313	190	0.782	2	0.025
New Zealand (1981)	27831	12354	0.444	11075	252	10823	0.876	1551	0.126	8814	0.796	608	0.392
Norway	514580	257023	0.499	205711	37055	168656	0.656	86185	0.335	204204	0.993	48143	0.559
Spain	32085	12522	0.390	11036	1360	9676	0.773	1636	0.131	8650	0.784	671	0.410
Sweden	934	553	0.592	407	55	352	0.637	242	0.438	318	0.781	138	0.570
Switzerland* (1984)	214100	80659	0.377	44859	5492	39367	0.488	44503	0.552	41793	0.932	26909	0.605
United Kingdom	377460	168923	0.448	148338	22481	125857	0.745	48488	0.287	128366	0.865	15731	0.324
United States*	4194	1549	0.369	1032	101	931	0.601	621	0.401	745	0.722	290	0.467

Source: IMF, Government Statistics, 1988 and International Financial Statistics, 1988

Note:
* in local government data state/provincial government figures are included.

Table 14.3: Summary statistics and correlation coefficient

Series	Mean	S.D.	Maximum	Minimum
REVGDP	0.4452632	0.0796854	0.5950000	0.3330000
EXPGDP	0.4747368	0.0835177	0.5950000	0.3690000
NCETEX	0.6916316	0.1483094	0.9170000	0.4450000
CRETRE	0.7858947	0.1513153	1.0020000	0.4730000
CTACEX	0.8276316	0.1055226	0.9950000	0.6180000
LEXTEX	0.3290000	0.1788202	0.7160000	0.0370000
LRETRE	0.2195263	0.1478796	0.5270000	0.0310000
LTALEX	0.4151053	0.1943470	0.7220000	0.0250000

Correlation		
REVGDP, REVGDP	1.0000000
REVGDP, NCETEX	−0.1834154
REVGDP, CRETRE	0.1213135
REVGDP, CTACEX	0.4022190
REVGDP, LEXTEX	0.1638086
REVGDP, LRETRE	−0.0124541
REVGDP, LTALEX	0.0844402
EXPGDP, EXPGDP	1.0000000
EXPGDP, NCETEX	0.2245156
EXPGDP, CRETRE	0.4048289
EXPGDP, CTACEX	−0.2009835
EXPGDP, LEXTEX	−0.2784092
EXPGDP, LRETRE	−0.3943292
EXPGDP, LTALEX	−0.3942372

variables as given by the correlation coefficient. The correlation between the size of public sector (EXPGDP) and the extent of centralization and decentralization is strong in some cases and almost always respectively positive and negative. This result is as expected for the indicators representing the centralization phenomenon (NCETEX and CRETRE) as well as for the decentralization indicators (LEXTEX, LRETRE, LTALEX), showing that local governments, especially when they are accountable, may exert negative effects on public spending. No plausible explanation can be found for the negative relation linking EXPGDP to CTACEX nor for the results obtained when the correlation between the size of public revenue and the above-mentioned variables is investigated. However, the fact that REVGDP does not take into account the size of the public-sector deficit – which differs in the various countries in the sample – might provide a biased measure of the size of the public sector in a cross-section analysis. So far, therefore, no clear relation seems to be established between the degree of centralization (decentralization) in the public sector and government size.

Looking at the regression analysis, some comments are in order. Analogous conclusions, so far, can be reached on the basis of the regression results presented in Table 14.4.

Table 14.4: *Estimated regression equations*

(1)	EXPGDP	=	−0.68	+	0.19	NCETEX	$\bar{R}^2$ =	0.003
			(8.06)		(1.02)		F =	1.05
(2)	EXPGDP	=	−0.66	+	0.37	CRETRE	$\bar{R}^2$ =	0.14
			(10.82)		(1.99)		F =	3.98
(3)	EXPGDP	=	0.81	−	0.24	CTACEX	$\bar{R}^2$ =	0.03
			(10.56)		(0.74)		F =	0.55
(4)	EXPGDP	=	−0.82	−	0.05	LEXTEX	$\bar{R}^2$ =	0.03
			(12.66)		(1.28)		F =	1.63
(5)	EXPGDP	=	−0.92	−	0.09	LRETRE	$\bar{R}^2$ =	0.12
			(9.75)		(1.86)		F =	3.48
(6)	EXPGDP	=	−0.87	−	0.10	LTALEX*	$\bar{R}^2$ =	0.19
			(14.54)		(2.27)		F =	5.17
(7)	EXPGDP	=	−0.89	+	0.19	DUMMY*	$\bar{R}^2$ =	0.21
			(13.78)		(2.41)		F =	5.80
(8)	REVGDP	=	−0.87	−	0.12	NCETEX	$\bar{R}^2$ =	0.04
			(10.07)		(0.60)		F =	0.35
(9)	REVGDP	=	−0.79	+	0.14	CRETRE	$\bar{R}^2$ =	0.03
			(11.75)		(0.67)		F =	0.44
(10)	REVGDP	=	−0.72	+	0.55	CTACEX	$\bar{R}^2$ =	0.11
			(10.08)		(1.81)		F =	3.29
(11)	REVGDP	=	−0.76	+	0.04	LEXTEX	$\bar{R}^2$ =	0.03
			(11.66)		(1.22)		F =	1.48
(12)	REVGDP	=	−0.80	+	0.01	LRETRE	$\bar{R}^2$ =	0.05
			(7.75)		(0.25)		F =	0.06
(13)	REVGDP	=	−0.84	−	0.015	LTALEX	$\bar{R}^2$ =	0.05
			(12.41)		(0.31)		F =	0.09
(14)	REVGDP	=	−0.92	+	0.14	DUMMY	$\bar{R}^2$ =	0.10
			(13.38)		(1.71)		F =	2.92

Note:
The numbers in parentheses below the estimated coefficients are the absolute values of the t-statistic. An asterisk indicates that the estimated coefficient is statistically significant at the 0.05 level (using a two-tail test). All the equations are in logarithmic form.

To explore alternative ways of testing another variable, that is, the existence of a federal constitution, as a proxy for the fiscal autonomy of decentralized governments, has been added to the above-mentioned indicators. A dummy variable has been used equal to zero for federal countries and equal to one for unitary countries. (See equation 14, Table 14.4.) Looking at the equations 1 to 6, where government size is measured in terms of expenditure, the only results providing some support to our hypothesis are equation 5, 6 and 7 which tells us that accountable local governments, indeed, may imply a limit to government growth. Equation 3 shows counter-intuitive results; in other equations explanatory variables exhibit the correct sign but are not significant. More controversial results are obtained when government size is measured in terms of revenue. The variables with the expected sign (equations 9, 10, 13, 14) are not significant while the others (equations 8, 11 and 12) are neither significant nor correct in sign. Thus, no clear conclusion can be drawn from the above results.

CONCLUDING REMARK

The results reached so far neither contradict our hypothesis nor support it. Some further problems ought to be outlined. The overall explanatory power of the equations is poor as well as their significance. Low values of R^2 are common in most cross-section studies and can be justified on the grounds that only one explanatory variable is employed. (Analogous problems are present in Oates's study for the equations when only one variable is used.) Moreover, some problems of testing may originate with the small number of observations used; therefore, from the above OLS results the conclusions must be drawn with caution, because of the lack of degrees of freedom. To improve the analysis further developments might take three forms:

(a) Other variables should be included in the equation given that the low values of F and R^2 would suggest that some relevant variables have been omitted. We have begun preliminary work on constructing regression equations which take account of such influences as past values of the size of the public sector (LAGEXP), income per capita (INCPC) and population (POPULA). The introduction of INCPC and POPULA as additional variables in the Table 14.4 equations does not improve explanatory power. However, equation performance improves markedly if EXPGDP becomes a function of LEXTEC, ITALEX and LAGEXP. Combined with LAGEXP, ITALEX outperforms LEXTEX, suggesting that decentralization has a constraining influence on growth of governnment expenditure when local expenditure has to be locally financed, that is, when local governments are accountable to the local electorate.

(b) More satisfactory indicators might be found to express the concentration (decentralization) phenomenon.

(c) The sample size should be enlarged.

Perhaps Peltzman is correct in his conclusion based on CRETRE only, that 'neither the extent of centralization nor small changes in centralization seem to explain much of the growth of government'. Our own findings lead us to reserve judgement.

Appendix. Mark Blaug: Bibliography, 1956–90

BOOKS

(A) Economic Theory, History of Economic Thought, Economic Methodology

Ricardian Economics. A Historical Study, New Haven, Conn.: Yale University Press, 1958. Reprinted Westport, Conn.: Greenwood Press, 1974. Translation in Japanese, with special preface, Tokyo: Bokutakusha, 1981.

Economic Theory in Retrospect, Homewood, Ill.: Richard D. Irwin, 1962. London: Heinemann Educational Books, 1964. Translation in Japanese as *Keizai riron no rekishi*, Tokyo: Keizai Shimpo Sha, 3 vols, 1966–71. Translation in Spanish, Barcelona: Editoria Luis Miracle, 1968. Second English edition, 1968. Translation in Italian as *Storia e Critica della Teoria Economica*, Turino: Editore Boringhieri, 1970. Translation in German as *Systematische Theoriegeschichte der Okonomie*, Munich: Nymphen-burger Verlagshandlung, 3 vols, 1971–5. Translation in Portuguese, Lisbon: A. M. Teizeira, 1976. Third English edition, Cambridge University Press, 1979. Translation in Japanese, Tokyo: Keizai Shimpo Sha, 3 vols, 1981–3. Translation in French as *La Pensée economique: origine et developpement*, Paris: Economica, 1981. Translation in Spanish, Madrid: Fondo de Cultura Economica, 1984. Translation in Portuguese, Lisbon Publicaco Dom Quixote Lda, 1985. Fourth English edition, Cambridge University Press, 1985. Translation in French, Paris: Economica, 1986; Translation in Portuguese, Lisbon: Publicacoes Dom Quixote, 1989.

Cambridge Revolution? A Critical Analysis of Cambridge Theories of Value and Distribution, London: Institute of Economic Affairs, 1974, 1975. Translation in Japanese, Tokyo: Toyo Keizai Shimpo Sha, 1977. Translation in Italian, Rome: Liguori Editore, 1978.

The Cambridge Debate on the Theory of Capital and Distribution, ed. G. Caravale, Perugia: Universita degli Studi di Perugia, Estratto N. 4, 1978. Reprinted in *The Crisis in Economic Theories*, ed. G. Caravale, Milan: Franco Angeli Editore, 1983.

A Methodological Appraisal of Marxian Economics, De Vries Foundation Lectures, 1979, Amsterdam: North-Holland, 1980.

The Methodology of Economics, or How Economists Explain, Cambridge: Cambridge University Press, 1980. Translation in French, Paris: Economica, 1982. Translation in Spanish, Madrid: Alianza Editorial, 1985.

(with P. Sturges), *Who's Who in Economics: A Biographical Dictionary of Major Economists, 1700–1980*, Brighton, Sussex: Harvester Press, 1982. Cambridge, Mass.: MIT Press, 1982. Second edition, 1986.

Great Economists since Keynes: An Introduction to the Lives and Works of 100 Modern

Economists, Brighton, Sussex: Harvester Press; New York: Barnes & Noble, 1985; New York: Cambridge University Press, 1988.

Great Economists before Keynes: An Introduction to the Lives and Works of 100 Economists of the Past, Brighton, Sussex: Harvester Press, 1986; Atlantic Highlands, N.J.: Humanities Press International, 1986; Cambridge: Cambridge University Press, 1988.

Economic History and the History of Economics, Brighton, Sussex: Harvester Press; New York: New York University Press, 1986. Aldershot, Hants: Edward Elgar, 1987.

Economics through the Looking Glass: The Distorted Perspective of Economics. The New Palgrave Dictionary, London: Institute of Economic Affairs, 1988.

Keynes: Life, Ideas, Legacy, London: Macmillan, 1989.

Economic Theories: True or False? Aldershot, Hants: Edward Elgar, 1990.

(B)   Economics of the Arts

Editor, *The Economics of the Arts*, with a preface by W. J. Baumol, London: Martin Robertson, 1976; New York: Praeger Books, 1976.

(C)   Economics of Education

Economics of Education: A Selected Annotated Bibliography. London: Pergamon Press, 1967. Second enlarged edition, 1970. Third enlarged edition, 1978.

(with M. H. Peston and A. Ziderman) *The Utilisation of Educated Manpower in Industry*, London: Oliver & Boyd, 1967.

Special Consulting Editor, *World Yearbook of Education, 1967. Educational Planning*, ed. J. A. Lauwerys, G. Z. F. Bereday and M. Blaug, London: Evans, 1967.

Editor, *Penguin Modern Economics: Economics of Education 1, 2*, London: Penguin Books, 1969, 1970. Spanish translation, Madrid: Editorial Tecnos, 1972.

(with P. R. G. Layard and M. A. Woodhall) *The Causes of Graduate Unemployment in India*, London: Allen Lane, The Penguin Press, 1969.

An Introduction to the Economics of Education, London: Allen Lane, The Penguin Press, 1970; Penguin Books, 1972. Translation in Portuguese, Lisbon: Editora Globo, 1975. Reprinted as Open University Setbook, 1977. Translation in Spanish, Mexico City: Biblioteca Aguilar, 1982.

(with B. Ahamad) *The Practice of Manpower Forecasting: A Collection of Case Studies*, Amsterdam: Elsevier, 1972.

Education and the Employment Problem in Developing Countries, Geneva: ILO and Macmillan Company of India, 1973. Translation in French, Geneva: ILO, 1974.

(with Inter-Agency Team) *Employment and Unemployment in Ethiopia, Report of an Exploratory Mission*, Geneva: ILO, 1974.

(with Inter-Agency Team, headed by G. Ranis), *A Programme of Employment, Equity and Growth for the Philippines*, Geneva: ILO, 1974.

(with Inter-Agency Team, headed by J. Faaland) *Growth, Employment and Equity. A Comprehensive Development Strategy for the Sudan*, Geneva: ILO, 1976.

(with ILO Team, headed by S. Nigam) *Lesotho, Options for a Dependent Economy*, Addis Ababa: JASPA Employment Advisory Mission, 1979.

Educacion y Empleo, Madrid: Instituto de Estudios Economicos, 1981.

Economics of Education and the Education of an Economist, Aldershot, Hants: Edward Elgar, 1987.

ARTICLES AND PAMPHLETS

(A)   Economic Theory, History of Economic Thought, Economic Methodology

'The Empirical Content of Ricardian Economics', *Journal of Political Economy*, February
  1956; reprinted in *David Ricardo: Critical Assessments*, ed. J. C. Wood (London:
  Croom Helm, 1985).
'The Classical Economists and the Factory Acts: a Re-examination', *Quarterly Journal of
  Economics*, May 1959; reprinted in *The Classical Economists and Economic Policy*,
  ed. A. W. Coats, London: Methuen, 1971.
'Welfare Indices in the Wealth of Nations', *Southern Economic Journal*, October 1959;
  reprinted in *Adam Smith: Critical Assessments*, ed. J. C. Wood, London: Croom Helm,
  1984.
'Technical Change in Marxian Economics', *Kyklos*, xiii, (4), 1960; reprinted in *Marx and
  Modern Economics*, ed. D. Horowitz, London: McGibbon & Kee, 1968.
'Economic Imperialism Revisited', *Yale Review*, Spring 1961; reprinted in *Problem i
  Varldekonomius Historia*, ed. R. Bunte and L. Jorberg, Lund: Gleerups, 1969; and
  Economic Imperialism: A Book of Readings, ed. K. E. Boulding and T. Mukerjee,
  Ann Arbor, Mich.: University of Michigan Press, 1972.
'A Survey of the Theory of Process Innovation', *Economica*, February 1963, reprinted in
  Penguin Modern Economics: Economics of Technological Change, ed. N. Rosenberg,
  London: Penguin Books, 1971.
'A Case of Emperor's Clothes: Perroux's Theories of Economic Domination', *Kyklos*,
  xvii, (4), 1964.
Introduction to Irwin Paperback Classics in Economics: *A. Smith, The Wealth of Nations;
  T. R. Malthus, An Essay on the Principles of Population*, Homewood: Ill.: Richard D.
  Irwin, 1964.
'Economic Theory and Economic History in Great Britain, 1650–1776', *Past and
  Present*, Summer 1965.
'David Ricardo', 'John Ramsay McCulloch' and 'Thomas Robert Malthus', *International
  Encyclopedia of the Social Sciences*, ed. D. L. Sills, London and New York: Macmillan,
  1968.
'Was There a Marginal Revolution?', *History of Political Economy*, Fall 1972; reprinted
  in *The Marginal Revolution in Economics*, ed. R. D. C. Black, A. W. Coats, C. D. W.
  Goodwin, Durham, N.C.: Duke University Press, 1973. Translation in Japanese,
  Tokyo: Keiza Shimpo Sha, 1974.
'Economics', *Encyclopedia Britannica, Macropaedia*, vol. vi, fifteenth edition, Chicago:
  Encyclopedia Britannica, 1974.
'The Economics of Education in English Classical Political Economy: a Re-examination',
  in *Essays on Adam Smith*, ed. T. Wilson and A. S. Skinner, Oxford: Clarendon Press,
  1976. Translation in German in *Ethik, Wirtschaft und Staat. Adam Smith's Politische
  Okonomie Heute*, ed. H. C. Recktenwald, Darmstadt: Wissenschaftliche Besuchgesell-
  schaft, 1985.
'Kuhn vs. Lakatos, or Paradigms vs. Research Programmes in the History of Economics',
  History of Political Economy, January 1976; reprinted in *Method and Appraisal in
  Economics*, ed. S. Latsis, Cambridge: Cambridge University Press, 1976. Spanish
  translation, *Revista Espanola de Economica*, March–April 1976.
'Discussion – The Reappraisal of Keynes' Economics: an Appraisal', in *Current Economic*

Problems, ed. M. Parkin and A. R. Nobay, Manchester: Manchester University Press, 1976.

'The German Hegemony of Location Theory: a Puzzle in the History of Economic Thought', *History of Political Economy*, Spring 1979.

'Economic Methodology in One Easy Lesson', *British Review of Economic Issues*, May 1980.

'Economics of David Ricardo', *The Times Literary Supplement*, 11 July 1980.

'Cambridge School', 'Comparative Advantage Theory', 'Labor Theory of Value' and 'Manchester School, in *Encyclopedia of Economics*, ed. D. Greenwald, New York: McGraw-Hill, 1982.

'Another Look at the Labour Reduction Problem in Marx', in *Classical and Marxian Political Economy: Essays in Honour of Ronald L. Meek*, ed. I. Bradley and M. Howard, London: Macmillan, 1982.

'Ricardo e il problema della politica economica', *Revista di Politica Economica*, May 1983. English translation in *Gli Economisti e la Politica Economica*, ed. P. Roggi, Naples: Edizione Scientifiche Italiane, 1985.

'Marx, Schumpeter y la teoria del empresario', *Revista de Occidente*, February–March 1983.

'A Methodological Appraisal of Radical Economics', in *Methodological Controversy in Economics: Historical Essays in Honor of T. W. Hutchison*, ed. A. W. Coats, Greenwich, Conn.: JAI Press, 1983.

'Our Methodological Crisis: Discussion', in *Economics in Disarray*, ed. G. Routh and P. J. D. Wiles, Oxford: Basil Blackwell, 1985.

'The Economics of Johann von Thunen', in *Research in the History of Economic Thought and Methodology*, vol. 3, ed. W. J. Samuels, Greenwich, Conn.: JAI Press, 1985.

'What Ricardo Said and What Ricardo Meant', in *The Legacy of Ricardo*, ed. G. A. Caravale, Oxford: Basil Blackwell, 1985.

'Marginal Cost Pricing: No Empty Box', in *Public Choice, Public Finance and Public Policy*, ed. D. Greenaway and G. K. Shaw, Oxford: Blackwell, 1985.

'Comment on D. W. Hands, *Karl Popper and Economic Methodology: A New Look*', *Economics and Philosophy*, I, (2), October 1985.

'The Entrepreneur in Marx and Schumpeter', in *Marx, Schumpeter, Keynes: A Centenary Celebration of Dissent*, ed. S. W. Helburn and D. Bramhall, New York: M. E. Sharpe, 1986. Translation in Japanese in *Keizai-hyoron*, September 1985.

'Classical Economics', 'Circulating Capital', 'Iron Law of Wages', 'Productive and Unproductive Consumption', 'Hutcheson, Terence Wilmot' and 'Storch, Heinrich Friedrich von', in *The New Palgrave: A Dictionary of Economic Theory and Doctrine*, ed. J. Eatwell, M. Millgate and P. Newman, London: Macmillan, 1987.

'On a Severe Case of Paranoia in the History of Economic Thought', *History of Economic Thought Newsletter*, 38, Spring 1987.

'Commentary', in *Classical Political Economy: A Survey of Recent Literature*, ed. W. O. Thweatt, Boston, Mass.: Kluwer, 1987.

'Second Thoughts on the Keynesian Revolution', *Rassegna Economics*, 4, 1988.

'John Hicks and the Methodology of Economics', in *The Popperian Legacy in Economics*, ed. N. de Marchi, London: Cambridge University Press, 1988.

'Das Walrasianische Gleichgewicht – Fortschritt Odes Sackgasse?', in *Vadeinecum Zu einem Zentralen Klassiker der Okomiscben Statik*, ed. H. C. Recktenwald *et al.*, Dusseldorf: Verlag Wirtschaft und Finanzen, 1988.

'Nicholas Kaldor, 1908–86', in *Pioneers of Modern Economics in Britain*, vol. II, ed. D. A. Greenaway and J. R. Presley, London: Macmillan, 1989.

(B)   Economic History

'The Productivity of Capital in the Lancashire Cotton Industry During the Nineteenth Century', *Economic History Review*, April 1961; reprinted in *Business History: Selected Readings*, ed. K. A. Tucker, London: Frank Cass, 1977.
'The Myth of the Old Poor Law and the Making of the New', *Journal of Economic History*, June 1963; reprinted in *Essays in Social History*, ed. M. W. Flinn and T. C. Smout, Oxford: Clarendon Press, 1974.
'The Poor Law Report Re-examined', *Journal of Economic History*, June 1964.

(C)   Economics of the Arts

(with K. King) 'Does the Arts Council Know What it is Doing? An Inquiry into Public Patronage of the Arts', *Encounter*, September 1973; 'Reply to Comments', ibid., December 1973; reprinted in *The Economics of the Arts*, ed. M. Blaug, London: Martin Robertson, 1976.
(with K. King) 'Is the Arts Council Cost-Effective?', *New Society*, 3 January 1974.
'Rationalising Public Expenditure – The Arts', in *Public Expenditure: Allocation between Competing Ends*, ed. M. V. Posner, London: Cambridge University Press, 1977; reprinted in *The Economics of the Arts*, ed. M. Blaug, London: Martin Robertson, 1976.
'Why Are Covent Garden Seat Prices So High?', London: Royal Opera House, 1976; reprinted in *Journal of Cultural Economics*, June 1978.
'A Postscript to the Edinburgh Conference on Cultural Economics', in *Economic Policy for the Arts*, ed. W. S. Hendon, V. S. Shanahan, A. J. MacDonald, Cambridge, Mass.: ABT Books, 1980.
'Justification for Subsidies to the Arts: a reply to F. F. Ridley', *Journal of Cultural Economics*, June 1983.

(D)   Economics of Education

(with M. Woodhall) 'Productivity Trends in British University Education, 1938–62', *Minerva*, Summer 1965; reprinted in *Economics of Education*, ed. D. C. Rogers and H. C. Richlin, New York: The Free Press, 1972.
'The Rate of Return on Investment in Education in Great Britain', *Manchester School*, September 1965; reprinted in *Nutzen–Kosten–Analyse und Programmbudget*, ed. H. C. Recktenwald, Tubingen: J. C. B. Mohr, 1970, and in *Penguin Modern Economics: Economics of Education 1*, ed. M. Blaug, London: Penguin Books, 1969.
'An Economic Interpretation of the Private Demand for Education', *Economica*, May 1966; reprinted in *Bildungsplanung: Ansatze, Modelle, Probleme*, ed. K. Hufner and J. Naumann, Stuttgart: Ernst Klett Verlag, 1971.
'Loans for Students?', *New Society*, October 1966.
'Literacy and Economic Development', *School Review*, Winter 1966.
'Economic Evaluation of Experimental Literacy Projects', Paris: UNESCO, 1966 (processed).

'The Role of Education in the Enlargement of the Exchange Economy in Middle Africa: the English-Speaking Countries', Paris: UNESCO, 1966 (processed).

'Economic Aspects for Vouchers for Education', in *Education: A Framework for Choice. Papers on Historical, Economic and Administrative Aspects of Choice in Education and its Finance*, London: Institute of Economic Affairs, 1967.

'Approaches to Educational Planning', *Economic Journal*, June 1967; reprinted in *Human Capital Formation and Manpower Development*, ed. R. A. Wykstra, London: Collier-Macmillan, 1971.

'The Private and the Social Returns on Investment in Education: Some Results for Great Britain', *Journal of Human Resources*, Summer 1967.

'A Cost-Benefit Approach to Educational Planning in Developing Countries', Report EC-157, Washington, D.C.: International Bank for Reconstruction and Development, 1967 (processed).

'Functional Literacy in Developing Countries: a Trend Report on Current Research Based on a Selective Annotated Bibliography', Paris: UNESCO, 1967 (processed).

(with M. Woodhall) 'Productivity Trends in British Secondary Education, 1950–63', *Sociology of Education*, Winter 1968.

'Loans', in *Crisis in the Classroom*, ed. N. Smart, London: Daily Mirror Books, 1968.

'The Productivity of Universities', in *Universities and Productivity. Universities' Conference, Spring 1968*, London: Association of University Teachers, 1968; reprinted in *Penguin Modern Economics: Economics of Education 2*, ed. M. Blaug, London: Penguin Books, 1970.

'Selectivity in Education', in *Social Services for All?*, Part 2, Fabian Tract 383, London: Fabian Society, 1968.

'Cost-Benefit and Cost-Effectiveness Analysis of Education', in *OECD Expert Meeting on Budgeting, Programme Analysis and Cost-Effectiveness in Educational Planning*, Paris: OECD, 1969.

(with M. Woodhall) 'Variations in Costs and Productivity of British Primary and Secondary Education', in *Economics of Education in Transition*, ed. K. Hufner and J. Naumann, Stuttgart: Ernst Klett Verlag, 1969.

(with K. Gannicott) 'Manpower Forecasting Since Robbins: a Science Lobby in Action', *Higher Education Review*, Autumn 1969; reprinted in *Planning of Higher Education*, ed. T. Burgess, London: Cornmarket Press, 1973.

'Raising the School Leaving Age: Bribery vs. Compulsion', *Higher Education Review*, Autumn 1970.

'Comments on the Work of OECD', in *Occupational and Educational Structures of the Labour Force and Levels of Economic Development*, Paris: OECD, 1970.

'Case Study of the United Kingdom. Comparative Analysis of Educational Expenditures in Member Countries since 1950', DAS/EID/69.4, Paris: OECD, 1970 (processed).

'A Post-Mortem of Manpower Forecasts in Thailand', *Journal of Development Studies*, October 1971.

'The Rate of Return on Investment in Education in Thailand. A Report to the National Planning Committee of Thailand'. Bangkok: National Council, 1971 (processed).

Chapter 2 in *Economic Situation and Prospects of India*, vol. i, *The Main Report*, Washington, D.C.: IBRD, South Asia Department, 1971.

'Education, Economic Situation and Prospects of India, 1971', *Bulletin of the Institute of Development Studies: Diplomas for Development?*, Brighton, Sussex: University of Sussex, June 1971.

'The Correlation between Education and Earnings: What Does it Signify?, *Higher Education*, February 1972. 'Reply to Comments', ibid., November 1972. French translation, *Revue Economique*, November 1971.

'Economics of Educational Planning in Developing Countries', *Prospects: UNESCO Quarterly Review of Education*, Winter 1972; 'Reply to Comments', ibid., Winter 1973.

'Educated Unemployment in Asia: a Contrast Between India and the Philippines', *Philippine Economic Journal*, xi, (1), 1972.

'Discussion – University Efficiency and University Finance', in *Essays in Modern Economics*, ed. M. Parkin and A. R. Nobay, London: McGraw-Hill, 1973.

'Environment, Genotype and the Luck of the Rich: Jencks' Inequality', *The Times Higher Education Supplement*, 22 June 1973.

'Employment and Unemployment in Ethiopia', *International Labour Review*, August 1974.

'An Economic Analysis of Personal Earnings in Thailand', *Economic Development and Cultural Change*, October 1974.

Taped interview, 'The Economics of Education', London: Sussex Tapes, 1974.

Taped debate (with G. Williams), 'The Economics of Education', London: Audio Learnings, 1974.

'Educational Policy and the Economics of Education: Some Practical Lessons for Educational Planners in Developing Countries', in *Education and Development Reconsidered: The Bellagio Conference Papers*, ed. F. C. Ward, New York: Praeger, 1974.

(with R. Dore) 'Education and Employment: Economic Survey of Asia and the Far East 1973', part 1. Colombo: UNECAFE, 1974.

'Nuevas Exploraciones Acerca del Valor Economico de la Educacion', *Revista de Economica Latinoamericana*, x, (39), 1974; and *Cuadernos de economia*, ii, (5), September–December 1974.

'Discussion – Cost-Benefit Analysis of Government Training Centres in Scotland: Appraisal', in *Contemporary Issues in Economics*, ed. M. Parkin and A. R. Nobay, Manchester: Manchester University Press, 1975.

'The Uses and Abuses of Manpower Planning', *New Society*, 31 July 1975.

'The Rate of Return on Investment in Education in Thailand', *Journal of Development Studies*, January 1976.

'The Empirical Status of Human Capital Theory: a Slightly Jaundiced Survey', *Journal of Economic Literature*, September 1976; reprinted in *Public Economics and Human Resources*, ed. V. Halberstadt and A. J. Culyer, Paris: Editions Cujas, 1977.

'Economic Criteria for Nonformal Education', Federal Republic of Germany: Bonn, Ministry for Economic Cooperation, 1976 (processed).

'Bowles and Gintis's "Schooling in Capitalist America: Educational Reform and the Contradictions of Economic Life" ', *Challenge*, July–August 1976.

'Jacob Mincer's Schooling, Experience and Earnings', *Economic Development and Cultural Change*, October 1976.

(with J. Mace) 'Recurrent Education – the New Jerusalem', *Higher Education*, Summer 1977.

'Educated Unemployment in Asia, with Special Reference to Bangladesh, India, and Sri Lanka', Bangkok: *UN Economic Bulletin for Asia and the Pacific*, December 1977.

'Economics of Education in Developing Countries: Current Trends and New Priorities. A Lecture on the Occasion of Professor Friedrich Edding's Emeritierung', Berlin:

Max-Planck-Institut für Bildungsforschung, 1978; reprinted in *Third World Quarterly*, January 1979.

(with R. Jolly and C. Colclough) 'Education and Employment in Africa', in *Survey of Economic and Social Conditions in Africa, 1976–1977*, Part 1, New York: UNECA, 1978.

(with M. Woodhall) 'Patterns of Subsidies to Higher Education in Europe', *Higher Education*, September 1979.

'Notes on Recurrent Education – Some Constructive Thoughts by a Skeptic', in *Transition from School to Work: An Intercountry Study*, ed. S. Mushkin and S. D. Nollen, Washington, D.C.: National Center for Education Statistics, 1979.

'The Quality of Population in Developing Countries, with Particular Reference to Education and Training', in *World Population and Development*, ed. P. M. Hauser, Syracuse, N.Y.: Syracuse University Press, 1979.

'A UNIDO Strategy for the Training of Industrial Manpower in the Third World', Vienna: UNIDO, 1980 (processed).

'Reforming Education in Latin America', CINTERPLAN (Centro Inter-americano de Estudios Investigaciones Para el Planeamiento de la Educacion) Conference Proceedings, Caracas, Venezuela: CINTERPLAN, 1980.

'Alcune reflessioni sul finanziamento dell'instruzione', in *I Costi dell'Instruzione*, Rome: Fondazione Luigi Einaudi, 1980.

'A Plain Man's Guide to the Finance of British Higher Education', Institute for Research on Educational Finance and Governance, School of Education, Stanford University, Program Report no. 80-B9, 1980 (processed). Translation in Spanish, *Revista Canaria de Estudios Ingleses*, 4 April 1982.

'Common Assumptions about Education and Employment', in *The Education Dilemma: Policy Issues for Developing Countries in the 1980s*, ed. J. Simmons, Oxford: Pergamon International Library, 1980.

'Student Loans and the NUS', *Journal of Economic Affairs*, October 1980.

'Student Grants: a Ham-Fisted Way to Aid Poor Students', *The Times Higher Education Supplement*, 19 December 1980.

'Grants and Awards: a Taxing Question', *The Times Higher Education Supplement*, 27 March 1981.

'The Economic Costs and Benefits of Overseas Students', in *The Overseas Students Question*, ed. P. Williams, London: Heinemann Educational Books, 1981.

'Can Independent Education be Suppressed?', *Journal of Economic Affairs*, October 1981.

'Comment on Recurrent Education', in *Collective Choice in Education*, ed. M. J. Bowman, Boston, Mass.: Kluwer Nijhoff, 1981.

'Thoughts on the Distribution of Schooling and the Distribution of Earnings in Developing Countries', in IIEP, *Planning Education for Reducing Inequalities*, Paris: UNESCO/IIEP, 1981.

'The Distributional Effects of Higher Education Subsidies', *Economics of Education Review*, II, (3), Summer 1982.

(with C. Dougherty and G. Psacharopoulos) 'The Distribution of Schooling and the Distribution of Earnings: Raising the School Leaving Age in 1972', *Manchester School*, March 1982.

'Where Are We Now in the Economics of Education?', OECD Directorate for Social Affairs, Manpower and Education, Study Group on Educational Development, 1982;

reprinted as Special Professiorial Lecture, University of London Institute of Education, 1983; and *Economics of Education Review*, IV, (1), 1985.

'Cost-Benefit Analysis Applied to the Concept of Economies of Scale in Higher Education', in *Economies of Scale in Higher Education*, ed. S. Goodlad, London: Society for Research into Higher Education, 1983.

'Declining Subsidies to Higher Education: an Economic Analysis', in *Reassessing the Role of Government in the Mixed Economy*, ed. H. Giersch, Kiel: Institut für Weltwirtschaft, 1983.

'Education Vouchers: a New Method of Financing Education', Madrid: Instituto de Economia de Mercado, 1984.

'Education Vouchers – It All Depends on What You Mean', in *Economics of Privatisation*, ed. J. Le Grand and R. Robinson, London: Weidenfeld & Nicolson, 1985.

'The "Pros" and "Cons" of Education Vouchers', *Economic Review*, IV, (5), May 1987.

(with G. K. Shaw) 'The University of Buckingham after Ten Years – a Tentative Evaluation', *Higher Education Quarterly*, Winter 1987.

(with R. Towse) 'The State of the Economics Profession in the UK', Royal Economic Society 1988 (cyclostyled).

'The Over-expansion of Higher Education in the Third World', in *Equity and Efficiency in Economic Development: Essays in Honour of Benjamin Higgins*, ed. D. V. Savoie, Montreal: McGill-Queens University Press, 1989.

'Ausbildungsgutschriften als markwirtscheftliche Alternative im erziehungswesen', *Neue Zurcher Zeitung*, nr. 241, 17 October 1989.

'The Economic Value of Higher Education', The Uhlenbeck Lecture, Wassaneer, The Netherlands: NIAS, 1990.

References

Ahamad, Bashir and Blaug, Mark (eds) (1973), *The Practice of Manpower Forecasting*, Amsterdam: Elsevier.

Akerlof, George (1970), 'The Market for "Lemons": Qualitative Uncertainty and the Market Mechanism' *Quarterly Journal of Economics*, **840** (August): 488–50.

Anonymous (1978), *Lecturer on Jurisprudence: Adam Smith's Glasgow Lectures*, Meek, R. L., Raphael. D. D. and Stein, P. G. (eds), Oxford: Oxford University Press.

Arrow, Kenneth and Debreu, Gerard (1954) 'Existence of an equilibrium for a competitive economy', *Econometrica*, **22**: 376–86.

Arrow, Kenneth and Hahn, Frank (1971), *General Competitive Analysis*, San Francisco: Holden Day.

Ashby, Eric (1963), 'A Landmark in Social History', *Observer*, 27 October.

Australia (1988) *Report of the Committee on Higher Education Funding* (the Wran Report), Canberra.

Baker, L.R. (1989), 'Instrumental Intentionality', *Philosophy of Science*, **56**: 30316.

Barnes, John and Barr, Nicolas (1988), *Strategies for Higher Education: The Alternative White Paper*, Aberdeen University Press, for the David Hume Institute, Edinburgh, and the Suntory-Toyota International Centre for Economics and Related Disciplines, London School of Economics.

Barr, Nicholas (1987), *The Economics of the Welfare State*, London: Weidenfeld and Nicolson, and Stanford, Conn.: Stanford University Press.

Barr, Nicholas (1989a), *Student Loans: The Next Steps*, Aberdeen University Press, for the David Hume Institute, Edinburgh, and the Suntory-Toyota International Centre for Economics and Related Disciplines, London School of Economics.

Barr, Nicholas (1989b), 'Baker's Proposal: a Better Class of Drain', *Independent*, 22 June: 21.

Barr, Nicholas and Low, William (1988), *Student Grants and Student Poverty*, London School of Economics, Welfare State Programme, Discussion Paper no. 28, London: London School of Economics.

Barro, R. and Grossman, H. I. (1971), 'A General Disequilibrium Model of Income and Employment', *American Economic Review*, **61** (March): 82–93.

—— (1976), *Money, Employment and Inflation*, New York: Cambridge University Press.

Bartley, W. W. III (1984), *The Retreat to Commitment*, 2nd edn rev. and enl., New York: Alfred A. Knopf.

Baumol, William (1974), 'The Transformation of Values: What Marx "Really" Meant (an Interpretation)', *Journal of Economic Literature*, **12**: 51–62.

Becker, Gary (1964), *Human Capital: A Theoretical and Empirical Analysis with Special Reference to Education*, Princeton, N. J.: Princeton University Press.

Benassy, J. P. (1987), 'Disequilibrium Analysis', in *The New Palgrave: A Dictionary of Economics*, ed. J. Eatwell, M. Milgate and P. Newman, vol. 1, London: Macmillan, 858–63.

Ben-David, Joseph (1968–9), 'The Universities and the Growth of Science in Germany and the United States', *Minerva*, **7** (2): 24.

Berg, Maxine (1990), *Political Economy in the Twentieth Century*, London: Philip Allan.

Blaug, M. (1966), 'Loans for Students', *New Society*, 6 October: 538–9.

—— (1970), *An Introduction to the Economics of Education*, London: Penguin.

—— (1974), *The Cambridge Revolution; Success or Failure?* London: Institute of Economic Affairs.

—— (1976a), 'The Empirical Status of Human Capital Theory: a Slightly Jaundiced Survey', *Journal of Economic Literature*, September: 827–56; reprinted in Blaug (1987a): 100–28.

—— (1976b), 'Kuhn versus Lakatos or Paradigms versus Research Programmes in the History of Economics", in Spiro Latsis (ed.) (1976), 149–80.

—— (1978), *Economic Theory in Retrospect*, 3rd edn Cambridge: Cambridge University Press.

—— (1979), 'The Economics of Education in Developing Countries: Current Trends and New Priorities', *Third World Quarterly*, January: 73–83; reprinted in Blaug (1987a).

—— (1980a), *Methodology of Economics*, Cambridge: Cambridge University Press.

—— (1980b), 'Student Loans and the NUS', *Economic Affairs*, October: 827–56.

—— (1981), 'The Economic Costs and Benefits of Overseas Students' in *The Overseas Student Question: Studies for a Policy*, ed. Peter Williams, London: Heinemann.

—— (1982), 'The Distributional Effects of Higher Education Subsidies', *Economics of Education Review*, **2**, (3): 209–31; reprinted in Blaug (1987): 204–26.

—— (1983), 'A Methodological Appraisal of Radical Economics', in *Methodological Controversy in Economics: Historical Essays in Honor of T. W. Hutchison*, ed. A. W. Coats, Greenwood, Conn.: JAI Press.

—— (1985a), 'Where Are We Now in the Economics of Education?', *Economics of Education Review*, **4**, (1) 17–28; reprinted in Blaug (1987a): 129–40.

—— (1985b), 'Comment on D. Wade Hands, "Karl Popper and Economic Methodology: A New Look" ', *Economics and Philosophy*, **I**, October: 286–8.

—— (1985c), *Economic Theory in Retrospect*, Cambridge: Cambridge University Press.

—— (1987a), *The Economics of Education and the Education of an Economist*, Aldershot: Edward Elgar.

—— (1987b), 'Second Thoughts on the Keynesian Revolution,' mimeographed English version, of 'Ripensamenti Sulla Rivoluzione Keynesiana', *Rassegna Economica*, **51**: 605–34.

—— (1989), 'Review of Economics of Education: Research and Studies', *Journal of Human Resources*, **24**, (2): 331–5.

—— (1990a), 'Reply to Hands, "Second Thoughts on 'Second Thoughts': Reconsidering the Lakatosian Progress of The General Theory" ', *Review of Political Economy*, **2**, (1): 102–4.

—— (1990b), *The Economic Value of Higher Education*, Uhlenbeck-Lecture VIII, Wassenaar: Netherlands Institute for Advanced Study in the Humanities and Social Sciences (NIAS).

—— (1990c), 'On the Historiography of Economics', *Journal of the History of Economic Thought*, **12**: 27–38.

—— (1992), 'Second Thoughts on the Keynesian Revolution', *History of Political Economy*, forthcoming.

—— and de Marchi, Neil (eds) (1991), *Appraising Economic Theories: Studies in Application of the Methodology of Research Programmes*, Cheltenham: Edward Elgar.

—— and Sturges, Paul (1983), *Who's Who in Economics*, 1st edn, Cambridge, Mass.: MIT Press; 2nd edn, 1986.

Boland, Lawrence, A. (1982), *The Foundations of Economic Method*, London: Allen and Unwin.

Booth, Alan (1983), 'The Keynesian Revolution in Economic Policy Making', *Economic History Review*, **36**, February: 102–3.

Bortkiewicz, L. von (1907), 'On the Correction of Marx's Fundamental Theoretical Construction in the Third Volume of Capital', English translation by P. Sweezy, New York: Augustus M. Kelley, 1949.

Bosworth, Barry, Carron, Andrew and Rhyne, Elizabeth (1987), *The Economics of Federal Credit Programs*, Washington D.C.: The Brookings Institution.

Breton, A. and Scott, A. (1978), *The Economic Constitution of Federal States*, Toronto: University of Toronto Press.

Buchanan, James (1985), 'Constitutional Economics' , in *Explorations into Constitutional Economics*, College Station: Texas A & M University Press.

Buroway, Michael (1979), *Manufacturing Consent*, Chicago Ill.: University of Chicago Press.

Butterfield, Herbert (1949), *The Origins of Modern Science 1300–1800*, London: G. Bell.

Caldwell, Bruce (1982), *Beyond Positivism: Economic Methodology in the Twentieth Century*, London: Allen & Unwin.

—— (1986), 'Towards a Broader Conception of Criticism', *History of Political Economy*, **18**, (4), Winter: 675–81.

—— 'The Case for Pluralism', in *The Popperian Legacy in Economics*, ed. Neil de Marchi, Cambridge: Cambridge University Press: 231–44.

—— (1989), 'Post-Keynesian Methodology: an Assessment', *Review of Political Economy*, **I**, (1), March: 43–64.

—— (1990), 'Human Molecules: a Comment on Nelson', in *The Methodology of Economics*, ed. Neil de Marchi Boston, Mass.: Kluwer.

—— (1991), 'Clarifying Popper', *Journal of Economic Literature*, forthcoming.

Callaghan, James (1987), *Time and Chance*, London: Collins.

Cassell, Gustav (1925), *Fundamental Thoughts in Economics*, New York: Harcourt, Brace.

Catalogue of the Goldsmith's Library of Economic Literature (1981), vol. II. *1801–50*, London: Athlone Library.

Chapman, Bruce (1988), 'An Economic Analysis of the Higher Education Contribution Scheme of the Wran Report', *Economic Analysis and Policy*, **18**, (2): 171–88.

—— and Chia, Tai-Tee (1989), 'Financing Higher Education: Private Rates of Return and Externalities in the Context of the Tertiary Tax' Australian National University, Centre for Economic Policy Research, Discussion Paper no. 213.

Checkland, S. G. (1951), 'The Advent of Academic Economics in England', *The Manchester School*, **19**, January.

Churchland, P. M. (1984), *Matter and Consciousness*, Cambridge, Mass.: MIT Press.

Churchland, P. S. (1986), *Neurophilosophy*, Cambridge, Mass.: MIT Press.

Clapham, Sir J. (1944), *The Bank of England: a history*, 2 vols, Cambridge: Cambridge University Press.

Coats, A. W. *et al.* (1981), 'Economists in Government', *History of Political Economy*, **13** (3), Fall: 365–694.

Cohen R. S., Feyerabend, P. K. and Wartofsky, M. W. (eds) (1976), *Essays in Memory of Imre Lakatos*, Dorarecht, Holland: D. Reidel.

Coleman, Williams (1990), 'The Defect in Ricardo's Argument for the 93 Per Cent Labour Theory of Value', *Australian Economic Papers*, **27**: 101–6.

Cooper, R. and John, A. (1988), 'Coordinating Coordination Failures in Keynesian Models', *Quarterly Journal of Economics*, **103** August: 441–63.

Court, Andrew T. (1939), 'Hedonic Price Indexes with Automotive Examples', in *The Dynamics of Automobile Demand*, New York: General Motors Corp.: 99–117.

Crick, W. F and Wadsworth, J. E. (1936), 'Some New Light on Thomas Joplin', *Economica*, NS **3**: 323–6.

Dante, Alighieri (1316?/1949), *The Divine Comedy – 1. Hell*, trans. Dorothy Sayers, London: Penguin.

de Marchi, Neil (1991), 'Introduction: Using MSRP', in Blaug and de Marchi (forthcoming).

Denison, Edward (1962), *The Sources of Economic Growth in the United States and the Alternatives Before Us*, New York: Committee for Economic Development.

Dennett, D. C. (1978), *Brainstorms: Philosophical Essays on Mind and Psychology*, Cambridge, Mass.: MIT Press.

Department of Education and Science (1988), *Top-Up Loans for Students*, CM 520, London: Her Majesty's Stationery Office.

—— (1989), *Shifting the Balance of Public Funding of Higher Education to Fees: A Consultation Paper*, London: Department of Education and Science.

Desai, Menghad (1979a), *Marxian Economics*, Oxford: Basil Blackwell.

—— (1979b), 'The Scourge of the Monetarists: Kaldor on Monetarism and Money', *Cambridge Journal of Economics*, March.

—— (1991), 'Kaldor between Hayek and Keynes, or Did Nicky Kill Capital Theory', forthcoming in *Kaldor Memorial Volume*, ed. E. Nell.

Dictionary of National Biography (1908–9), ed. L. Stephen and S. Lee, 22 vols and supplements, reprinted Oxford: Oxford University Press, 1921–2.

Domar, E. (1946), 'Capital Expansion, Rate of Growth, and Employment, *Econometrica*, **14** (April): 137–47.

Dorfman, Joseph (1946–59), *The Economic Mind in American Civilization*, 5 vols, New York: Viking.

Dougherty, C. R. S. (1985), 'Manpower Forecasting and Manpower-Development Planning in the United Kingdom', in *Forecasting Skilled Manpower Needs: The Experience of Eleven Countries*', Youdi, R. V. and Hinchliffe, Keith. Paris: UNESCO: International Institute for Educational Planning.

Douglas, Mary and Isherwood, Baron (1979), *The World of Goods*, New York: Basic Books.

Dwyer, J. and Bruce, J. (1988), *A Home Divided*, Stanford, Conn.: Stanford University Press.

Eatwell, J. and Milgate, M. (1983), *Keynes's Economics and the Theory of Value and Distribution*, London: Duckworth.

Economics Institute (1975, 1979), *Guide to Graduate Study in Economics and Agricultural Economics*, Homewood, Ill.: Richard Irwin.

Ellis, A. (1933), *Bold Adventure*, London: National Provincial Bank.

Encyclopedia of the Social Sciences (1930–5), 15 vols, New York: Macmillan.

Farr, J. (1983), 'Popper's Hermeneutics', *Philosophy of the Social Sciences*, *13*: 157–76.

Feinstein, C. (ed.) (1967), *Socialism, Capitalism and Economic Development, Essays in Honour of Maurice Dobb, Cambridge*: Cambridge University Press.

Fetter, F. W. (1953), 'The Authorship of Economic Articles in the *Edinburgh Review, 1802–47', Journal of Political Economy*, **61**: 232–59.

—— (1958a), 'The Economic Articles in the *Quarterly Review* and Their Authors, 1809–52', *Journal of Political Economy*, **66** (February), Part I: 47–64.

—— (1958b) 'The Economic Articles in the *Quarterly Review* and Their Authors, 1809–52', *Journal of Political Economy*, **66** (April) Part II: 154–70.

—— (1960), 'The Economic Articles in *Blackwood's Edinburgh Magazine* and Their Authors, 1817–1853', *Scottish JPE*, **7** (June), Part I: 85–107; **7**, (November), Part II: 213–31.

—— (1962), 'Economic Articles in the *Westminster Review* and Their Authors, 1824–51', *Journal of Political Economy*, **70** (December): 570–96.

—— (1965), 'Economic Controversy in the British Reviews, 1802–1850', *Economica*, **32** (November): 424–37.

Fischer, S. (1988), 'Recent Developments in Macroeconomics', *Economic Journal*, **98** (June): 294–339.

Fleming, J. M. (1962), 'Domestic Financial Policies Under Fixed and Under Floating Exchange Rates', *International Monetary Fund: Staff Papers*, **9** (November): 369–79.

Folbre, Nancy (1982), 'Exploitation Comes Home: a Critique of the Marxian Theory of Labour Power', *Cambridge Journal of Economics*, **6**, (4), 318–29.

Fox Keller, Evelyn (1983), 'Feminism and Science', in *The Signs Reader: Women, Gender and Scholarship*, ed. Elizabeth Abel and Emily K. Abel, Chicago, Ill.: University of Chicago Press.

Fraschini, A. and Rizzo, I. (1987), 'Definizione e Misurazione del Grado di Decentramento: Probleme Teorici e Tentativi di Quantifizione', *Rivista di Diritto Finanziario e Scienza delle Finanze*, (September).

Frey, B. (1985), 'Are there Natural Limits to Government Growth?', in *Public Expenditure and Government Growth*, ed. F. Forte and A. T. Peacock, Oxford: Basil Blackwell.

Friedman, Milton (1953), 'The Methodology of Positive Economics', in his *Essays in Positive Economics*, Chicago: University of Chicago Press: 3–43.

—— (1956), 'The Quantity Theory of Money – A Restatement', in *Studies in the Quantity Theory of Money*, ed. M. Friedman, Chicago, Ill.: University of Chicago Press; 3–21.

—— (1961), 'The Lag in Effect of Monetary Policy', *Journal of Political Economy*, **69** (October): 447–66; reprinted in Friedman (1969): 237–60.

—— (1962), *Capitalism and Freedom*, Chicago, Ill.: University of Chicago Press.

—— (1968a), 'Money: Quantity Theory', in *International Encyclopedia of the Social Sciences*, ed. D. L. Sills, New York: Macmillan and Free Press, **10**: 432–47.

—— (1968b), 'The Role of Monetary Policy', *American Economic Review*, **58** (March): 1–17; reprinted in Friedman (1969): 95–110.

—— (1969), *The Optimum Quantity of Money, and Other Essays*, Chicago, Ill.: University of Chicago Press.

Garegnani, Pierro (1978) 'Notes on Consumption, Investment and Effective Demand', *Cambridge Journal of Economics*, **2** and **3**, also in Eatwell and Milgate (1983).

Gavroglu, K., Goudaroulis, Y. and Nicolacopoulos, P. (eds) (1989), *Imre Lakatos and Theories of Scientific Change*, Boston, Mass.: Kluwer.

Gilbart, J. W. (1865), *Works*, 6 vols, London: Bell and Daldy.

Glennerster, Howard, Merrett, Stephen and Wilson, Gail (1968), 'A Graduate Tax', *Higher Education Review*, **1**, (1).

Goodwin, R. M. (1967), 'A Growth Cycle', in Feinstein (1967).

—— Krueger, M. and Vercelli, A. (1984), *Nonlinear Models of Fluctuating Growth*, Berlin: Springer Verlag.

Gregory, Sir T. E., (1926), 'One Hundred Years of Joint Stock Banking, *Banker*, (April/May): 336–345.

—— (1936), *The Westminster Bank Through a Century*, 2 vols, London: Oxford University Press/Milford.

Greig, James A. (1948), *Francis Jeffrey*, London: Oliver & Boyd.

Hahn, Frank (1982), *Money and Inflation*, Oxford: Basil Blackwell.

—— (1984), *Equilibrium and Macroeconomics*, Oxford: Basil Blackwell.

—— and Negishi, T. (1962), 'A Theorem on Non-Tâtonnement Stability', *Econometrica*, **30**; 463–9.

Hands, D.W. (1985a), 'Karl Popper and Economic Methodology: a New Look', *Economics and Philosophy*, **1**, (1), (April): 83–99.

—— (1985b), 'Second Thoughts on Lakatos', *History of Political Economy*, **17**, (1), (Spring): 1–16.

—— (1990), 'Second Thoughts on "Second Thoughts": Reconsidering the Lakatosian Progress of *The General Theory*', *Review of Political Economy*, **2**, (1): 69–81.

—— (1991a), 'Falsification, Situational Analysis, and Scientific Research Programs: the Popperian Tradition in Economic Methodology', in *The Methodology of Economics*, ed. Neil de Marchi, Boston, Mass: Kluwer.

—— (1991b), 'The Problem of Excess Content: Economics, Novelty, and a Long Popperian Tale', in Blaug and de Marchi (1991).

Handwörterbuch der Staatswissenshaften (1923, 1956), Jena, Germany: Verlag von Gustav Fischer.

Haraway, Donna (1988), 'Situated Knowledges: the Science Question in Feminism and the Privilege of Partial Perspective', *Feminist Studies*, **14**, (3), (Fall): 575–97.

Harcourt, G. (1990), 'On the Contribution of Joan Robinson and Piero Sraffa to Economic Theory', in Berg (1990).

Harding, Sandra (1986a), 'The Instability of Analytical Categories of Feminist Theory', *Signs*, **11**, (4).

—— (1986b), *The Science Question in Feminism*, Ithaca, N.Y.: Cornell University Press.

Harrod, R. F. (1939), 'An Essay in Dynamic Theory', *Economic Journal*, **49** (March): 14–33.

—— (1951), *The Life of John Maynard Keynes*, London: Macmillan; reprinted, New York: Augustus M. Kelley, 1969.

Hartmann, Heidi (1981), 'The Family as the Locus of Gender, Class and Political Struggle: the Example of Housework'. *Signs*, **6** (3): 366–94.

Hausman, Daniel (1981), *Capital, Prices and Profits*, New York: Columbia University Press.

Hayek, F. A. (1945), 'The Use of Knowledge in Society', *American Economic Review*, (September).

—— (1946), 'The London School of Economics, 1895–1945', *Economica*, **13** (February): 1–31.

Hempel, C. G. (1962), 'Rational Action', *Proceedings and Addresses of the American Philosophical Association*, **35**: 5–23.

—— (1965), *Aspects of Scientific Explanation*, New York: The Free Press.

—— and Oppenheim, P. (1948), 'Studies in the Logic of Explanation', *Philosophy of Science*, **15**: 135–75.

Hennings, Klaus (1988), 'Aspekte der Institutionalisserung der Okonomie an deutschen Universitäten', in *Die Institutionalislerung der Nationalökonomie an Deutschen Universitäten* ed. N. Waszek, (Scripta Mercaturae).

Herbst, Jurgen (1965), *The German Historical School in American Scholarship*, Ithaca, N.Y.: Cornell University Press.

Hicks, J. R. (1937), 'Mr Keynes and the "Classics": a Suggested Interpretation', *Econometrica*, **5**, (April): 147–59.

—— (1974), *The Crisis in Keynesian Economics* (Oxford: Basil Blackwell).

Hirschman, Albert O. (1977), *The Passions and the Interests*, Princeton, N. J.: Princeton University Press.

Hodder, E. (1891), *George Fife Angas*, London: Hodder & Stoughton.

Hollander, Samuel (1980), 'On Professor Samuelson's Canonical Model of Political Economics', *Journal of Economic Literature*, **18**: 559–74.

—— (1987), *Classical Economics*, Oxford: Basil Blackwell.

Hollis, Martin and Nell, E. J. (1975), *Rational Economic Man: A Philosophical Critique of Neo-Classical Economics*, Cambridge: Cambridge University Press.

Hope, Julie and Miller, Paul (1988), 'Financing Tertiary Education: an Examination of the Issues', *Australian Economic Review*, **4**: 37–57.

Howitt, P. (1986a), 'Conversations with Economists: a Review Essay', *Journal of Monetary Economics*, **18** (July): 1–16.

—— (1986b), 'The Keynesian Recovery', *Canadian Journal of Economics*, **19** (November): 626–41.

Hume, David (1985), 'On the Independency of Parliament', in *Essays, Moral Political, and Literary*, Liberty Classics.

Hutchinson, T. W. (1938), *The Significance and Basic Postulates of Economic Theory*, reprinted 1960, New York: Kelley.

—— (1968), *Economics and Economic Policy in Britain, 1946–1966: Some Aspects of Their Inter-relations*, London: George Allen & Unwin.

International Monetary Fund (1988), *Government Finance Statistics Yearbook*, Washington, D.C.: IMF.

Johnstone, Bruce (1986), *Sharing the Costs of Higher Education: Student Financial Assistance in the United Kingdom, the Federal Republic of Germany, France, Sweden and the United States*, New York: College Entrance Examination Board.

Jones, Lyle V. *et al.* (eds) (1982), *An Assessment of Research-Doctorate Programs in the United States: Social and Behavioral Sciences*, prepared by a committee of the Conference Board of Associated Research Councils, Washington, D.C.: National Academy Press.

Joplin, T. (1822), 'On the General Principles and Present Practice of Banking, in England and Scotland', *The Pamphleteer*, **24**, (48): 529–79.

—— (1823a), *Outlines of a System of Political Economy*, London: Baldwin, Cradock and Joy.

—— (1823b), *An Essay on the General Principles and Present Practice of Banking, in England and Scotland*, 4th edn, privately printed, Newcastle-upon-Tyne.

—— (1825), *An Illustration of Mr. Joplin's Views on Currency, and Plan for Its Improvement*, London: Baldwin, Cradock and Joy.

—— (1826), *Views on the Subject of Corn and Currency*, London: Baldwin, Cradock and Joy, and T. Ridgway.

—— (1827), *An Essay on the General Principles and Present Practice of Banking*, 6th edn, London: Baldwin, Cradock and Joy.

—— (1828), *Views on the Corn Bill of 1827*, London: Ridgway, and Baldwin, Cradock and Joy.

—— (1830), *An Examination of the Principles of an Improved System of Banking*, London: Ruffy.

—— (1831a), *An Examination of the Principles of an Improved System of Banking*, 2nd edn, London: Ruffy.

—— (1831b), *The Plan of a National Establishment for Country Banking, and the Principles by which it is Recommended*, London: Ruffy.

—— (1832), *An Analysis and History of the Currency Question*, London: Ridgway.

—— (1833), *A Digest of the Evidence on the Bank Charter taken before the Committee of 1832*, London: Ridgway.

—— (1833–4), *Cases for Parliamentary Inquiry, into the Circumstances of the Panic: in a Letter to Thomas Gisbourne, Esq., M.P.*, London: Ridgway.

—— (1837), *An Examination of the Report of the Joint Stock Bank Committee*, 4th edn, London: Ridgway.

—— (1838), *Articles on Banking and Currency From 'The Economist' Newspaper*, London: Ridgway.

—— (1839), *On Our Monetary System*, London: Ridgway.

—— (1840), *Prospectus of an Association to Promote the Establishment of a Uniform Currency under One General Head*, London: Ridgway.

—— (1841), *The Cause and Cure of Our Commercial Embarrassments*, London: Ridgway.

—— (1844a), *Currency Reform: Improvement not Depreciation*, London: Richardson.

—— (1844b), *An Examination of Sir Robert Peel's Currency Bill of 1844*, London: Richardson.

—— (1845a), *An Examination of Sir Robert Peel's Currency Bill, Second Edition With Supplementary Observations*, London: Richardson.

—— (1845b), *Mr. Joplin's Circular to the Directors and Managers of the Joint Stock Banks*, London: Richardson.

—— (1846), 'Memoir of Mr. Thomas Joplin', *Bankers Magazine*, **6**: 70–80.

Judd, J. P. and Scadding, J.L. (1982), 'The Search for a Stable Money Demand Function', *Journal of Economic Literature*, **20**, (September): 993–1023.

Kaldor, N. (1960) 'Monetary Policy, Economic Stability and Growth', Memorandum of Evidence submitted to the Radcliffe Committee on the Workings of the Monetary System, *Principal Memoranda of Evidence*, vol. 3, London: Her Majesty's Stationery Office.

Katz, L. F. (1988), 'Some Recent Developments in Labor Economics and Their Implications for Macroeconomics', *Journal of Money, Credit and Banking*, **20** (August, part 2): 507–22.

Keynes, John Maynard, *Collected Writings*, vols I–VI (1971), vols VII–VIII (1973), vols IX–X (1972), vols XI–XII (1983), vols XIII–XIV (1973), vols XV–XVI (1971), vols xvii–xviii (1978), vols xix–xx (1981), vol. xxi (1982), vol. xxii (1978), vols xxiii–xxiv (1979), vols xxv–xxvii (1980), vol xxix (1979), vol. xxx (Bibliography and Index, forthcoming), London: Macmillan, for the Royal Economic Society.

—— (1923), *A Tract on Monetary Reform*, as reprinted in Keynes, *Collected Writings*, vol. iv.

—— (1925), *The Economic Consequences of Mr. Churchill*, as reprinted in Keynes, *Collected Writings*, vol. ix, 207–30.

—— (1930a), *A Treatise on Money*, vol. i: *The Pure Theory of Money*, as reprinted in Keynes, *Collected Writings*, vol. v.

—— (1930b), *A Treatise on Money*, vol. ii: *The Applied Theory of Money*, as reprinted in Keynes, *Collected Writings*, vol. vi.

—— (1931), *Essays in Persuasion*, as reprinted with additions in Keynes, *Collected Writings*, vol. ix.

—— (1936), *The General Theory of Employment, Interest and Money*, London: Macmillan.

—— (1937), 'Alternative Theories of the Rate of Interest', *Economic Journal*, **47** (June): 241–52, as reprinted in Keynes, *Collected Writings*, vol. xiv: 109–23.

—— (1940), *How to Pay for the War*, as reprinted in Keynes, *Collected Writings*, vol. ix: 367–439.

—— (1946), 'The Balance of Payments in the United States', *Economic Journal*, **56** (June): 172–89; as reprinted in Keynes, *Collected Writings*, vol. xxvii: 427–46.

—— *The General Theory and After. Part I: Preparation*, Donald Moggridge, vol. xiii of Keynes, *Collected Writings*.

—— *The General Theory and After. Part II: Defence and Development*, ed. Donald Moggridge, vol. xiv of Keynes, *Collected Writings*.

—— *Activities, 1940–1946: Shaping the Post-War World: Employment and Commodities*, ed. Donald Moggridge, vol. xxvii of Keynes, *Collected Writings*.

—— *The General Theory and After: A Supplement*, ed. Donald Moggridge, vol. xxix of Keynes, *Collected Writings*.

Kirchgassner, G. and Pommerehne, W. W. (1988), 'Government Spending in Federal Systems: a Comparison between Switzerland and Germany', in *Explaining the Growth of Government*, ed. J. A. Lybeck and M. Henrekson, Amsterdam: North Holland.

Kitcher, P. (1989), Explanatory Unification and the Causal Structure of the World', in *Scientific Explanation: Minnesota Studies in the Philosophy of Science*, vol. xiii, ed. P. Kitcher and W. C. Salmon, Minneapolis: University of Minnesota Press: 410–505.

Klamer, Arjo (1984), *New Classical Macroeconomics: Conversations with New Classical Economists and their Opponents*, Brighton, Sussex: Wheatsheaf.

—— (1991), 'Towards the Native Point of View; or, How to Change the Conversation', in *Economics and Hermeneutics*, ed. Don Lavoie, London: Routledge.

—— Colander, David (1990), *The Making of an Economist*, Boulder, Col.: Westview Press.

—— Donald McCloskey and Robert Solow (eds) (1988), *The Consequences of Economic Rhetoric*, New York: Cambridge University Press.

Klappholz, Kurt and Agassi, J. A. (1959), 'Methodological Prescriptions in Economics', *Economica*, NS **26**, (101), (February): 60–74.

Klein, Lawrence (1947), *The Keynesian Revolution*, New York: Macmillan.

Koertge, N. (1974), 'On Popper's Philosophy of Social Science', in *Philosophy of the Social Sciences 1972*, ed. K. F. Schaffner and R. S. Cohen, Dordrecht, Holland: D. Reidel: 195–207.

—— (1975), Popper's Metaphysical Research Program for the Human Sciences', *Inquiry*, **19**: 437–62.

—— (1979), 'The Methodological Status of Popper's Rationality Principle', *Theory and Decision*, **10**: 83–95.

—— (1985), 'On Explaining Beliefs', *Erkenntnis*, **22**: 175–86.

Kuhn, Thomas (1962), *The Structure of Scientific Revolutions*, 2nd enl. edn, 1970, Chicago, Ill.: University of Chicago Press.

—— (1970), *The Structure of Scientific Revolutions*, 2nd enl. edn, Chicago, Ill.: University of Chicago Press.

Kurdas, Cigdem (1988), 'The "Whig Historian" Adam Smith: Paul Samuelson's Canonical Classical Model', *History of Economics Society Bulletin*, **10**: 13–23.

Lagueux, M. (1990), 'Popper and the Rationality Principle', paper presented at the Annual Congress of the Canadian Philosophical Association, Victoria, B.C., May.

Lakatos, Imre (1970), 'Falsification and the Methodology of Scientific Research Programmes', in *Criticism and the Growth of Knowledge*, ed. Imre Lakatos and Alan Musgrave, Cambridge: Cambridge University Press: 91–196.

—— (1971), 'History of Science and its Rational Reconstruction' in *PSA 1970, In Memory of Rudolf Carnap: Boston Studies in the Philosophy of Science*, ed. R. Buck and R. Cohen, Dordrecht, Holland: D. Reidel: 91–139.

—— (1976), *Proofs and Refutations: The Logic of Mathematical Discovery*, ed. John Worrall and Elie Zahar, Cambridge: Cambridge University Press.

Latsis, Spiro (1972), 'Situational Determinism in Economics', *British Journal for the Philosophy of Science*, **23**: 207–45.

—— (1976), *Method and Appraisal in Economics*, Cambridge: Cambridge University Press.

—— (1983), 'The Role and Status of the Rationality Principle in the Social Sciences', in *Epistemology, Methodology and the Social Sciences*, ed. R. S. Cohen and M. W. Wartofsky, Dordrecht, Holland: D. Reidel: 123–51.

Laudan, Larry (1977), *Progress and Its Problems*, Berkeley, Cal.: University of California Press.

Lavoie, Don (ed.) (forthcoming), *Economics and Hermeneutics*, London: Routledge.

Leach, J. J. (1968), 'The Logic of the Situation', *Philosophy of Science*, **35**: 258–73.

Le Grand, Julian and Robinson, Ray (1984), *The Economics of Social Problems*, 2nd edn, London: Macmillan.

Leijonhufvud, Axel (1968), *On Keynesian Economics and the Economics of Keynes*, New York: Oxford University Press.

Lekachman, Robert (ed.) (1964), *Keynes' General Theory: Reports of Three Decades*, New York: St Martins Press.

Leslie, L. and Brinkman, P. (1988), *The Economic Value of Higher Education*, New York: American Council on Education.

Losee, John (1987), *Philosophy of Science and Historical Enquiry*, Oxford: Clarendon Press.

Lucas, R. E. Jr (1973), 'Some International Evidence on Output–Inflation Tradeoffs', *American Economic Review*, **63** (June): 326–34.

McCloskey, Donald (1985), *The Rhetoric of Economics*, Madison, Wis.: University of Wisconsin Press.

—— (1988), 'Some Consequences for a Feminine Economics, unpublished MS, Project in Rhetoric of Inquiry.

McConnell, John W. (1943), *The Basic Teachings of The Great Economists*, New York: Home Library.

Machlup, F. (1939), 'Period Analysis and the Multiplier Theory', *Quarterly Journal of Economics*, **54** (November): 1–27.

—— (1978), *Methodology of Economics and Other Social Sciences*, New York: Academic Press.

Mackie, J. L. (1974), *The Cement of the Universe*, Oxford: Oxford University Press.

Mai, Ludwig H. (1975), *Men and Ideas in Economics*, Totowa, N.J.: Littlefield Adams.

Mankiw, N. G. (1988), 'Recent Developments in Macroeconomics: a Very Quick Refresher Course', *Journal of Money, Credit and Banking*, **20** (August, part 2): 436–49.

Marshall, Alfred (1920), *Principles of Economics*, 8th edn, London: Macmillan.

Marx, Karl *Capital*, vol. I (1867); vol. II (1885); vol. III (1894), Chicago, Ill.: Charles H. Kerr, 1909.

Maynard, Alan (1975), *Experiment with Choice in Education*, London: Institute for Economic Affairs.

Meade, J. E. (1951), *The Theory of International Economic Policy*, vol. 1: *The Balance of Payments*, London: Oxford University Press.

Miller, R. (1987), *Fact and Method: Explanation, Confirmation and Reality in the Natural and the Social Sciences*, Princeton, N. J.: Princeton University Press.

Mirowski, Philip (1989), *More Heat than Light*, Cambridge: Cambridge University Press.

Mises, Ludwig von (1949), *Human Action: A Treatise on Economics*, 3rd rev. edn, 1966, Chicago, Ill.: Contemporary Books.

Modigliani, F. (1944), 'Liquidity Preference and the Theory of Interest and Money', *Econometrica*, **12** (January): 45–88.

Moggridge, D. E. (1980), *Keynes*, 2nd edn, London; Macmillan.

Morishima, M. (1973), *Marx's Economics*, Cambridge: Cambridge University Press.

Morris, Martin (1989), 'Student Aid in Sweden: Recent Experience and Reforms' in *Financial Support for Students: Grants, Loans or Graduate Tax?* ed. Maureen Woodhall, London: Kogan Page.

Mundell, R. A. (1963), 'Capital Mobility and Stabilization Policy under Fixed and Flexible Exchange Rates', *Canadian Journal of Economics and Political Science*, **29** (November): 475–85.

Murphy, K. M. and Topel, R. H. (1987), 'The Evolution of Unemployment in the United States: 1968–1985', in *NBER: Macroeconomics Annual*, ed. S. Fischer, Cambridge, Mass. MIT Press: 11–58.

Nadeau, R. (1990), 'Confuting Popper on the Rationality Principles', paper presented at the Annual Congress of the Canadian Philosophical Association, Victoria, B.C., May.

Nelson, Alan (1986a), 'Review of Hahn, Equilibrium and Macroeconomics', *Economics and Philosophy*.

—— (1986b), 'Explanation and Justification in Political Philosophy', *Ethics*, **97**.

—— (1990), 'Social Science and the Mental', *Midwest Studies in Philosophy*, **15**.

Nelson, Julie (1989a), 'A Picture of Gender', unpublished paper, University of California, Davis.

—— (1989b), 'Sex, Gender, and Economic Research', unpublished paper, University of California, Davis.

Neumann, M. (1978) 'Comments' (on Oates, W. sopra.) *Secular Trends of the Public Sector*, ed. Horst Claus Recktenwald, Proceedings of the 32nd Congress of the IIPF, Edinburgh 1976, Paris: Editions Cujas.

New Zealand (1989), *Learning for Life: 2: Education and Training beyond the Age of Fifteen*, Wellington: Department of Education.

Nola, R. (1987), 'The Status of Popper's Theory of Scientific Method', *British Journal for the Philosophy of Science*, **38**: 441–80.

Nozick, Robert (1975), *Anarchy State and Utopia,* Oxford: Basil Blackwell.

Oates, W. (1978) 'The Changing Structure of Intergovernmental Relations', in Recktenwald, op. cit.

—— (1985), 'Searching for Leviathan: an Empirical Study', *American Economic Review*, **75**, (4): 748–57.

O'Brien, D. P. (1971), *The Correspondence of Lord Overstone*, 3 vols, Cambridge: Cambridge University Press.

Organisation for Economic Co-operation and Development (OECD) (1990), *Changing Patterns of Finance in Higher Education*, Paris: OECD.

Overseas Students Trust (OST) (1987), *The Next Steps: Overseas Student Policy in the 1990s*, London: Overseas Students Trust.

Parrish, J. B. (1967), 'Rise of Economics as an Academic Discipline: the Formative Years to 1900', *Southern Economic Journal*, **34**, 1.

Patinkin, Don (1956), *Money, Interest and Prices: An Integration of Monetary and Value Theory*, Evanston, Ill.: Row, Peterson.

—— (1965), *Money, Interest and Prices: An Integration of Monetary and Value Theory*, 2nd edn, New York: Harper and Row.

—— (1969), 'The Chicago Tradition, the Quantity Theory, and Friedman', *Journal of Money, Credit and Banking,* **1**, (February): 46–70, as reprinted in Patinkin (1981): 241–64.

—— (1972), 'Friedman on the Quantity Theory and Keynesian Economics', *Journal of Political Economy*, **80** (September – October): 883–905.

—— (1974), 'Keynesian Monetary Theory and the Cambridge School', in *Issues in Monetary Economics*, ed. H. G. Johnson and A. R. Nobay, Oxford: Oxford University Press: 3–30; as reprinted in Patinkin (1982): ch. 6.

—— (1976a), *Keynes' Monetary Thought: A Study of Its Development*, Durham, N.C.: Duke University Press.

—— (1976b), 'Keynes and Econometrics: On the Interaction Between the Macroeconomic Revolutions of the Interwar Period' *Econometrica*, **44** (November): 1091–123; as reprinted with minor changes and a postscript in Patinkin (1982): ch. 9.

—— (1981), *Essays On and In the Chicago Tradition*, Durham, N.C.: Duke University Press.

—— (1982), *Anticipations of the General Theory? and Other Essays on Keynes*, Chicago, Ill.: University of Chicago Press.

—— (1984), 'Keynes and Economics Today', *American Economic Review*, **74** (May): 97–102.

—— (1987), 'John Maynard Keynes', in *The New Palgrave: A Dictionary of Economics*, ed. J. Eatwell, M. Milgate and P. Newman, London: Macmillan, vol. III: 639–44.

Peacock, A. T. (forthcoming), *Public Choice in Historical Perspective* – the Mattioli Lectures 1989, Cambridge: Cambridge University Press, Lecture 2.

—— and Wiseman, J. (1961), *The Growth of Public Expenditure in the United Kingdom*, New York: National Bureau of Economic Research, and Princeton, N.J.: Princeton University Press, chs 2 and 6.

—— and —— (1962), 'The Economics of Higher Education', in *Higher Education:*

Evidence – Part Two: Documentary Evidence, Cmnd 2154–xɪɪ, London: Her Majesty's Stationery Office: 129–38.

Peltzman, S. (1980), 'The Growth of Government', *Journal of Law and Economics*, **23**, (2).

Pepin, B. (1990), 'Hands on Popper: a Critique', paper presented at the Annual Congress of the Canadian Philosophical Association, Victoria, B.C., May.

Phelps, Edmund S. (1967), 'Phillips Curves, Expectations of Inflation and Optimal Unemployment over Time', *Economica*, **34** (August): 254–81.

—— (1972), *Inflation Policy and Unemployment Theory: The Cost-Benefit Approach to Monetary Planning*, New York: Norton.

Phillips, A. W. (1958), 'The Relation between Unemployment and the Rate of Change of Money Wage Rates in the United Kingdom, 1861–1957', *Economica*, **25** (November): 283–99.

Phillips, M. (1984), *A History of Banks, Bankers, and Banking in Northumberland, Durham and North Yorkshire*, London: Effingham Wilson.

Pitt, J. C. (ed.) (1988), *Theories of Explanation*, New York: Oxford University Press.

Pommerehne, W. (1977), 'Quantitative Aspects of Federalism' in *The Political Economy of Federalism*, ed. Wallace E. Oates, Lexington, Mass.: D. C. Heath.

Popper, K. R. (1961), *The Poverty of Historicism*, 3rd edn, New York: Harper and Row.

—— (1965), *Conjectures and Refutations*, 2nd edn, New York: Harper and Row.

—— (1966), *The Open Society and its Enemies*, vol. ɪɪ, 2nd edn, New York: Harper and Row.

—— (1967), 'La Rationalité et le statut de principe de rationalité', in *Les Fondements philosophiques des systèmes economiques*, ed. E. M. Classen, Paris: Payot: 142–50. (For translation, see Popper 1985.)

—— (1968), *The Logic of Scientific Discovery*, 2nd edn, New York: Harper and Row.

—— (1972), *Objective Knowledge*, Oxford: Oxford University Press.

—— (1976a), 'The Logic of the Social Sciences', in *The Positivist Dispute in German Sociology*, ed. T. W. Adorno *et al.*, trans. G. Adey and D. Frisby, New York: Harper and Row: 87–104.

—— (1976b), *Unended Quest*, LaSalle, Ill.: Open Court.

—— (1983), *Realism and the Aim of Science*, ed. W. W. Bartley ɪɪɪ, Totowa, N. J.: Rowman & Littlefield.

—— (1985), 'The Rationality Principle', English translation of Popper (1967), in *Popper Selections*, ed. D. Miller, Princeton, N. J.: Princeton University Press.

Prest, Alan (1962), 'The Finance of University Education in Great Britain', in *Higher Education: Evidence – Part Two: Documentary Evidence*, Cmnd 2154–xɪɪ, London: Her Majesty's Stationery Office: 139–52.

Quirk, J. and Saposnik, R. (1968), *Introduction to General Equilibrium and Welfare Economics*, New York: McGraw-Hill: 198–9.

Rabinow, Paul and Sullivan, William M. (eds) (1979), *Interpretive Social Science: A Reader*, Berkeley, Cal.: University of California Press.

Rashid, Salim (1989), 'Does a Famous Economist Deserve Special Standards? A Critical Note on Adam Smith Scholarship', *History of Economics Society Bulletin*, **11**: 190–209.

Reder, Melvin (1982), 'Chicago Economics: Permanence and Change', *Journal of Economic Literature*, **20**, (1), (March): 1–38.

Redman, Deborah (1989), *Economic Methodology: A Bibliography with References to Works in the Philosophy of Science, 1860–1988*, New York: Greenwood Press.

Recktenwald, Horst Claus (ed.) (1978), *Sector Trends of the Public Sector*, Proceedings of the 32nd Congress of the IIPF, Edinburgh 1976, Paris: Editions Cujas.

Reischauer, Robert (1989), 'HELP: A Student Loan Program for the Twenty-First Century', in *Radical Reform or Incremental Change? Student Loan Policies for the Federal Government*, ed. Lawrence E. Gladieux, New York: College Entrance Examination Board.

Renton, Timothy (1985), *Government Policy on Overseas Students*, London Conference on Overseas Students, First Annual Lecture, 21 February.

Report of the Universities' Review Committee (1987), *New Zealand's Universities: Partners in National Development* (The Watts Report), Wellington: New Zealand Vice Chancellors' Committee.

Report of the Working Group on Postcompulsory Education and Training in New Zealand (1988) (the Hawke Report), Wellington.

Ricardo, David (1951), *The Principles of Political Economy and Taxation*, ed. P. Sraffa, Cambridge: Cambridge University Press.

Robbins, Lionel (1952), *The Theory of Economic Policy in English Classical Political Economy*, London: Macmillan.

—— (1980), *Higher Education Revisited*, London: Macmillan.

Robbins Report (1963), *Higher Education*: Report of the Committee under the Chairmanship of Lord Robbins, Cmnd 2154, London: Her Majesty's Stationery Office.

Robinson, J. (1937), *Essays in the Theory of Employment*, Oxford: Basil Blackwell.

Roley, V. V. (1985), 'Money Demand Predictability', *Journal of Money, Credit and Banking*, **17**, (November): 611–41.

Rooney, Phyllis (1989), 'Gendered Reason: Sex Metaphor and Conceptions of Reasons', unpublished manuscript, Iowa City.

Roos, Charles F. (1934), *Dynamic Economics*, Principia Press.

Rosenberg, Alexander (1976), *Microeconomic Laws: A Philosophical Analysis*, Pittsburgh, Pa: University of Pittsburgh Press.

—— (1980), *Sociobiology and the Pre-emption of Social Science*, Baltimore, Md: Johns Hopkins University Press.

—— (1983), 'If Economics Isn't Science, What Is It?, *Philosophical Forum*, **14**: 296–314.

—— (1986), 'The Explanatory Role of Existence Proofs', *Ethics*, **97**: 177–87.

—— (1988), *Philosophy of Social Science*, Boulder, Col.: Westview Press.

—— (1989), 'Are Generic Predictions Enough?', *Erkentniss*, **30**: 43–68.

Round Table (1989), 'Overseas Students: Private/Public Sector Interaction, (1) Government and British Council Support', mimeographed paper prepared for Round Table on Overseas Student Policy.

Ruskin, John (1860), *Unto This Last*, London: Penguin, 1985.

Salmon, W. C. (1988), 'Deductivism Visited and Revisited', in *The Limitations of Deductivism*, ed. A. Grunbaum and W. C. Salmon, Berkeley, Cal.: University of California Press: 95–127.

—— (1989), 'Four Decades of Scientific Explanation', in *Scientific Explanation: Minnesota Studies in the Philosophy of Science*, vol XIII, ed. P. Kitcher and W. C. Salmon, Minneapolis: University of Minnesota Press: 3–219.

Samuelson, Paul A. *The Collected Scientific Papers of Paul A. Samuelson*, 5 vols, Cambridge, Mass.: MIT Press.

—— (1968), 'What Classical and Neoclassical Monetary Theory Really Was', *Canadian Journal of Economics*, **1**: 1–15; also in *Collected Scientific Papers*, 529–43.

—— (1971), 'Understanding the Marxian Theory of Exploitation: a Summary of the So-called Transformation Problem', *Journal of Economic Literature*, **9**: 399–431; also in *Collected Scientific Papers*, **3**: 276–308.

—— (1974a), 'Marx as Mathematical Economist: Steady-State and Exponential Growth Equilibrium', in G. Horwich and P. Samuelson, eds. *Trade, Stability, and Macroeconomics: Essays in Honor of Lloyd A. Metzler*, ed. G.Horwich and P. Samuelson, New York: Academic Press; also in *Collected Scientific Papers*, **4**: 231–269.

—— (1974b), 'Insight and Detour in the Theory of Exploitation: a Reply to Baumol', *Journal of Economic Literature*, **12**: 62–70; also in *Collected Scientific Papers*, **4**: 289–97.

—— (1974c), 'Rejoinder: Merlin Unclothed, a Final Word', *Journal of Economic Literature*, **12**: 75–7; also in *Collected Scientific Papers*, **4**: 298–301.

—— (1978), 'The Canonical Classical Model of Political Economy', *Journal of Economic Literature*, **16**: 1415–34; also in *Collected Scientific Papers*, **5**: 598–617.

—— (1980), 'Noise and Signal in Debates Among Classical Economists: a Reply [to Hollander], *Journal of Economic Literature*, **18**: 575–8; also in *Collected Scientific Papers*, **5**: 618–21.

—— (1987), 'Out of the Closet: a Program for the Whig History of Economic Science', *History of Economics Society Bulletin*, **9**: 51–60.

—— (1988), 'Keeping Whig History Honest', *History of Economics Society Bulletin*, **10**: 161–7.

—— (1990a), 'Revisionist Findings on Sraffa', in *Essays on Piero Sraffa*, ed. K. Bharadwaj and B. Schefold, London: Unwin Hyman.

—— (1990b), 'Trimming Consumers' Surplus Down to Size', in *A Century of Economics: 100 Years of the Royal Economic Society and the Economic Journal*, ed. John Hey and Donald Winch, Oxford: Basil Blackwell.

— and Solow, R. M. (1960) 'Analytical Aspects of Anti-Inflation Policies', *American Economic Review*, **50** (May): 177–94.

Schmid, M. (1988), 'The Idea of Rationality and its Relationship to Social Science: Comments on Popper's Philosophy of the Social Sciences', *Inquiry*, **31**: 451–69.

Schultz, Theodore (1961), 'Investment in Human Capital', *American Economic Review*, **51**, (2): 1–17.

Scotto, A. (1950), 'Di Un Indice de Decentramento Finanziario', in *Finanza Pubblica Contemporanea*, Bari: Gius. Laterza.

Seiz, Janet (forthcoming), 'Gender and Economic Language and Research', in *The Methodology of Economics*, ed. Neil de Marchi, Boston, Mass.: Kluwer.

Seligman, E. R. A. (1925), *Essays in Economics*, New York: Macmillan.

Shackle, G. L. S. (1966), *The Nature of Economic Thought*, Cambridge: Cambridge University Press.

Skidelsky, R. (1983), *John Maynard Keynes*, vol. 1: Hopes Betrayed, 1883–1920, London: Macmillan.

—— (1989), *John Maynard Keynes*, vol. 2: *The Economist as Prince, 1920–1937*, London: Macmillan.

Smith, Adam (1959), *The Theory of Moral Sentiments*, London: Andrew Millar; last [sixth] edition 1790, the previous five editions entailing no alterations.

—— (1776), *An Inquiry into the Nature and Causes of the Wealth of Nations*, New York: Modern Library Edition, 1937.

Spence, Michael (1973), 'Job Market Signalling', *Quarterly Journal of Economics*, **87**, (August): 355–74.

Sraffa, Piero (1926), 'The Laws of Return under Competitive Conditions', *Economic Journal*, **36**: 535–50.

—— (1951), 'Introduction', in *The Principles of Political Economy and Taxation*, Cambridge: Cambridge University Press.

—— (1960), *The Production of Commodities by Means of Commodities*, Cambridge: Cambridge University Press.

Stager, David (1989), *Focus on Fees: Alternative Policies for University Tuition Fees*, Toronto: Council of Ontario Universities.

Stich, S. P. (1983), *From Folk Psychology and Cognitive Science*, Cambridge, Mass.: MIT Press.

Stigler, George J. (1958), 'Ricardo and the 93% Labor Theory of Value', *American Economic Review*, **48**: 357–67.

—— (1964), 'Statistical Studies in the History of Economic Thought', reprinted in Stigler (1965).

—— (1965), *Essays in the History of Economics*, Chicago, Ill.: University of Chicago Press.

—— (1976), 'Do Economists Matter?', *Southern Economics Journal*, **42**: 347–54.

Throsby, C. D. (1985), *Trade and Aid in Australian Post-Secondary Education*, Australian National University, Development Studies Centre Working Paper no. 85/8.

—— (1986), 'Economic Aspects of the Foreign Student Question', *Economic Record*, **62**, (179): 400–14.

UK (1960), *Grants to Students* (the Anderson Report), Report to the Committee Appointed by the Minister of Education and the Secretary of State for Scotland, Cmnd 1051, London: Her Majesty's Stationery Office.

——. Department of Education and Science (1988), *Top-Up Loans for Students*, Cm 520, London: Her Majesty's Stationery Office.

—— —— (1989), *Aspects of Higher Education in the United States of America: A Commentary by Her Majesty's Inspectorate*, London: Her Majesty's Stationery Office.

USA (1988), *Budget of the United States Government: Fiscal Year 1988, Appendix*, Washington D.C.: Government Printing Office.

—— Bureau of the Census (1960), *Historical Statistics of the United States, Colonial Times to 1957*, Washington D.C.: Government Printing Office.

van Fraassen, B. C. (1980), *The Scientific Image*, Oxford: Clarendon Press.

Varian, Hal (1984), *Microeconomic Analysis*, 2nd edn, New York: Norton.

Viner, Jacob (1937), *Studies in the Theory of International Trade*, New York: Harper.

—— (1972), *The Place of Providence in the Social Order*, Philadelphia, Pa: American Philosophical Society.

Wadhwani, S. B. (1985), 'Inflation, Bankruptcy, Default Premia and the Stockmarket', Discussion Paper no. 194, Centre for Labour Economics, London School of Economics.

Watkins, J. (1979), 'Imperfect Rationality', in *Explanation in the Behavioral Sciences*, ed. R. Borger and F. Cioffi, Cambridge: Cambridge University Press: 91–121.

—— (1984), *Science and Skepticism*, Princeton, N.J.: Princeton University Press.

Weintraub, E. Roy (1985a), 'Appraising General Equilibrium Analysis', *Economics and Philosophy*, **1**, (1), (April): 23–27.

—— (1985b), *General Equilibrium Analysis*, Cambridge: Cambridge University Press.

—— (forthcoming), *Stabilizing Dynamics: Constructing Economic Knowledge*, Cambridge: Cambridge University Press.

Wicksell, Knut (1898), *Interest and Prices*, reprinted New York: Kelley, 1963, from the 1936 translation by R. F. Kahn.

Williams, Gareth (ed.) (1991), *New Funding Mechanisms in Higher Education*, Milton Keynes: Open University Press, forthcoming.

—— and Gordon, Adrian (1981), 'Perceived Earnings Functions and Ex Ante Rates of Return to Post-Compulsory Education in England', *Higher Education*, **10**, (2): 199–227.

——, Woodhall, Maureen and O'Brien, Una (1986), *Overseas Students and Their Place of Study*, London: Overseas Students Trust.

Williams, Peter (ed.) (1981), *The Overseas Student Question: Studies for a Policy*, London: Heinemann.

Wilson, T. (1948), *Fluctuations in Income and Employment*, London: Pitman.

Winkler, D. R. (1983), 'The Costs and Benefits of Foreign Students in US Higher Education', *Journal of Public Policy*, **4**: 115–38.

Wiseman, J. (1989), *Cost, Choice and Political Economy*, Aldershot, Hants: Edward Elgar.

Withers, H. (1933), *National Provincial Bank: 1833 to 1933*, London: National Provincial Bank.

Wood, J. C. (ed.) (1983), *John Maynard Keynes: Critical Assessments*, vol. II, London: Croom Helm.

Woodhall, Maureen, (1982) *Student Loans: Lessons from International Experience*, Policy Studies Institute, London.

World Bank (1986) *Financing Education in Developing Countries: An Exploration of Policy Options* World Bank, Washington D.C.

World Bank (1988) *Education in Sub-Saharan Africa* World Bank, Washington.

Index